THE COUNTESS FROM KIRRIBILLI

Joyce Morgan is a former arts editor of the *Sydney Morning Herald*. She is the author of *Martin Sharp: His life and times*, which was long-listed for the 2018 Stella Prize, and *Journeys on the Silk Road*, about the discovery of the world's oldest printed book. Joyce has written on arts and culture for more than three decades and has worked as a journalist in London, Hong Kong and Sydney. She is a Getty arts journalism fellow and Huntington Library fellow. British-born, she has travelled widely and lives in Sydney.

THE COUNTESS FROM KIRRIBILLI

The mysterious and
free-spirited literary sensation
who beguiled the world.

JOYCE MORGAN

For my twin, Brenda

First published in 2021

Allen & Unwin
83 Alexander Street
Crows Nest NSW 2065
Australia
Phone: (61 2) 8425 0100
Email: info@allenandunwin.com
Web: www.allenandunwin.com

A catalogue record for this book is available from the National Library of Australia

ISBN 978 1 76087 517 6

Set in 11.5/17 pt Minion Pro by Midland Typesetters, Australia
Printed and bound in Australia by Griffin Press, part of Ovato

10 9 8 7 6 5 4 3 2 1

The paper in this book is FSC® certified. FSC® promotes environmentally responsible, socially beneficial and economically viable management of the world's forests.

CONTENTS

Prologue		vii
Chapter 1	SETTING SAIL	1
Chapter 2	A PERT, UNLOVABLE CHILD	11
Chapter 3	SMOTHERED IN BABIES	25
Chapter 4	A POMERANIAN COUNTESS	36
Chapter 5	DOVE AND SERPENT	50
Chapter 6	TORMENTING THE TUTORS	63
Chapter 7	THE GYPSY QUEEN	80
Chapter 8	EMOTIONS AFTER BREAKFAST	94
Chapter 9	THE WICKED EARL	107
Chapter 10	A FAMILY FRACTURED	122
Chapter 11	THE DREGS OF MISERY	137
Chapter 12	'ALICE' IN PROPAGANDA-LAND	153
Chapter 13	MOUNTAIN SOLACE	170
Chapter 14	DO NOT MARRY A NOVELIST	185
Chapter 15	COUSIN KATHERINE	200
Chapter 16	MORTAL LONGINGS	214
Chapter 17	A WORMY BUSINESS	227

Chapter 18 A VULGAR LITTLE MIND 242
Chapter 19 DOG DAYS 256
Chapter 20 HELL IS LOOSE 272
Chapter 21 LIFE BENEATH THE SMILES 288
Appendix THE BEAUCHAMPS AND THE LASSETTERS 307
Acknowledgements 314
Bibliography 317
Notes 320
Index 336

PROLOGUE

April 1939

The wisteria was heavy with blossom; the roses scrambled around the windows of the old French farmhouse. A medlar tree spread its branches, giving shade from the unusually hot spring sun. From the rosemary bushes, an anti-aircraft gun pointed skyward.

A slim, small woman sat at her wooden desk within a little outbuilding. She reached for her fountain pen. Oh, Tuppence. The starving mutt she had found wandering a few weeks earlier had chewed the pen's cap. She shouldn't have left the dog alone in her writing room. At least he hadn't eaten her manuscript.

She had been working on it for two years. Writing had become an act of defiance. Hitler would not come between her and her work, she resolved. But it was getting harder to concentrate, with thirty soldiers bunking in the garage and officers in the spare rooms. Mas des Roses, as she'd named her farmhouse, was looking more like Mas des Regiment.

She wrote her books in looping cursive, before having them typed.

But her typist was about to leave for England. So were many of her Riviera friends.

They always vanished from their villas in spring, before the Mediterranean summer began. But this year they were not just fleeing the heat. Europe was again on the cusp of war. She understood every word of the Führer's bellicose speeches as she listened to her crackly wireless. As a bride in Pomerania, she had learned the language of her first and now long-dead husband.

But she would not flee. She had a plan. This was to be her home forever. She had called the pink house Mas des Roses as an act of faith in the future, back when she had yet to plant a single rose in the dirt. She had created the house and verdant garden near the village of Mougins, in the hills behind Cannes, by herself. No husband, lover or inheritance had contributed.

The house was built on the success of her novels; it was the crown of her long career. She had been writing her witty bestsellers for four decades, and the public knew her simply as 'Elizabeth'. She had called one of her most popular novels *The Enchanted April*. It was April now, but far from enchanted.

She would stay put. She had been uprooted so many times. From her Sydney birthplace; from England, Germany and Switzerland. Twice she had fled for her life—from a war and from a husband. Little wonder her stories were full of women on the run. 'Charming' was how her books were often blithely described. But they deceived, much like her fragrant rosemary. There was always something darker, more steely peeping through.

She had no fear of death; there were times she would have welcomed it. She had seen so many taken too young—a daughter, a brother, nephews, and her cousin Katherine Mansfield. Would it matter if she also died before her time?

Chapter 1

SETTING SAIL

Sydneysiders devoured their breakfast of eggs and bacon with a side order of scandal on 31 August 1866. Their morning newspaper described how a body had been lowered into a Devonshire Street Cemetery plot in an oversized coffin. The deceased had been a large woman, the undertaker had claimed. And she'd died with her knees bent. They couldn't be straightened. But after questions were raised and the coffin was re-opened, it was found to contain three bodies, a court heard. The undertaker had been charged with fraud, refused bail and would be waking that morning behind bars.

Sydney was a raffish place in the middle of the nineteenth century, a wild colonial town on the edge of the earth. Its air of gentility was wafer-thin, its roots as an open-air jail for Britain's unwashed and unwanted not yet a distant memory.

Unlike the undertaker, Henry Herron Beauchamp had found orthodox ways to make money since he sailed through Sydney's Heads two decades earlier with a light heart and a thin pair of breeches.

The London-born merchant had then prospered enough to escape across the harbour from the scruffy town where raw sewage seeped straight into the water near where the Sydney Opera House stands today, and where dysentery and tuberculosis were ever-present and deadly realities.

Reached only by boat, Kirribilli Point was one of Sydney's most arcadian places. It was barely a ten-minute row across the water, but a world away from the town's filth, stench and crime. A handful of elegant mercantile villas had sprung up by the middle of the nineteenth century to house those who had flourished in the infant colony. With manicured lawns and lush gardens, these were the trophies of success, built on the traditional land of the Cammeraygal people.

From the Point, Henry could look across to Circular Quay and the ships that brought the cargo on which his fortunes rested. But fortunes turned with the tide. Henry was worried about his own fate on this day as his sixth child was being born. He had little time to savour either his daughter's arrival or the morning paper. Henry was in a panic. He feared all he had built was about to be lost as the ripples of a major London bank collapse were being felt even in distant Sydney. And now he had another mouth to feed.

The newborn girl, who would become world-famous for a book about her garden, arrived on the cusp of spring. A topsy-turvy spring for her English father, but not for her Tasmanian-born mother, Louey (Elizabeth) Beauchamp. For the once-impoverished Louey—who knew plenty about fickle fortunes—the baby's arrival ushered in the end of more than a decade of childbearing, during which she had produced six living children. That was enough.

Although Louey and Henry named their daughter Mary Annette Beauchamp, they never called her that. They dubbed her May. In time, she would be known by another name entirely, Elizabeth von Arnim, but for many years before that she was simply Mary Beauchamp.

Her birthplace was registered only as Kirribilli Point. *The Sydney Morning Herald* announced that Louey delivered her daughter 'at her residence', but the exact residence wasn't specified. The restless Beauchamps moved from villa to villa on Kirribilli Point in the 1860s. Not until 1910 did that newspaper state that her birthplace was the waterfront villa called Beulah. Certainly, she lived there by the time she was old enough to take her first steps.

Beulah was a gracious six-bedroom sandstone home with a colonnaded veranda, floor-to-ceiling windows and sweeping views sloping down to the rocky shoreline and across the sparkling harbour to the town. Despite its Biblical-sounding name, Beulah had been built by a well-connected scoundrel. William Gibbes had been a libertine who sired numerous illegitimate children; he was a bankrupt and convicted smuggler. Wicked Willy, as he was dubbed, built the elegant residence from the proceeds of his nefarious activities. Mary Beauchamp would grow up with an eye for duplicitous dealings and create a cast of wealthy, dubious men under her pen-name.

As an infant, Mary didn't lack for playmates at Beulah. She was surrounded by her older sister, Charlotte, and her four older brothers, Ralph, Sydney, Walter and Harry. She was within shouting distance of her Lassetter cousins, who lived at Kirribilli Point's most splendid villa, Wotonga. Her uncle, Frederic Lassetter, was one of Sydney's richest men. The fates of the Beauchamps and the Lassetters were intertwined.

Wotonga, the only one of the villas still standing, is now part of Admiralty House, the governor-general's Sydney residence, where visiting heads of state are entertained in grand style. Beulah was demolished and its grounds subdivided and auctioned in 1905, decades before the Sydney Harbour Bridge planted its northern pylon about a ten-minute walk away. For young Mary, today's vice-regal domain was simply a part of her childhood playground.

The Beauchamp and Lassetter families gathered for harbourside picnics on Saturdays and holidays, when oysters were chipped at low tide from the rocky foreshore. Kirribilli was rich in seafood, its name likely derived from the Aboriginal word *kiarabilli*, which meant a good fishing spot.

The diminutive, fun-loving Louey led a privileged life at Beulah, with staff to cook, sew and tend the laundry and garden—a far cry from her desperately poor life as a young girl on a farm outside Launceston. Louey and her sister had almost been abandoned after their mother died and they were left in the neglectful care of their erratic father, Matthew Lassetter.

When news arrived that the motherless girls, in their early teens, were living in squalor, a Melbourne relative crossed the Tasman to see for herself. She was horrified at the sight that greeted her. Louey opened the door with her hair unkempt and her clothes as filthy as the house. The relative took the two girls with her, back to Melbourne. Meanwhile, their father soon left for the goldfields of California.

Louey eventually came to Sydney, where her older brother Frederic had prospered. The former farm boy was on his way to becoming a retail magnate. Eventually his city store, Lassetters, would cover an area bigger than Harrods.

To Frederic's dismay, Louey began courting a young shipping merchant called Henry Beauchamp. He did not want his sister hitched to a non-Wesleyan. He quizzed Henry about his religious beliefs, but could make little of them. Henry argued that as long as he kept the Ten Commandments all would be well. Frederic relented and nineteen-year-old Louey married Henry, the son of a London silversmith, in 1855.

Life on the Point was not without its perils for the Beauchamps and Lassetters. Louey and her brother Frederic were once chased by a bull that escaped from a nearby paddock. A gardener helped herd the beast into a paddock at Beulah where it was shot with a muzzle-loader and its carcass dumped in the water off Kirribilli Point.

But Mary's infancy, with its companionship of her cousins, was about to change. Frederic Lassetter wanted to visit England. The Lassetters quit Wotonga and left for London in 1869. Writing from there, Frederic encouraged Henry to join them for a year's holiday, after which, he suggested, the two families would return to Australia. He believed that their wives would enjoy themselves together, the family's health would improve, and they could all travel to the Continent. He sent Louey £200 to help with her outfits and proposed that the two large families should live together.

A year-long adventure would have appealed to Henry's restless spirit and may have suited his wallet. Henry had become a director of several maritime companies, including chairman of the Australasian Steam Navigation Company, where he had presented a gloomy report to shareholders in 1867 after a drop in profits. He decided to sell up.

Sydney's cashed-up and curious made their way to Beulah in early 1870 for an auction of 'every requisite for a gentleman's family'. Among the goods going under the hammer were a pianoforte, cut glass, and furniture, as well as a 'quiet and good Milch Cow'.

Three-year-old Mary was the youngest of the Beauchamp party who boarded the wooden three-masted sailing ship *La Hogue*, berthed at Circular Quay, a week later. The group comprised her parents and her five siblings; a cousin, Emma Beauchamp; the children's nurse; and a governess, Miss Miles. The oldest member of the group was Mary's grandfather—the father who'd left his children behind when he'd sailed off to California.

Matthew Lassetter was a man with a chequered past. He was a Somerset farmer and lay preacher who was known as Reverend, although he had not been ordained. Disgrace had dogged him after he arrived in Tasmania with his wife in the 1830s and where he initially ran an infants' school. Money was always short. He tried his hand as a baker, but was accused of selling underweight loaves and dubbed Reverend Mr Lightweight.

He hit the bottle and the Launceston Wesleyans expelled him for drunkenness. He sobered up, became chair of the local Teetotal Society, returned to farming and the Wesleyan fold before his wife died and he left for San Francisco. If he had hoped to strike gold in California, riches eluded him. He returned to Australia about a year before Mary was born and continued lay preaching.

In time, Mary would rarely write a book without the appearance of a cleric. They were seldom treated kindly. Reverends, parsons and bishops were among her favoured satirical targets. Mary's grandfather may have offered the feckless prototype.

Soon after sunrise on 12 January, *La Hogue* hoisted sail. Within minutes, it glided past Beulah, the only home Mary had known. By 7 a.m., the vessel was riding a fair breeze out through the protective embrace of Sydney Heads and on to the rolling Pacific Ocean. 'Made money, lost a great deal, saved a little,' Henry observed as the town passed from view.

Henry was a witty observer of life aboard, attuned to its intrigues, frictions and dramas. His astringent commentary in his journals, with its eye for detail and keen sense of humour, showed many of the traits that would later be evident in the writing of his daughter. The 'Beauchamp waggishness' is how the celebrated author, Elizabeth von Arnim, would later describe it to Bertrand Russell.

Henry was a gregarious, exuberant man with a thirst for adventure and novelty, but whose mood could change with the weather. Louey was flirtatious and capable of dissembling, a woman whose 'sweet, twining ways' proved irresistible to Henry and others.

Louey quickly became seasick, as did the children. Within days, the queasiness gave way to jokes about their ability to eat without chucking up. The more robust Henry, an experienced sailor, cast an appreciative eye over the finer things the ship had to offer—champagne on Sundays and Thursdays—as well as the more attractive women, including a 'frisky little widow uncommonly lively and agreeable'. He spent his days chatting with passengers and the ship's 35-year-old Captain Goddard, from whom he learned much about the intrigues of Sydney's social set. His fellow passengers seemed a pleasing bunch. It was early days.

The family settled into a routine in which Reverend Matthew Lassetter read a chapter of scripture each night at eight in his little cabin that Henry had dubbed The Vicarage. By week two, the weather turned bitter and the family were again seasick. Famished by the cold and finding the ship's rations inadequate, Henry regretted leaving Sydney. He yearned for 'an hour on the sunny side of George Street on a hot wind day'.

Worse was to come. A sickly young Englishman, who had been unwell since boarding, died. Mary watched in driving rain as the young man was buried at sea. She inquired curiously, 'Pa, are him bellied?' The sea burial raised a question in young Mary's mind and Henry noted her first recorded comment. As an adult, Mary loathed the ocean and sea voyages. 'All my nightmares [. . .] are about ships, me inside them,' she wrote many years later. Although she became a great traveller, she rarely boarded a ship willingly. Her aversion may well have been ignited on her first voyage.

The young man's death underscored the perils of ocean travel, where sickness, death and disaster were constant companions. Henry knew the dangers of maritime travel well. He had been in Sydney when one of the country's worst maritime disasters unfolded as the *Dunbar* went down off the Heads in 1857, with the loss of 121 lives. Card games were suspended the night of the young man's sea burial, out of respect. Passengers instead 'chatted and did a little scandal'.

As Louey's health returned, so did her volatile temper. After she threw her napkin across the dining table and into the face of the governess, Miss Miles, the captain joked to Henry that he hoped her health would not improve further, lest she became unmanageable.

Temperatures warmed as the vessel sailed north, and romance was in the air. Henry observed 'a decided outbreak of lovemaking [. . .] but not much fear of it spreading as respectable eligible male material is wanting'.

Louey's flirtatious behaviour prompted rumours of an affair between her and the captain, gossip Henry treated with more amusement than jealousy: 'Poor old captain and Louey needlessly dejected at what the meanest vermin have the power of suggesting.' A remorseful matron, Mrs Plomer, sought Louey's forgiveness for spreading the rumours. How could Mrs Plomer have believed such 'vile slander'? Louey demanded. The matron's reply undercut her contrition: 'Well, certainly Mrs Beauchamp I thought it not improbable considering your *playful* disposition.' Henry dryly noted in his journal that the seventh commandment—thou shalt not commit adultery—should be amended to include 'or be playful'. Meanwhile, Louey relished the drama that placed her at the centre of scurrilous attention. So much so that she 'began to wish for a new slander once a week at least', Henry wrote.

The birth of a daughter to a steerage passenger prompted some explaining to Henry's curious young children, who had until then accepted the belief that baby girls were produced from a bed of parsley. The baby's arrival had 'shaken our children's faith (before so firm) in the "Parsley bed" theory and they are almost yielding to the belief that the little lady was brought on board during the night on the back of an enormous flying-fish'.

Louey's thirty-fourth birthday aboard brought her little cheer. She was again unwell and sick of shipboard life. Louey was not the only one weary of the long voyage. By early April, twelve weeks after leaving Sydney, people were increasingly bad-tempered and tired of each other. However, a Miss Scott managed to raise her own birthday spirits with a party and a punch that ended up 'intoxicating several ladies heretofore considered models of sobriety', Henry noted.

Changeable winds made it hard to assess how long the journey would take. At least the vessel was unlikely to run out of food. Aside from salted and preserved provisions, the ship still had a mobile larder that included a pig, seventeen sheep, two milch cows, several parrots, a wombat and a kangaroo.

La Hogue was off Penzance on the Cornish coast on England's south-western tip by late April and into calm waters. Henry was impatient with those who did not share his joy in such smooth sailing. 'Lovely placid day, and should feel perfectly happy but for the grumblings of my co-passengers who are actually dissatisfied with this superlatively delicious yachting. What; on water, or earth, would content them!'

The vessel followed the coastline close enough to land to see trees, windmills, haystacks and men ploughing fields. *La Hogue* turned into the Thames estuary. After more than three months at sea, on 24 April 1870, the Beauchamps stepped onto English soil.

Chapter 2

A PERT, UNLOVABLE CHILD

Plane trees had sprouted their youthful foliage and tulips, daffodils and bluebells raised their colourful heads as the Beauchamp party clip-clopped their way in hansom cabs through London's spring streets. Louey and the children were delighted at their first sight of strange European trees and shrubs. For Henry, it was a return to familiar flora. For Mary, who would develop a passion for gardens and landscapes, she could not have arrived at a more beautiful time of year.

The Beauchamps stayed at Belsize Park with Frederic Lassetter and his wife Charlotte. Henry visited relatives, renewed mercantile contacts, wandered through Kensington Gardens and attended the Haymarket Theatre. Amid his old haunts, his years in Australia began to feel like a dream.

Henry's oldest son Ralph contracted scarlet fever within weeks of arrival. Fearing contagion, Charlotte Lassetter sent her children to stay elsewhere for safety. Henry was uneasy at his brood having displaced the Lassetter children: 'Feel ourselves like cuckoos having taken possession of other birds' nests.' Not that Henry took the risk of contagion terribly seriously. He detected snobbishness in attitudes to the spread of infectious diseases on public transport: 'First [class], giving you Scarlet fever, (which is considered therefore respectable); the Second, Measles; and the Third, Small Pox!' Henry had little faith in medical advice—an attitude Mary would also share—and resented the fees. 'Our coming home is a fine thing for the medical profession,' he grumbled.

Henry leased a furnished house in Hampstead by mid-May, but the cost of moving and difficulties arranging servants saw his frustration boil over. The tetchy Henry cursed the high price of supplies from tradesmen and regretted leaving Sydney. 'Wished them all to Jericho and ourselves back in Australia.'

His fulminations were characteristically short-lived, and he was soon enjoying days out around London, often with Frederic. He attended Derby Day, revisited boyhood haunts and at a flower show he spotted the Prince of Wales looking puffy and overfed. Visitors called on Henry, including Captain Charles Constable, son of the painter John Constable, and *La Hogue*'s Captain Goddard, with whom he remained friends for years.

Louey often took to her bed with unspecified illnesses. One day, Henry returned home unexpectedly after having left her home in bed. He was surprised to find his wife miraculously recovered, all dressed up and awaiting the arrival of a carriage she had ordered.

Henry took his children on excursions to the Houses of Parliament, the British Museum, and the Lord Mayor's Show, but they were left behind when he and Louey when off on longer trips out of London. Henry could be impatient and exasperated with his young brood. Years later, Mary reflected: 'He wasn't a man who ought ever to have had any children, except grown-up ones. The cries of babies maddened him. He disliked little girls, who bounced in from the garden without wiping their shoes.'

About most of his children, Henry noted little beyond their childhood illnesses. Mary was the exception. Her early utterances sufficiently amused her father that he recorded her comments. After a Sunday church service, during which Mary had stared at the skullcap-wearing preacher, Henry asked his daughter her opinion of the man. 'Him's a rum one, Pa,' she told her father. It was Mary's first known comment about a clergyman, and Henry thought it a fair assessment of the man he considered a lugubrious old frog.

Henry's thoughts turned frequently to Sydney. As he sat in a gloomy church on a foggy early autumn day, he 'thought of the lovely month of September in Australia, the clear air, bright sunshine, and thousand odours of the full Spring'.

He kept in touch with friends visiting from Australia, wrote regularly to Australian associates and kept abreast of events there. Henry kept his eye too on events in Continental Europe, where France and Prussia were at war. Prussia would triumph and eventually a united Germany under Prussian King Wilhelm I would change the balance of power in Europe. He could not know that this would eventually have dramatic consequences for his youngest daughter.

A cold northern Christmas was a novelty for Mary and her siblings. Henry took them to Hampstead Heath on Christmas Eve where 'our Australians made their debut on the ice with many sore tumbles'.

Henry was getting restless in London. He dined with Captain Goddard aboard *La Hogue*, newly returned from Australia, and found himself wishing for another voyage. With the lease of the Hampstead home up in spring, Henry decided to uproot his family to Switzerland for an extended holiday.

In Lausanne, the Beauchamps moved into a hillside chalet with a view over Lake Geneva. Mary would recall years later the sight of her mother wrapped in a blue shawl, waving, as Mary played in nearby woods. Henry was delighted with the new environment, where the heat reminded him of Sydney. He felt he had the best of both worlds with Lausanne's 'Australian air and climate plus the fine European trees [. . .] & snow-topped mountains, good servants, & superior civilization'.

The Beauchamps were joined by Frederic and Charlotte Lassetter and their six children. The two families went on outings together, including a summer boat trip across Lake Geneva to the romantic Chillon Castle, from which Lord Byron and Henry James drew inspiration. Henry was impressed that hot day with five-year-old Mary's unflagging energy, which she would retain for most of her life.

The two oldest Beauchamp boys, fourteen-year-old Ralph and ten-year-old Sydney, were enrolled in a local school. Mary began lessons at home with Miss Miles, and Henry observed his daughter learning to write.

Henry's initial plan for just a year in Switzerland had already stretched to two years by the time he, Louey and the Lassetters left their children behind to tour Europe in the spring of 1872. As they approached Naples, Henry noticed a huge billowing cloud. He thought it similar to ones he had seen in Australia but, as their train drew closer, it was clear the cloud was unlike anything he'd ever seen.

Vesuvius had erupted. Streams of red-hot lava descended from the volcano, setting the base alight, as his party travelled through crowded, smoke-filled streets to their hotel. The mountain roared like thunder as it made its most dramatic eruption of the nineteenth century.

Henry and Louey did not return to their children in Switzerland for three months. They had been away long enough to notice how much Charlotte had grown in their absence. Indeed, Charlotte had matured more than anyone realised.

Henry's restlessness and his desire for a sea voyage increased. At nearly fifty, he resolved to travel to Australia and back, a journey that seems to have been motivated primarily by a thirst for adventure. He waved his family goodbye in November and was delighted to soon find himself aboard and in the company of fellow globetrotters.

Louey was left in sole charge of their six children in Lausanne. It may have suited her to be without Henry. It certainly suited Mary. She felt liberated without his dominating presence. She wrote of her father's long absences years later: 'Queer how sprightly life became, how roomy, with what wide margins, when my father, in those years, wasn't there. For my part, instead of taut I became happy-go-lucky; instead of minding my p's and q's and watching my steps, I ceased to mind or watch anything.'

In Melbourne, Henry stayed with his brother, Horatio, and on a bushwalk outside the city he delighted in wandering amid towering gums, colourful rosellas and laughing jackasses, as he called kookaburras. He longed to be twenty-one again and free of responsibilities. He felt as content back in Australia as he did in London. 'I can be happy in Belsize Park and go into raptures in the Australian bush.'

In Sydney, acquaintances stopped Henry so frequently on George Street that he felt as though his hands had been squeezed to jelly. He visited friends and crossed the harbour to Kirribilli. He looked wistfully on his graceful former home and wished he was again comfortably installed at Beulah.

Henry had some business to conduct in Sydney. He owned eighteen acres together with a villa, which he never occupied, at St Leonards (which was then the name of the whole area that stretched from present-day North Sydney to Gore Hill). Henry had intended that his family would eventually return to Sydney and live on the prime North Shore property he had bought in 1865. But now he decided to sell it instead.

He found a newly cashed-up buyer: Australia's most celebrated gold miner, Bernhardt Holtermann. The German immigrant had spent years mining for gold in New South Wales and had just struck it rich when Henry arrived back in Sydney. Holtermann discovered the world's largest specimen of reef gold at Hill End in October 1872. Known as the Holtermann Nugget, the 286-kilogram rock contained more than ninety kilograms of gold. Holtermann was famously photographed beside his find, with the nugget reaching his chin. He soon built a palatial mansion on Henry's former property, which is today part of the prestigious boys' school, Shore.

With his St Leonards property sold, Henry sailed out of Sydney. The journey was enlivened by an adventurous fellow passenger who came aboard in Hong Kong. Nicholas Miklouho-Maclay was a twenty-six-year-old Russian who had just spent more than a year in New Guinea. The anthropologist and explorer would later leave his mark on Australia, where he would live for years. He built the country's first marine biological research laboratory—a sandstone building that still stands at Sydney's Watsons Bay.

But that was in the future. In Hong Kong, the young man's scientific explorations were rather different. He had smoked prodigious amounts of opium—twenty-six pipes' worth in four hours—observed by a physician who monitored the young scientist's reactions. Henry was impressed and amused. '[Maclay] does not at all wonder at people forsaking home, wife, wealth, everything to indulge in it, the sensations are so beatific [. . .] a martyr to science!'

Henry issued orders to Louey as he travelled. She must not neglect attending church, must see that the children persevere with their studies and must undertake moderate exercise. He missed them and had a message for his youngest daughter. 'Darling little May! Tell her Papa is always thinking of her . . . and looks at her, and all your portraits, every day.' He repeatedly assured Louey that they would never again be parted. 'After sowing my wild oats, I promise you to settle down.' He hoped his darling wife was as well and frisky as he was. He had never felt better in his life.

Back in Lausanne, all was not well. Thirteen-year-old Charlotte was pregnant. She had likely conceived when Henry and Louey had left their children behind while they travelled the previous summer.

The physical risks of pregnancy to a girl barely into her teens were considerable. Nonetheless, Charlotte—known as Shad—gave birth to an apparently healthy son around the time of her fourteenth birthday in March 1873. Who fathered the child is not recorded, nor the infant's fate. The boy is never mentioned again. It is likely the birth was hushed up. This was made easier by the family being away from English relatives. The birth of an illegitimate child at that time would have been considered shameful.

Yet Henry's reaction was hardly that of a scandalised Victorian-era father. His response was both lighthearted and dismissive when he learned of the birth as he was sailing back to England. Henry wrote to Louey that he had received her 'happy intelligence of dear Shad's return to a decent figure by the advent of one more little mortal to this world of sin. Well; thank God, that's over!'

Charlotte's pregnancy did little to prompt Henry to hasten home. He sailed via Japan to the United States and Canada, reaching Lausanne in September after an eleven-month absence. Joyfully reunited with Louey and the children, Henry promised never to leave again. There was a reunion too with the Lassetters who had moved to the elegant Château de Coppet, near Geneva. The château had once been the home of the famous French writer, Madame de Staël, and it and its most celebrated occupant left a deep impression on young Mary.

After three years in Switzerland, a place Henry considered paradise on earth, he was ready to uproot his family again. The Beauchamps were going back to London.

Mary had just turned eight when she and Charlotte were enrolled in a girls' school, Blythewood House, near the family's Hampstead home. At a time when little store was put on girls' learning, Henry insisted his daughters were educated.

Mary's studies were interrupted within weeks of starting at the school when she contracted scarlet fever. She was quarantined from the family under the care of her cousin Emma. Far from disliking the isolation, as her father feared, Mary was delighted at her exile. She would grow into a woman content in her own company, for whom solitude and independence were essential. Mary did not waste away during her convalescence. When she returned home after seven weeks her father observed she had become fat. Henry disapproved of corpulence, in his children as much as in the Prince of Wales.

Henry became friends with Sir Sydney Waterlow, patriarch of one of London's wealthiest and most prominent families. Sir Sydney, who had recently hung up his robes as Lord Mayor of London, had built the wealth of the family company Waterlow and Sons, a large firm of printers and engravers. The Waterlows were a cultured and artistic dynasty who would in time produce British landscape painter Sir Ernest Waterlow and eminent art curator Nick Waterlow, and would settle in Australia in the twentieth century.

Henry and Louey dined regularly with Sir Sydney and Lady Waterlow. When the Waterlows' son George, then in his early twenties, visited Australia in late 1873, Henry likely provided introductions, including to his brother, Horatio Beauchamp, and to prosperous Sydney business contact Thomas Mort, whose company later became the agricultural brokers Goldsbrough Mort. George was a talented artist and among the watercolours painted on his voyage were Horatio's rambling country home north of Melbourne, the view from Thomas Mort's Double Bay home, and Sydney Heads. These works are now held by the State Library of New South Wales.

On his return to London, George Waterlow and Charlotte Beauchamp were often in each other's company and they became engaged in May 1875. It was a prestigious match for sixteen-year-old Charlotte.

With his eldest daughter betrothed, Henry's promise of no more long separations from his wife and family was forgotten. He again set sail for Australia in July 1875. Henry still had ideas of returning with his family to the southern hemisphere. One purpose of his second round-the-world trip was to look for places to live. In Sydney, he looked again at the house he most loved, Beulah, and sighed as he thought of Louey and the children, and the years when the elegant villa was their home.

But returning to Sydney seemed unrealistic. While squatters and landowners had prospered, mercantile men were going hungry, he observed. It was not just his business prospects that were less than glittering. 'Sunday in Sydney is terribly quiet which makes me think that the people must be dreadfully wicked all the week,' he quipped to Louey. Even if the Beauchamps and Lassetters—whom he included in his plans—did return, he could not imagine what Louey or her sister-in-law Charlotte Lassetter would do in Sydney. It was a measure of how close the two families were that he saw their futures as intertwined. 'I do not at all like the idea of the two families being separated. Perhaps I may find a suitable home for both in New Zealand,' Henry wrote to his wife.

Louey, meanwhile, was beset with doubts about what her husband was up to on his long voyage. She feared his wandering eye and that he might not return. Henry acknowledged he enjoyed lively company—male and female—but dismissed her suspicions as silly. 'If you would but love me for what I am, and not think ill of me because I am not what I might be! You talk about flirting—I assure you that you are the last person I had anything to do with in that line [. . .] you will find me a truly lovely husband when I return, if you will but appreciate me.'

Henry instructed Louey to ensure Mary concentrated on her studies. 'She has plenty of ability—and we must do all we can for her,' Henry wrote to Louey. A governess was engaged to teach the girl French, Latin and the piano.

Meanwhile, Henry sailed to New Zealand where two of his brothers had settled. Arthur Beauchamp in Whanganui had prospered as a stock salesman and auctioneer. Henry was impressed with his industrious nephew, seventeen-year-old Harold. In time, Harold would become chairman of the Bank of New Zealand. He would also become the father of Kathleen Beauchamp, who became known to the literary world as the writer Katherine Mansfield.

Henry's other brother Craddock had not fared well, eking out an existence on a farm at Anakiwa at the head of Queen Charlotte Sound with his wife and eight children. Arthur struck Henry as devoid of business ability, a dreamer unlikely to realise his golden visions of a comfortable future.

Henry left New Zealand for Melbourne, thinking Christchurch might be the best place to live. Henry agreed to act as chaperone to Horatio's daughter Connie Beauchamp on the voyage back to England, where the young woman was to continue her education. By the time Henry arrived home after nine months away, he had abandoned plans to settle in Christchurch—or anywhere else in the southern hemisphere. He decided instead to conduct his business from London.

With sprigs of orange blossom and myrtle in her hair, Charlotte Beauchamp walked down the aisle of St Saviour's, South Hampstead, to the strains of *Lohengrin*, trailed by seven bridesmaids. A fashionable crowd gathered to watch her marry George Waterlow on 1 August 1876.

Charlotte gave birth to a daughter, Zoe, nine months later and Henry and Louey rejoiced at becoming grandparents. But when Charlotte, George and the baby spent the Christmas season at the Beauchamps' home, the seven-month-old took ill. Her lungs were congested, and she struggled to breathe. The baby died just before the New Year. Charlotte, at eighteen, had given birth to two children but was yet to raise any. Ten-year-old Mary, who would later write frankly about marriage and motherhood, would have observed her sister's sorrow.

Mary was often her father's companion on trips around London. He took her to Westminster Abbey to listen to the organ and choir, walked with her on Hampstead Heath, took her to a flower show, and together they made pilgrimages—as he called them—to his old haunts. Music, walking in nature and gardens would become her lifelong passions. She too would revisit former houses and places that held strong memories for her, also calling them pilgrimages.

Henry took Mary to visit her aunts and she recalled as an adult how she must have appeared: 'A pert, unlovable child. My aunts, kindly and indulgent, merely looked at each other, and remarked, for perhaps the hundredth time, that I was a peculiar little thing.'

Henry, the self-made man, put little store by university education for his rapidly maturing sons, convinced this produced men too learned for commerce. Henry wanted practical young men, in his own image. Ralph joined a firm of tea brokers, Sydney was apprenticed to Waterlow and Sons, Walter joined a wool brokers, while Harry worked on farms.

The Beauchamps moved to Acton in west London in early 1881, where Henry rented a grand home, East Lodge, for seven years. Despite their appearance of affluence, Henry was again beset with financial worries. The price of grains in which he traded fell, and he invested heavily in gas shares—just as newfangled electricity was poised to boom.

The wisdom of past financial decisions returned to haunt him. He regretted selling his Sydney property at St Leonards. Its value had boomed, he learned. The property Henry sold to Holtermann eight years earlier for £1500 was now worth £20,000. Henry wished he had returned with his family to the colonies, where he was convinced his sons would have been more profitably employed than in Britain.

He still hankered for Sydney and maintained his Australian links. He attended a London banquet for Sir Henry Parkes, then New South Wales premier, and kept in touch with his many contacts. When a former business partner, Lancelot Threlkeld, died suddenly in England, Henry joined Frederic Lassetter and Australian newspaper baron James R. Fairfax at the funeral.

Sydney Beauchamp left his apprenticeship at Waterlow and Sons and began studying medicine at Cambridge. Walter decided to try his hand in Australia and Harry made plans to join him. Walter sailed back to his birthplace with his uncle Frederic Lassetter in 1883. 'All feeling acutely our loss of the first one out of the nest,' Henry noted.

By her mid-teens, Mary Beauchamp had long fair hair tied in a ribbon at her neck and brilliant blue eyes. She was petite, pretty and smart. At her local Ealing school, she topped a history exam against all the borough's schools. Her father was proud of his daughter's triumph.

As she prepared to sit her final school exams at the end of 1883, the usually robust Mary became ill. Dismayed that her illness meant she might miss sitting the exams, the seventeen-year-old rallied enough to complete some of them. She even penned an essay on flowers that impressed an examiner, but it wasn't enough. She failed. It was a sad end to her school days.

For a wealthy, eligible young woman, the next few years might have been a waiting game until a suitable match could be made. Instead, the musically gifted Mary began studying at the newly formed Royal College of Music. Violin, viola and piano were among the instruments she learned, but her main focus was the organ. She was blessed with highly talented musical mentors. Her teacher was

Walter Parratt, organist at St George's Chapel, Windsor. The college's director, Sir George Grove, would become the founding editor of *Grove's Dictionary of Music and Musicians*.

Mary's was a musical family. Her parents were frequently at the opera and music concerts. Her mother sang at family gatherings and there was a piano in every house they lived in. Her brother Harry played the cello and sang, and Mary accompanied him on piano. She was keen to see her farmer brother Harry develop his musical talents. She was so confident of his vocal abilities that she took him to sing before Parratt and Grove. As a result, Harry abandoned his plans to join his brother Walter in Australia. Harry remained in England to cultivate his voice instead of his fields.

Mary impressed at the Royal College of Music where she earned accolades and some money as an organist. Her musical abilities far exceeded what might have been expected of a well-brought-up girl able to entertain family and friends at parlour room gatherings.

Mary was surrounded by telegrams, notes and presents when she turned twenty-one on 31 August 1887. Her long hair had darkened to a thick wavy brunette and was soon worn swept up in the late Victorian fashion. Her festive coming of age was, her father recalled, 'very different from that of her birth when the 1866 panic caught me in "full sail" at Sydney and I was near ruined just as I was about retiring with a sufficiency after some 28 years of very hard toil'. The family's 'bright, industrious, good' baby was now a woman.

Chapter 3

SMOTHERED IN BABIES

On a January morning in 1889, Mary and her father boarded a train at London's Victoria Station. Both had been learning Italian in the months before departure for the Eternal City. The Continental tour was likely aimed at introducing his musical daughter to potential suitors. She was now twenty-two.

On arrival in Rome, Henry received a good omen. His son Walter in Sydney had married. Walter had made an excellent match in a local woman named Isabel Dean. The bride's father, Alexander Dean, was a prominent Sydney builder who would erect several of the city's landmark buildings, including the elegant Hotel Australia in Castlereagh Street and Sydney University's Macleay Museum.

Sir George Grove provided Mary in Rome with a letter of introduction to the Italian pianist and composer Giovanni Sgambati, who gave them a reception in late February. During the evening, a distinguished man appeared. He was splendidly dressed and on his way to a ball at the Quirinal Palace.

Count Henning August von Arnim-Schlagenthin was a Prussian aristocrat. He had soft features and pale, intelligent eyes. He wore a pince-nez and had a thick, well-groomed handlebar moustache. His receding hair emphasised his high forehead but made him look older than his thirty-seven years. He may have carried an air of sadness, as he was a recent widower. His wife, Countess Anna von Törring-Jettenbach, had died aged twenty-seven—a year earlier—as had their infant daughter.

Henning was Junker, a member of Prussia's landed gentry. His pedigree was impressive. Through his mother, Elise von Prillwitz, he was related to the imperial family. Her father was Prince Wilhelm Heinrich August of Prussia, brother of Frederick the Great. Through his mother, who died when he was three, Henning had inherited the Prussian estate of Schlagenthin and added its name to his branch of the Arnim family. His diplomat father, Count Harry von Arnim, had been the ambassador to Paris.

Henning was an accomplished pianist, having studied with Franz Liszt. Mary performed at subsequent receptions at Sgambati's; Henning attended them and no doubt appreciated her skilful playing. Henry noticed how attentive Henning was to his young daughter. Mary and Henning conversed together in French since she could not speak German and the count could not speak English.

Mary and her father left Rome for Florence in early April. Here, Henry installed Mary in accommodation and he took off for a few days alone. While Henry was away, Henning arrived in Florence. He was eager to show Mary the view from the top of the Duomo. Henning panted his way up the more than four hundred, steep, narrow stairs. He was no longer slim, nor as nimble as Mary, who was fifteen years younger than him. They reached the top of the cathedral and looked down on the Renaissance city. There, he abruptly announced his intentions.

'All girls like love. It is very agreeable. You will like it too. You shall marry me, and see,' he told her, in what sounded more like a command than a proposal. He suddenly embraced her, which she found more alarming than romantic. He pulled from his pocket a sapphire and diamond ring. Although it had belonged to his late wife, Mary was impressed with the sparkler.

By the time Henry returned to Florence a week later, followed by Louey from London, Mary was betrothed. Louey was impressed by Henning's devotion to her daughter—and by the match's advantages. 'What a rich woman I shall be when she gets married,' Louey wrote to a relative in London.

Henning took control of the Beauchamps' travel plans. Louey took charge of Mary's wardrobe. A new outfit with a green velvet collar and green sash was ordered ahead of their departure for Germany. Louey wanted her daughter to dazzle.

Henning wanted Mary to attend the operatic mecca, Bayreuth. For Mary, it was a trip to a musical Valhalla. It was also the epicentre of German high society, whose members flocked to the summer festival, and an opportunity for Henning to introduce his fiancée to his aristocratic milieu. The Bavarian town was newly synonymous with composer Richard Wagner, who had built his Festspielhaus to stage his operas. After Wagner died in 1883, his widow Cosima, daughter of the composer Liszt, took over the running of the festival. Henning was a friend of the formidable Cosima. As well as squiring Mary to opera performances, Henning introduced her to his social set.

Mary wore a cream evening dress when Henning took her and Louey to a reception at Cosima's home. Louey was overawed: 'I never was in such a lovely house or met so many distinguished people to all of whom we were introduced by the Count.'

Henning arranged for Mary to give an organ recital before Cosima Wagner. Although the organ was not particularly good, it was a way for Mary to meet—and impress—his friends. 'They say the way to Madam Wagner's heart is to play Liszt and May plays him very exquisitely,' Louey wrote. Henning continued to woo Mary at Bayreuth. She recalled, years later, 'there's not a tree anywhere within five miles that I haven't been kissed under!'

Louey's initial awe at the match turned to foreboding. She did not doubt Henning's devotion, but worried at the yawning class difference between the two lovers: 'The more I see of him and his whole set the more I feel the difference in our positions—he and his people are far too swell for us [. . .] it would be better for her if she married in her own set. I can't think this will be for her happiness.'

Prosperous as Louey's family had become, they were hardly old-money landed gentry. Her husband had climbed the social ladder from modest roots. Her brother Frederic had married a convict's daughter. Both men had made their money in the colonies, where even ex-convicts could prosper, and where class divisions were more porous than in Europe.

Louey's impoverished girlhood in distant Tasmania would have left a mark. Her prosperous middle-class London life was, geographically and socially, a world away from that. But the prospect of her daughter marrying into Prussian aristocracy—a society with strict, hidebound rules—was akin to entering a different galaxy.

Mary shared her mother's apprehensions. 'There are times when she does not feel quite sure of herself,' Louey wrote. 'And yet if he [Henning] is away for only a few hours she is lonely and wretched. Still she sees with me her life [as an aristocrat's wife] will be rather a difficult one. Every day he has Princes and Princesses or some distinguished people to meet us at lunch [. . .] we are having some cheering times, at others we are moved to tears at the prospect of all before us.' That prospect included a move far away from her family to a country whose language Mary did not speak.

An apartment was arranged in Dresden, where Mary could begin German lessons and learn about the culture and class into which she would marry. Louey remained as a chaperone while Henry returned to London. Within weeks, Louey was so anxious about her daughter's future that Henry hastily returned to Dresden. '[I] shall stay with them until this wretched affair of May's is settled one way or t'other,' he wrote to a relative. 'It is tearing Louey to pieces.'

The 'wretched affair' had complications. Henning was beset with financial problems. He had inherited his father's debts. Harry von Arnim had a spectacular fall from grace in his later years. In a complicated web of political intrigue while ambassador to Paris, he had fallen foul of the German Chancellor, Otto von Bismarck. Harry had been arrested in 1874 on charges of stealing state documents. The sensational case was widely reported, even as far away as Australia. Some viewed Harry as a potential rival to Bismarck and regarded the charges as a politically motivated crushing of the ambassador.

Harry was sentenced to nine months' jail, but fled the country. While in exile, he was accused of the more serious crime of treason, tried in his absence and sentenced to a further five years' jail. He attempted to return to Germany to take part in a new trial, but died in Nice. Years later, Henning attempted to clear his father's name—even threatening an ageing Bismarck to a duel.

Henning felt honour-bound to repay his father's debts. He intended to mortgage some of his estates to do so. This would take time, he told Henry. Mary, Louey and Henry returned to England, in autumn, without a wedding date set.

Mary entered the drawing room at Buckingham Palace in a floor-length gown from which flowed a three-yard train. Dress rules were strict and specific. In her hair, she was required to wear two ostrich feathers visible at the front, and two lappets of tulle or lace two yards long at the back.

Mary curtseyed as Queen Victoria extended her hand. Being presented at court was a greatly anticipated rite of passage for well-bred young women in Victorian England and allowed those eligible an entrée into fashionable society. This included attendance at court functions, balls and parties—with the potential these glittering events offered for the women to harvest well-bred, well-heeled husbands.

By late in Victoria's reign, the ritual was not limited to daughters of the aristocracy. With the right connections, even those from the merchant class could gain admittance to Her Majesty's drawing room.

Mary's court debut in March 1890 may have been a means to raise her status, an insurance policy lest the romance with Henning toppled. It had been nearly a year since the count proposed, and a wedding date had not yet been set.

In summer, Mary moved with her maid to Hazel Cottage in the village of Goring-on-Thames in Oxfordshire. Louey was installed as chaperone when the count arrived from Berlin to visit. Having had one daughter give birth out of wedlock, Louey would not leave their youngest daughter unsupervised. Mary's reputation was increasingly at risk as months passed and still Henning had not set a date. Decisive action was needed. Mary and her father discussed her position in late November. Mary wrote to Henning and broke off her engagement.

Mary's letter may have been a means to force Henning's hand. If so, it brought swift results. Within weeks, Henning settled his financial affairs and renewed his request to marry her.

Mary walked up the aisle of St Stephen's, Gloucester Road, on her father's arm on 21 February 1891. It was the damp, gloomy end of winter, and Mary may well have shivered in her ivory satin gown. Her dress was draped with old lace, a gift from Henning, and had a spray of orange blossom fastened with a diamond broach. She wore a tulle veil.

Her brother Sydney, newly qualified as a doctor, was best man. The guests included members of the Waterlow family, prominent engineer Sir Bradford Leslie, who was a relative, and Sydney-born barrister and politician Sir James Garrick. After a reception at the Kensington home of a cousin, Mary changed into warm travelling clothes. She stepped out of the house in a heliotrope outfit trimmed with black velvet, a black bonnet edged with beaver, and a fur boa and muff. The newlyweds left on an afternoon train for Berlin.

Miss Mary Beauchamp was now Mary, Countess von Arnim. Most who knew her celebrated her elevated social status. One man did not. Sir George Grove lamented this loss to the world of music. He considered it irrelevant that this rare, capable female musician had landed a Prussian count. To him, her marriage meant 'a promising artist gone!'

As the young bride began her married life with Henning in Berlin, the political tectonic plates shifted in her new homeland. Bismarck, the 'Iron Chancellor' who had dominated European affairs for three decades, resigned. He was forced out by the new Emperor and King of Prussia, Kaiser Wilhelm II. Bismarck had unified Germany's principalities and made the country one of Europe's most powerful. Vengeful as Bismarck was—not least in his treatment of Harry von Arnim—he had maintained peace across the continent.

The new Kaiser would chart a different course. He was a grandson of Queen Victoria, but this was no guarantee of continuing cordial relations between Britain and Germany. Under the Kaiser, Germany would develop an expansionist, imperialist and increasingly bellicose foreign policy that would have far-reaching consequences for Europe and beyond. In time, it would tear Mary's life apart.

But the political shift did not weigh heavy on Mary's mind. She was preoccupied with adjusting to her new status as a wife and countess, or *Gräfin*. The social conventions were more codified than in Britain. As an aristocratic Prussian Junker, she had to learn the rules of behaviour, including who she could and couldn't socialise with—a task that took her longer than learning German.

She struggled to control her household. Although she had grown up with servants, she had not overseen them. She felt ill-equipped and too young to give orders. Her youth was underscored by the infantilising pet name Henning gave her: Dollie.

A little dog helped relieve her anxieties. Like her engagement ring, Mary inherited the dachshund from Henning's first wife. Mary doted on the dog, named Cornelia, even as her husband chided her in the maxims that peppered his speech: 'Do not kiss the dog. No dog should be kissed. I have provided you, for kissing purposes, with myself.'

As she adjusted to marriage and life far from her family, a bigger change was to come. Within weeks of her wedding, Mary was pregnant. She endured a painful labour and was refused the anaesthetic for which she begged. German mothers were expected to deliver their children without pain relief, her (male) doctor told her. To do otherwise was unpatriotic and morally lax. Mary gave birth to Eva, known as Evi, on 8 December 1891.

Mary's dachshund delivered a litter of pups around the same time. While the dog was up and lively within a week, Mary was not. Mary was weak, and the baby cried frequently. The newborn greedily 'casts herself on her poor mother as a shark his prey' was how Henning described his new family in a letter to Henry. Mary was unwell for weeks afterwards, with an unnamed illness—possibly mastitis—alluded to only as 'awkward'.

She never forgot her agonising experience. When she wrote her novel *The Pastor's Wife* years later, with its harrowing account of childbirth, she had her own ordeal to draw on.

Within six months of giving birth, Mary was pregnant again. This time, she was determined to have her sister Charlotte, who was by then the mother of three surviving children, by her side for the birth. Charlotte was with Mary in Germany when her second daughter, named Elizabeth but known as Liebet, was born on 15 February 1893. Liebet, too, cried constantly.

In Berlin, Mary's oldest daughter Evi became ill after a vaccination in October. Mary took Evi and the baby to London. There, Evi was seen by Mary's doctor brother, Sydney. One further aspect may have prompted the trip to London. Mary was pregnant for the third time.

She wanted no more unsympathetic German doctors tending to her. Although she was only in the early stages of her pregnancy, she did not return to Berlin. In London, she and her daughters stayed with her parents before taking a flat in nearby Kensington.

There, Sydney Beauchamp oversaw the birth of Mary's third daughter Beatrix, known as Trix, on 3 April 1894. Henning, who had longed for a boy, arrived from Berlin for a brief visit. He soon returned home alone. Mary was in no rush to join him.

Three children in less than three years was more than Mary could cope with. 'Poor little May smothered in babies,' was Henry's succinct comment. When Mary eventually returned to Berlin in July, she left her middle child Liebet in London with her parents for nine months.

Mary was overwhelmed with the demands of motherhood. Henning desperately wanted a son and heir. Mary desperately did not want any more children. The physical demands of repeated pregnancies were immense on her slight frame. She was barely one and a half metres tall and weighed just fifty kilograms. Mary, like her mother and sister, had little trouble becoming pregnant. With no reliable form of contraception, marital relations came to a halt. When Henning joined Mary on a subsequent visit to London to stay with her parents, he was consigned to a spare bedroom.

With balls, the opera, embassy receptions and dinner parties, Mary's daily life in Berlin involved constant social engagements. She called on Berlin high society, or its members called on her. 'Haven't a notion who he is,' she wrote of one baron who left a calling card. Between social calls, Mary walked in the Tiergarten or rode a bicycle. The latter was considered a controversial activity for a woman, being associated with feminism and scandalously short skirts.

Mary's oldest surviving journal, from 1896, chronicles constant daily activity and outings, much like her father's diaries. But her journal also flags something far more significant. Mary had begun to write. Her first entry for New Year's Day read simply: 'Wrote F.W. am.' In the early months of that year, the words 'wrote F.W.' recur. In her journals, Mary often referred to her works-in-progress simply by their initials or by condensing their titles. Her journals, which she kept for most of her life, were handwritten in haste and full of abbreviations and crossings out, with words missing or truncated.

What 'F.W.' stood for is unknown—no such manuscript has so far been uncovered—but it is clear that by 1896 she was regularly spending part of her days writing. However, in Berlin, her writing was squeezed between an unceasing round of social obligations. On the cusp of thirty, Mary was suffocating under their weight. She was ripe for change.

Chapter 4

A POMERANIAN COUNTESS

The wind whipped at Mary and Henning as their horse-drawn carriage passed by Pomeranian farms and forests and at last reached the stone pillars at the entrance to Nassenheide. They had set out early that March morning by train from Berlin to the town of Stettin, about 150 kilometres north. From there, Henning's remote estate near the Baltic Sea lay two hours away by open road.

The carriage drew up near a once grand house. The schloss had been a convent during the early seventeenth century. An aristocratic botanist and traveller had owned the estate in the eighteenth century and brought back rare seeds and plants for its grounds. Henning's father bought the 8000-acre estate from the botanist's heirs.

An imposing front door opened onto a vaulted hall which had once been the convent's chapel. Near the door was written in Greek: 'Venus, Eros, the Graces, the Muses, Dionysus, Apollo, swore to each other that they would live here.' The evocation of ancient deities was not written by Christian nuns but by a classically inclined early owner. The words resonated with Mary. In years to come, she would have them inscribed in other houses.

The schloss was dilapidated and had not been lived in for a quarter of a century. Nonetheless, Mary was captivated by the estate and wanted to make Nassenheide her home rather than Berlin. She set about transforming the house. She travelled between Nassenheide and Berlin for the next couple of months, buying baths and carpet for the house and seeds for the garden. She hired workmen and began creating a garden. The first cuckoo of spring filled her with joy, as did her newly sown beds of sweet peas, hollyhocks, clematis and roses.

She had come to loathe Berlin, where she often felt lonely despite, or perhaps because of, the relentless social rounds. In Nassenheide, she relished the solitude she had rarely known either as the youngest child in a large family or as an aristocrat's wife in the city.

She walked alone, meditated and read. She was a voracious reader, including of William Wordsworth, Edmund Spenser and Shakespeare. She read works by and about women, including Mrs Gaskell's *The Life of Charlotte Brontë*, and Dorothy Wordsworth's journal. She became so enamoured of a work called *The Garden that I Love* that she wrote its author Alfred Austin a fan letter, although she did not post it. Austin was an English writer, who followed Tennyson as poet laureate, and the book was a lighthearted work about the pleasures and pains of his garden and his whimsical encounters with those close to him. His book may have planted an imaginative seed in Mary's mind.

Henning spent much of his time in Berlin. He paid occasional visits to Nassenheide, where Mary had brought their three daughters. Time away from Berlin and her husband suited Mary. Yet her marriage to Henning was not without moments of joy, including one evening at Nassenheide when Henning was helping her water the plants and she felt 'we were like Adam & Eve in our innocent enjoyment'.

There was a playful quality in her relationship with Henning, evident in a photograph in Nassenheide's garden. Mary sits on Henning's knee, and his face shows a candid mix of surprise and amusement. Mary's face is half-hidden as she appears to plant a kiss or whisper teasingly into his ear. There's a spontaneity about the image that suggests Mary has interrupted her sedate, middle-aged husband quietly smoking his cigar. The young woman, long dark hair piled high, has tossed aside her parasol, which lies upturned near a dog.

She was enchanted by the remote estate, its woodlands, lake and nearby forests, and her feeling for her garden took on a spiritual dimension. 'I can't express the love & grace & fellowship that is with me whenever I go into my garden (which has grown to be the presence of God to me). It is a benediction every time I go into it, & there alone can I realise what is meant by the peace which passeth understanding.'

Her peace in the garden contrasted with ructions indoors. She had trouble with the servants. A housekeeper she referred to as 'the Popess' she found demanding and overbearing. She had difficulty acquiring a cook. When she did, the arrangement was short-lived. After a man was found in the cook's room at night, the pair were sent packing. Another was caught thieving and was jailed. She loathed having to discipline staff. She even had to contend with problems of a supernatural dimension when several maids became convinced the house was haunted.

Soon, there was also friction on the marital front. Mary wanted to attend the summer wedding in England of her musical brother Harry. But she needed Henning's permission. His refusal prompted 'disgraceful scenes' between them. Henning was unrelenting and stymied her attempt to leave in time for the wedding.

A dramatic, if fanciful, account in a 1986 biography of her says she slipped away in secret later that night, walking many kilometres in the dark to a railway station. Her diaries tell otherwise. Frustrated and depressed, Mary had to content herself reading letters about the wedding she had missed.

She was still at Nassenheide three weeks later when her daughter Evi became ill. The doctor ordered Mary to take the girl to Berlin for treatment. There were further scenes 'as usual' with Henning in Berlin—disagreements were becoming commonplace. Once Evi had recovered, Mary travelled with her to London. 'H. very nasty but we managed to get away.'

For the next five days in London, Mary wrote little in her journal each day but the word 'Happy'. She stayed with her parents, spent days with Charlotte, and attended services at St Paul's with Ralph, relishing the divine music. It was nearly a month before Henning followed her to London. He arrived in a bad mood but in time for Mary's thirtieth birthday. Her father noted the day was less than celebratory: 'Praise-worthy attempt to celebrate it German fashion with somewhat feeble results.' Mary confided to her journal on her birthday that she felt 'painfully old'.

Although she and Henning mostly kept their fights behind closed doors, they rowed in public as they readied to leave England by train in mid-September. Mary arrived at Nassenheide where her sorrow at leaving England was allayed by her joy at seeing her daughters, who greeted her with bouquets after her eight-week absence. Long separations would become a feature of their childhood.

Mary convinced Henning to relinquish their Berlin apartment and make Nassenheide their home. As winter set in, the days were filled with sleigh rides, skating on a lake and the arrival for Christmas of some English relatives and a female friend she nicknamed Mouse. Mary was enchanted by the sight of her three little daughters, who looked like fairies in their white dresses and sashes on Christmas Eve. Candles were lit on trees, carols sung and the health of absent relatives toasted.

But family life was not as pretty as a Christmas card. Mary and Henning returned from a peaceful walk together one day and events took a disturbing turn: 'Came home & being too playful and hurting him accidentally he fell upon me with his fist & much thumping. Much grieved & shocked.'

On a cold day in early May 1897, as the damp trees dripped, Mary picked up her pen and started the book that would launch her career: 'Began to write "In a German Garden", sitting among the raindrops & owls.'

Written as a diary, it chronicles a year in the life of a young woman of unspecified nationality married to a wealthy German. It begins on 7 May, the same day Mary picked up her pen. The first-person narrator tells how, after five years bored and miserable in a flat in town, she has moved to a former convent in rural Germany with her three children—the April, May and June babies as she calls them—and her husband, known only as the Man of Wrath. The house has stood empty for twenty-five years and the garden has run to seed. But she is overjoyed, living in a world of 'dandelions and delights'.

Her journals of the time provide an unvarnished basis for the book. Indeed, Mary's works were invariably semi-autobiographical; she mined her life for the raw material from which she constructed situations, characters and incidents.

The diarist, like Mary, is happiest outdoors. 'The garden is the place I go to for refuge and shelter, not the house. In the house are duties and annoyances, servants to exhort and admonish.' The garden was where she felt protected, where 'every flower and weed is a friend and every tree a lover'.

The Man of Wrath is frequently absent, which suits her. The narrator tells how she writes to him regularly, sends her love but cannot manage to 'fret and yearn'. The narrator is self-possessed, content in her solitude. She is as happy to see guests go as arrive, sometimes happier. And she values robust strength, and not only in flora. 'I never could see that delicacy of constitution is pretty, either in plants or women.'

Although much of the plotless book has to do with her garden, the pen-portraits of people and her observations provide humour and insight. She pokes fun at the local parson who, as winter progresses, adds so many coats he swells prodigiously: 'We know when spring is coming by the reduction in his figure.' A formidable former governess is conjured economically as 'an enemy of day-dreams'.

The Man of Wrath, despite his name, is a figure of fun. When he insists her garden cannot be her duty because it is her pleasure, she remarks: 'What a comfort it is to have such wells of wisdom constantly at my disposal! Anybody can have a husband, but to few is it given to have a sage.'

The book's tone is lighthearted, but there are hints of darker undercurrents. 'Far from innocuous,' is how writer Frank Swinnerton described the book years later. The narrator is horrified at how local women farm workers return to their fields the day they give birth. But the Man of Wrath is devoid of sympathy, telling her they did not suffer because they had never worn corsets. Little wonder the narrator finds herself 'wondering at the vast and impassable distance that separates one's own soul from the soul of the person sitting in the next chair'.

Henning had been cross for days when Mary began her book. The reason, for once, had nothing to do with her. He was engaged in a fight with the managers of the bank where he was chief director. Henning believed the managers were incompetent and cheats. He wanted them sacked.

Although the combative Henning seemingly got his way—crowing in a letter to Henry Beauchamp about how he had scalped his enemies—he made powerful adversaries and was attacked in the newspapers. Henry congratulated his son-in-law on the triumph. He wished Henning had been the director of an Australian bank when Henry had faced financial ruin. Henry was still recovering from financial losses from an Australian banking crisis four years earlier in which the Federal Bank of Australia collapsed.

Despite the arcadian picture of life at Nassenheide that Mary painted in letters to her mother, the reality was otherwise. Conflicts between Mary and Henning had increased after the birth of their third daughter. Henning still wanted a son. 'H & I quarrelled, he wanting a baby & I not seeing it.' They likely kept their differences from Henry when he visited Nassenheide in September. Henry was impressed with the estate's prosperous appearance and how Henning had transformed it. Land that had been underwater when Henning's father bought it had been reclaimed and made usable.

Henning ran cattle and sold about 400 fattened beasts annually. The dairy produced milk and enough butter to send 150 kilograms of it to market each week. Henning's potatoes were converted into alcohol by the estate's distilleries. It was not a bad life for a man in his prime, Henry thought. The estate was largely self-sufficient and stocked with deer, partridges and hares and the family ate sumptuously each day. Henry was a keen gardener and saw how devoted Mary was to her own.

Mary continued to work on her garden-inspired book throughout the year. She was simultaneously penning another work called *The Tea Rose*, about a young couple and a possessive mother. Mary became convinced that her German garden book was the more promising work. She dismissed *The Tea Rose* as crude and locked it away.

Early in 1898, she showed Henning sections of her German garden manuscript. To Mary's dismay, he insisted some parts should be removed: 'greatly upset and couldn't sleep because it will mean rewriting', she confided to her journal. It is possible that what Henning objected to were sections that risked identifying Mary, himself or Nassenheide.

As the wife of a German aristocrat, Mary could not be known publicly as an author nor associated with an enterprise as commercial as writing a book. It was a matter of family honour. Pomeranian countesses did not sully their hands earning money. When she posted her manuscript to London publisher Macmillan on 3 March, she wrote a covering letter: 'It is the first thing I have done, and would have to be, for private reasons, *strictly* anonymous.'

Within a month, she received momentous news. Her manuscript had been accepted for publication. Yet beyond briefly noting 'Got answer re G.G. accepting it', her day's journal was given to more mundane matters—the cloudy weather, bicycling and a visit from her head gardener. There is no hint of her excitement that she would soon be a published author.

Mary's bloodless remark surprised her when, four decades later, she reflected on that day's entry: 'I note I make no comment on this, to me, great news, but I vividly remember my heavenly happiness that day at the family luncheon, hugging my secret. I think this was perhaps the most purely happy moment of my life.'

Her book was titled *Elizabeth and Her German Garden*, but published without the author's name. Mary had suggested the pseudonym of E. Careless. Macmillan disagreed and suggested dropping the nom de plume. She was happy to do so. And so the fiction of 'Elizabeth' was born. For the rest of her literary life, her name never appeared on any of her books. Their covers read: 'By the author of *Elizabeth and Her German Garden*' or later as 'By Elizabeth'.

Her first book, with a simple green cover and gold lettering, was published in England in September 1898 and reviewed widely. 'Great jubilation' was her response when she read her first review in *The Scotsman*. The paper praised her contrasting treatment of English and German character, which she 'managed with the skill of a woman arranging flowers in a bowl for effect'. *The Times* found the book bright and humorous while noting the acidic comments put in the mouth of the Man of Wrath. *The Manchester Guardian* observed that: 'A whimsical personality betrays itself on every page; an absence of convention, a manner of speaking the truth quite simply.'

In her birthplace, *The Sydney Morning Herald* compared the book with Alfred Austin's *The Garden that I love*. 'English people will enjoy the sly quips which she can now and then launch at the national peculiarities [. . .] It is a book of wit and urbane observation, complicated with occasional platitudes.' But one critic disapproved and wanted less chatter and more gardening tips. The public devoured it and within eighteen months it had been reprinted twenty-one times.

Mary refused to have the book translated into German. She acknowledged it mildly satirised the Germans but insisted—disingenuously—the book would be of no interest to the German public. She would have known her portrayal of Germans would have been seen as insulting. Some might have recognised themselves and trace the trail of authorial breadcrumbs back to her.

Speculation soon began about who had written the anonymous book. Was the author English? German? *Punch* speculated: 'She sedulously cultivates the assumption that she herself is of the German race. But no German is gifted with the particular kind of humour that sparkles over these pages.' Others wondered about the author's gender. 'The anonymous author—he is a gentleman, not a lady we feel sure,' *The Derby Mercury* asserted.

Mary was visiting England when the first reviews appeared and where, for a week, she again wrote little in her journal other than 'Happy'. Her father shared her joy. 'May chirrupy on favourable criticisms of her book of which I have recklessly ordered six copies it being to me good, original, refreshing, clever and altogether delightful.'

It is likely one of those six copies soon ended up in New Zealand. On the day Mary's book appeared, her father farewelled his nephew Harold and Harold's wife Annie as they left to sail home from England after a six-month visit. Henry no doubt shared the good news of his daughter's achievement with Harold, and may well have given him one of his copies as a farewell gift. According to family legend, Harold gave the book to his ten-year-old daughter, the future Katherine Mansfield, who read it and afterwards insisted that she too wanted to be a writer.

Back in Germany, Mary summed up the year that saw her debut as a writer. 'Chief thing that happened as far as I'm concerned [is the] appearance of "Elizabeth" with fair success—more, a good deal—than it deserved.'

Mary sat in her writing room upstairs at Nassenheide, where she kept a photograph of her father on her desk. She loved his cheerful, encouraging expression as he looked directly at her. She paused to look at the photograph before she took up her pen.

She was overjoyed that *Elizabeth and Her German Garden* had earned her father's approval. 'What you say & think of *Elizabeth* is more to me than any other criticism, and if the next one gives *you* pleasure then all my torments in writing it will be made up for. For it is poor stuff I fancy, but I hope I may be wrong,' she wrote to him in January 1899.

She had already begun her next book, *The Solitary Summer*, before her first had even been published. It is a sequel, in which the narrator flags her intention in her opening lines: 'I want to be alone for a whole summer, and get to the very dregs of life. I want to be as idle as I can, so that my soul may have time to grow. Nobody shall be invited to stay with me, and if any one calls they will be told that I am out, or away, or sick.'

In reality, Mary's efforts at peace and seclusion herself were not so successful. She had many arguments with Henning, and after one as heated as the August day, she locked herself in her writing room to work on her book. When Henning discovered the door was locked, he broke in and threw a pencil at her. Mary was frozen with fury. The pair did not speak to each other for days. She never forgot his intrusion.

Much of *The Solitary Summer* reflects on the narrator's summer reading and how she seeks out the ideal environments in which to devour her favourite authors. Mornings with Thoreau by a pond, afternoons in the garden with Goethe, Keats for forests and evenings with Boswell in her lamplit library. Walt Whitman, Jane Austen, Emily Brontë, Charles Lamb, Thomas Carlyle—the list flags a narrator with an intellectual and poetic disposition. Although the narrator creates the impression she is German, Goethe aside, her reading is largely devoid of German writers.

The book satirises German authority figures, from parsons to military men—'a lieutenant is a bright and beautiful being who admires no one so much as himself'. She also pokes fun at herself and her fickle generosity. Philanthropy seizes her 'like a cold in the head whenever the weather is chilly. On warm days my bump of benevolence melts away.' Despite her real-life tensions with Henning, she dedicated the book to the Man of Wrath—'with some apologies and much love'—who is depicted with greater affection, but is no less opinionated than in the first book. She finished *The Solitary Summer* in early 1899. As she read it through, she had a crisis of confidence. 'Mixed feelings—chiefly disgust. Futility that cannot be uttered. Am after all a poor fool.'

On the eve of its appearance, Mary opened the English literary journal *The Athenaeum* and recoiled in shock. In its literary gossip section, a small item read: 'The author of *Elizabeth and Her German Garden*, who promises a new volume shortly, is said to be Miss May Beauchamp, now Countess von Arnim.' She wanted the genie back in the bottle and asked Macmillan to issue a denial. The retraction appeared in *The Athenaeum*'s next issue.

Who leaked her identity is not known. But the article referred to her as May, her family nickname, not Mary. Was someone within the family the source? Dismayed at her exposure, Mary wrote to her mother. But Louey had little sympathy for her daughter's plight and wrote back 'disgusted with me for being disgusted at *The Athenaeum's* conduct'.

The Solitary Summer was published in May 1899 without a name on the cover; simply as 'by the Author of *Elizabeth and Her German Garden*'. Why she picked 'Elizabeth' as her literary persona remains a matter of speculation. Her friend, the author Frank Swinnerton, suggested years later that she may have adopted the name of the witty heroine of Jane Austen's *Pride and Prejudice*, Elizabeth Bennett. Others have suggested she may have Anglicised the name of Bettina von Arnim, her literary ancestor by marriage. There may have been a simpler reason—Elizabeth was the name of her mother and grandmother.

The book proved popular and was reprinted seven times within four months. The *Daily Mail* called the book a 'literary event'. The work was reviewed across the English-speaking world, including in America, India and Australia, where her acerbic wit appealed to *The Sydney Morning Herald*: 'Our author has a knack of saying the unkindest things in the kindest way.'

The Athenaeum's item about her identity was ignored or overlooked by other British journals and newspapers. Not one of the many reviews of *The Solitary Summer* referred to it. But some reviewers did question the fiction of the German narrator. *The Times* found the pretence 'a little too thin'.

But in far-off Melbourne, the literary journal *The Book Lover* had some intelligence about the identity of 'Elizabeth': 'I hear the anonymous writer of the delightful garden books "Elizabeth" and "[The] Solitary Summer" [. . .] is an Australian native, educated in Germany and married to a German count.' The popular author was related to Sydney's prominent Lassetter family, the article noted. 'Her books cannot be supplied fast enough [. . .] importers have failed to satisfy the demand.'

Despite the glowing reviews, Mary was dismayed to learn that the critic whose opinion she valued most was not impressed with her second book. 'Got a letter from Pa about [*The Solitary Summer*] from which I gather he does not care for it—spent the day in tears consequently, for I had been so sure that just Pa would like it.' She might have been more consoled had she read his journal at that time. In it, he wrote approvingly that her book, 'should help to open the eyes of many to the beauties God so bountifully scatters abroad for all'.

Her creativity was not all that occupied her. Mary was pregnant again. Yet she makes no reference to another pregnancy, which she had been determined to avoid, in writing. The only reference to her fourth pregnancy is in her semi-autobiography *All the Dogs of My Life* written years later in which she breezily links her conception to the death of her dog Ingraban, who was accidentally shot: 'Ingraban's death had shocked me very much, and my husband, seeing this, began comforting me, and one thing led to another in the way things do, and before I knew where I was I was caught once more in the toils of childbearing.'

And once more, she was determined not to give birth in Germany. Heavily pregnant, she arrived in London in June 1899, where she was joined by Henning. He busied himself buying a herd of swine for his estate and did not stay for the birth. If he had, he probably could not have hidden his disappointment.

Daughter number four, called Felicitas, arrived on 29 July. The baby was 'weighed in balance and found wanting', was Henry's sad comment. Without a male heir, Mary knew the pressure to produce one would continue. On her thirty-third birthday she, 'Wept much without any apparent reason'.

Chapter 5
DOVE AND SERPENT

Shortly after lunch on a warm September day, Henning prepared to spend the afternoon shooting rabbits at Nassenheide. Mary had been home just three days with her new-born daughter when officials arrived at the schloss.

Henning was arrested, taken to Stettin and jailed. He was accused of fraud in connection with the collapse of the Pomeranian bank of which he was a director. Henning, with others, was alleged to have defrauded the failed Pomeranian National Hypothekbank. The charge was serious, but Henning suspected it was driven by revenge. As a director of the bank, he had fallen foul of a government official. It is possible the incident two years earlier—when he moved to sack dishonest and incompetent bank officials—had returned to haunt him.

Whatever lay behind the case, Mary was left with her new baby and three small daughters and the running of a vast estate. For the first but not the last time in her life—when she faced overwhelming troubles—her diary fell silent. She was utterly alone. She had no morale-boosting visits from her father or sister. And no one to accompany her as she visited Henning in jail.

Amid it all, Mary worked on a new book. It may have afforded an escape from the pressures around her—as well as income ahead of an expensive trial. *The April Baby's Book of Tunes* would be Mary's only children's book. It wove tales of her three fictionalised daughters from her two previous books—dubbed the April, May and June babies—with nursery rhymes and music. The book featured colour illustrations by Kate Greenaway, of the little girls in blue dresses, white smocks and cherry red coats with bonnets trimmed with fur. Released just before Christmas 1900, it presented a romanticised Victorian childhood amid a joyful world of sleigh rides, Easter egg hunts and tea parties. The contrast with Mary's life at the time could not be starker. As she faced the most trying period of her married life—confronting financial ruin and social disgrace—her book painted a rosy picture of a happy family.

Henning's trial began in Stettin in January 1900. He was eventually acquitted in July. In its wake, Henning wrote to Henry in a mix of fury at the proceedings and triumph at defeating what he was adamant were trumped-up charges. Henning's alleged crimes ran to hundreds of pages, 'each page containing at least one big crime, and crimes of such select quality that it is rather a pity they have never been committed,' he wrote.

He slammed the prosecutor as an imbecile overseeing a trial that ended with a 'brilliant victory' for the pugnacious Henning, who crowed: 'As I am a fighting cock, I will probably not swallow all the injustice I had to suffer without kicking; you know perhaps Henning is the name of the cock in Germany nursery tales and I can't behave like a hen.'

Mary's response was more sanguine. She took solace in words from the poet Edmund Spenser, whom she cited (a little incorrectly) in a letter to her father as: 'Sleep after toil, porte after stormie seas / Rest after war, death after life doth greatly please.'

She could not get the lines out of her head.

As the storm over Henning's trial abated, speculation about the author of the bestselling 'Elizabeth' books gathered pace in the summer of 1900. *The New York Times* claimed it had confirmed rumours sweeping British high society: the mysterious author was Princess Henry of Pless.

The princess was a British blue blood, born Mary Theresa Olivia Cornwallis-West at Ruthin Castle in Wales in 1873. Known as Daisy, the aristocratic beauty had married Prince Henry of Pless in 1891. He was one of imperial Germany's wealthiest men, with vast estates and a couple of castles in Silesia, now in Poland.

Royal romances were a Cornwallis-West tradition. Daisy's ambitious mother was the mistress of the Prince of Wales, later King Edward VII, and she ensured her three children married well. Daisy's brother George married Lady Randolph Churchill, the mother of Winston Churchill, and her sister Shelagh married the Duke of Westminster, one of Britain's largest landowners.

The New York Times claimed Princess Henry's authorship of the 'Elizabeth' books had been unwittingly revealed in an 'unguarded moment by her husband who, it is said, is wont to make fun of his wife's attempt at amateur gardening on those Baltic estates.' But 'Elizabeth's' publisher remained non-committal, the paper added a week later. It noted that new editions of *Elizabeth and Her German*

Garden and *The Solitary Summer* would be published in October but 'owing to the author's persistent modesty, or for other reasons' these would not carry her name.

The prominent New York literary journal *The Critic* devoted two pages to the identity of 'Elizabeth' in its August issue, publishing what it claimed was a portrait of the author. The full-page photograph on its frontispiece depicted Princess Henry of Pless, dressed in a long embroidered ballgown, fan in her hand and a crown on her head. The journal claimed that among Prince Henry's estates was a 'fine old place in Pomerania' on the Baltic shores that was home to Elizabeth's garden. *The Critic*'s columnist gushed: 'It would be superfluous to say that the Princess Henry is clever. One need only read her books to be convinced of that. They strike a new note in literature, and one that rings strong and true. For a young woman without any special training to master such a delightful literary style is certainly remarkable. Such books as the "German Garden" make life worth living.'

The Critic claimed the publisher Macmillan planned to disclose the authorship in autumn ahead of new illustrated editions. 'If these books are illustrated with *bona fide* views of the "Garden" it will not be very difficult to locate the scene; that once done, the author stands revealed, so *The Critic* is merely a little ahead of time.'

The interest in the identity of 'Elizabeth' was not confined to literary pages or smart literary journals. The issue was reported everywhere from *The Chicago Daily Tribune* and *The Washington Post* to *The Irish Times* and *The Australian Star.* Most simply rehashed *The Critic*'s story and credited it with solving the mystery—overlooking *The New York Times*'s 'scoop' a month earlier.

But some questioned whether the mystery was solved. In London, the literary journal *The Academy* raised an arch and quizzical eyebrow, taking issue with what it saw as *The Critic*'s flimsy evidence.

Merely pointing to the books' merits and Princess Henry's cleverness did not prove her authorship, 'they merely prove that the person who wrote them is clever,' *The Academy* argued.

The New York Times again weighed in. Beneath the headline 'At last! The author of *Elizabeth and Her German Garden*', the paper published a letter from what it claimed was a trustworthy source. The anonymous correspondent, who signed themself Magnolia of Mass, wrote:

> In your own ear, Mr Editor, I will tell you, (or possibly you know and are in the secret) I know her. She is Countess von Arnim, (née Beauchamp, Mary, daughter of Henry Beauchamp, Esq., of England.) She married the son of Count von Arnim, who was persecuted by Bismarck. She lives with her husband and children in a lonely schloss. And all she writes is very much as her life is there.

The correspondent claimed the true identity of 'Elizabeth' was well known to her friends. The fragrant Magnolia of Mass found it ridiculous that the book's publishers kept up the mystery and were likely driven by a belief that sales would benefit if the public believed the author was royal.

The New York Times hedged its bets and added a comment on the letter. It was 'inclined' to believe Magnolia, but took exception to Magnolia's claim that the publisher had perpetuated the mystery. The publisher's silence was demanded by the author. 'Just as they would neither confirm nor deny the Princess Henry of Pless story, so they are now non-committal concerning that of the Countess von Arnim.'

The paper had seen photographs for the new editions of the books, complete with images of the garden; the schloss, including its interior; as well as the April, May and June babies. With the publication of these photos it was unlikely the author could remain incognito 'even though she still persists in keeping her name from the title page, and her publishers continue to remain obdurate'.

The Critic could hardly ignore *The New York Times*'s claims in Magnolia's letter. But if the journal was feeling red-faced at having trumpeted the Princess Henry theory, it wasn't about to show it. Instead, its columnist feigned indifference. 'I care little whether it be the Princess or the Countess who wrote the books. To me the writer is "Elizabeth," and that is quite sufficient.' As argument continued on both sides of the Atlantic about the identity of 'Elizabeth', *The Academy* had a new snippet: Countess von Arnim was an Australian.

The New York Times soon had more from Magnolia on the author's Australian background and family. Her mother was Australian, her father a London man. The family had lived for years in Australia. And it detailed Henry's English relatives. 'I think with these relatives on her father's side, "Elizabeth" may be called an Englishwoman, or perhaps cosmopolitan, as she had an Australian mother.'

The Critic received a message from 'Elizabeth' via her publishers: Princess Henry of Pless was not the author. In a nonsensical piece of logic, the journal claimed 'Elizabeth' had issued the denial as she wanted the delightful fan letters she received to go to her and not to Princess Henry of Pless. And *The Critic*'s columnist doubled-down on his own mistake. 'The fact that I published my misinformation has resulted in unearthing the real "Elizabeth".'

It was not the end of the matter. Far from it.

The popular press on both sides of the Atlantic was soon devoting full pages to the literary mystery. Papers were determined to root out the author's identity in much the same way as in recent times the media worked so hard to uncover the identity of the Italian novelist 'Elena Ferrante'.

'Who really wrote the now famous "Elizabeth and Her German Garden"? The *San Francisco Examiner* wanted to know. It threw a third, even loftier, name into the ring: Princess Henry of Prussia. She was Queen Victoria's German-born granddaughter who had married her first cousin, a son of the late German emperor Frederick III, in 1881. Princess Henry of Prussia outranked Countess von Arnim and Princess Henry of Pless.

The story had little to offer in support of its claim other than that the blue blood was intelligent, thoughtful and often alone on her husband's Baltic estate. Photographs depicted the three women, with the two princesses in tiaras and revealing abundant décolletage. The Countess von Arnim revealed less flesh and was dressed in a high-necked gown, redolent of Hans Christian Andersen's *The Snow Queen*.

It gave potted histories of the three contenders for the authorial crown, including a disdainful depiction of the Countess von Arnim: 'She has not had a train of suitors that are her slaves in public. She has a reputation for eccentricity.' Mary was not amused. But she pasted a copy of the syndicated story into her scrapbook and annotated it as 'yellow' journalism.

In England, the *Daily Mail* elevated the speculation. 'Author Unknown! The Great Literary Mystery of the Year' was the paper's headline a few weeks later. The paper rehashed much of the American story and favoured Princess Henry of Prussia as author. It dismissed Princess Henry of Pless as a contender and noted that the Countess von Arnim's publishers Macmillan had denied she was the author. 'This may be a diplomatic denial [. . .] but it is bound to have weight.'

A cut-price publisher capitalised on the confusion by releasing an edition of *Elizabeth and Her German Garden.* In place of an author's name the Chicago publisher used a large question mark—and a drawing of Princess Henry of Pless it captioned 'the supposed author'.

Princess Henry of Pless wrote in her 1930s memoir that she admired the writings of 'Elizabeth', particularly *Elizabeth and Her German Garden*, and she was flattered that authorship of 'this charming book' had been attributed to her. She had read aloud to her children *The April Baby's Book of Tunes* and wished she had met 'Elizabeth'. Even in her memoir, the princess remained ignorant of the author's nationality, believing her an American married to a German.

Meanwhile, the satirical magazine *Punch* poked fun at the controversy in a poem that offered humorous advice to ambitious authors:

> . . . whatever the temptation to behold your name in print,
> It is vital that the title-page should have no author in't [. . .]
> How can books without a mystery expect to make a fuss?
> People grovel to a novel if it is anonymous.

Henry Beauchamp was overjoyed at how well his daughter looked when she visited England in early 1901. Henry had not seen her for more than a year, since just after her fourth daughter was born and shortly before Henning was arrested. Henry thought Mary looked like a seventeen-year-old, so bright and charming did she appear at the Beauchamps' Bexley home. Henry wrote to Henning to share his delight and to express his gratitude for this dramatic change, which he attributed to Nassenheide and the Man of Wrath, as Henry referred to him.

His daughter was, he acknowledged to Henning, a 'rare and fascinating combination of dove and serpent'. Henry's astute observation may have resonated with Mary. Years later she would draw on the description in one of her most significant books.

In the wake of Henning's woes, the dove in Mary took wing and there was a thaw in their relationship. Mary resumed her journal, but absent was any mention of the arguments that had previously filled its pages. Indeed, Mary was ecstatic when she arrived in Berlin from London and 'dear H' was there to meet her. 'Oh so happy to get back again! Oh, oh, oh!'

She returned to Nassenheide in time for Henning's fiftieth birthday, for which she arranged their little daughters to present him with bouquets, and to sing and recite poetry, before they all walked together on the warm spring day.

Mary was in bed a few days later when she heard cries of alarm. Fire illuminated the night sky. From her bedroom window, she could see flames consuming a nearby building. Initially, she thought the stables were on fire. She and Henning rushed out to discover it was not the stables but a house occupied by staff, including a family with children. Although no one was killed, a woman staff member was injured jumping from a bedroom window to escape the blaze which burned her house to the ground.

The inferno would soon provide material for a pivotal scene in the new book Mary was working on. *The Benefactress* would transform Mary from a fictional diarist into a novelist. It tells of a penniless young Englishwoman, Anna Estcourt, who inherits a property in Pomerania. Her windfall allows her to escape her dependent, stultifying existence living with her relatives. Resolving never to marry, Anna fills her German house with miserable but well-bred women who have fallen on hard times. Determined to restore their happiness, Anna is instead preyed upon by them. Along the way, she rejects romantic overtures from her wealthy German neighbour who is jailed on trumped-up charges following a fire on his property. She visits him in prison, realises she is in love with him and hauls down her 'flag of independent womanhood'.

The novel is a satire in which the folly of well-meaning compassion without wisdom intertwines with social snobbery and questions of female independence. The latter issue would become central to her writing as she repeatedly challenged women's position in society as well as marriage and domesticity as a woman's life goal. The novel hints too at a theme fleshed out in later novels, German anti-Semitism.

The darkest element in the otherwise frothy tone of the book is the imprisonment of the landowner Axel von Lohm, repeatedly pacing in a gloomy, five-by-three yard cell with its heavy locked door. Mary had the horror of Henning's recent imprisonment and her visits to him to draw on. Just as Henning directed his invective at the prosecutor in his case, so Mary portrays the book's prosecutor as driven by zeal and ambition.

But her evolution into a novelist would not be easy. Mary had little confidence about her ability to do so, as she grappled with plot, character development, pacing and a shift from the first to the third person. At times, her efforts depressed her.

'[I] saw its weaknesses depressingly clearly. It is so ill-balanced—the first part so leisurely and the end so rapid—alack, alack, I am done for I fear. But I won't take it seriously, and must set to and try to do better next time,' she wrote in her journal when copies of *The Benefactress* arrived in early October. She feared the book 'will fall very flat because it is bad'.

The first reviews cheered her. *The Spectator*, which made *The Benefactress* its book of the week, found it 'agreeably malicious' with her insights into the '"mean streets" of the human, and especially the feminine, heart'. One reviewer likened her to Jane Austen, a writer with whom she would often be compared, while another declared her 'the unknown genius'.

But *The Athenaeum* slammed the book. Its plot was indifferent and its characters lacked depth. Mary was stung by its verdict, even as she thought it just. 'And however one may protest one is always really conceited down at one's dregs, so the better part of me is gloomily rejoiced at seeing the viler part of me curling up.'

The critic whose view she most valued approved. Her father thought the book would 'more than support her previous reputation'. She was irritated that the book's darker undercurrents were overlooked by reviewers, who focused on its light tone. Mary confided to her father: 'I keep getting reviews that talk about froth and trifles [. . .] If ever I write a second novel, which won't be ever, it shall be steeped to the top of its pages in blood. I might kill H. in it and give a detailed account of how he looked disembowelled and call it "The Murder of the Man of Wrath"'.

The release of *The Benefactress* prompted renewed speculation over her identity, with a fourth name raised. This time it was not another glamorous European aristocrat with no writing credentials, but a published author with a literary pedigree: Anne Thackeray Ritchie, whose works included *The Story of Elizabeth*, published in 1863. She was the novelist daughter of William Makepeace Thackeray, author of *Vanity Fair*. A letter writer to *The New York Times* saw a similarity in style and atmosphere and noted that Thackeray Ritchie's first heroine was called Elizabeth.

Mary stepped off the ferry from the mainland and into her horse-drawn carriage. With the sapphire sea on her right, she rode amid cornfields and beech woods under a dappled summer sky to a coastal village on the island of Rügen. The Baltic island off the Pomeranian coast had long drawn artists to its shores. Its white chalk cliffs had inspired Brahms' craggy first symphony and Caspar David Friedrich's paintings, while Thomas Mann, Albert Einstein and later Christopher Isherwood enjoyed its breathtaking beauty.

Mary planned a new book based on a journey around the island. She wanted to return to the diary form that had served her well. And she wanted again to conjure her best-known figure. In the summer of 1901, Mary spent two weeks gathering material for a book that is part-diary, part-travelogue. The narrator of *The Adventures of Elizabeth in Rügen* tells how she has been inspired to make the journey by a book by Marianne North.

North was an intrepid English adventurer, botanical artist and writer who travelled the world including, at Charles Darwin's suggestion, to Australia in 1880 where she painted extensively. As a young woman, North had travelled to Rügen. Mary—like her fictional alter ego—had a copy of North's popular memoir *Recollections of a Happy Life* in her Nassenheide library and saw in the solitary, independent-minded North a kindred spirit. North eschewed marriage, motherhood and domesticity, commenting: 'I prefer vegetables.'

After Mary's return from Rügen, blissfully alone after her house guests and Henning had departed, she re-read North. She saw in North a happy soul, content in her solitude and indifferent to the opinions of those who might consider her selfish.

In her own book, Mary incorporated some incidents from her journey around Rügen. Her narrator is again a witty and candid companion who announces that 'there is nothing so absolutely bracing for the soul as the frequent turning of one's back on duties'. A woman fleeing domestic constraints would become central to Mary's writing and her life.

The book includes a subplot in which the narrator encounters a long-lost cousin, Charlotte. Oxford-educated Charlotte has abandoned her elderly German professor husband, become 'emancipated' and gives lectures on women's rights. The narrator, who attempts to reconcile the couple, is 'thunderstruck' when she learns her cousin has applied for a separation.

The demise of the fictional Charlotte's marriage coincided with the unravelling of the marriage of Mary's older sister to George Waterlow. Charlotte moved from her marital home Uplands to a rented house in London, 'her troubles going with her,' observed Henry Beauchamp.

Mary struggled to focus on her new book. She wrote it fitfully, usually in the evenings. 'Can't get on with my Rügen book—feel a complete failure,' she wrote in her journal. Mary's moods shifted with the weather, such as on one sparkling, crisp, December day: 'What a lovely world to be alive in—and yet, in sober moments, that is on wet, windy days, my calm opinion made in cold blood is that life on the whole is more like a bad joke at one's expense.'

She was working on her book in the spring of 1902 when she was filled with anxiety. 'Suddenly dawned on me that I hadn't had my "season" last week. Full of foreboding of a horrible kind,' she wrote. She attempted to induce her period using a common, if unproven, method. 'Took hot footbath but resultless.' Over the next fortnight, blizzards, gales and storms matched her wretched mood. Amid her deepening despair, her journal fell silent.

Chapter 6
TORMENTING THE TUTORS

'The author of *Elizabeth and Her German Garden* and *The Solitary Summer* has revealed so much of herself in those books that it may not be indiscreet to lift another corner of the veil.' So began an article in the London literary journal *The Pall Mall Magazine* in September of 1902.

The veil the journal lifted was that the author—whose identity was still a matter of speculation—was indeed the Countess von Arnim. It detailed how the former Miss Beauchamp met in Rome the older Count von Arnim. 'Between them was a certain difference of age, at which love laughs. They were married, and the German took his English wife to live in Berlin in one of those stately but sombre palaces, and amid a stately but sombre society, which she did not like. Her heart was in the country, with the flowers and blue skies and fine forests.' Her move to his Baltic estate prompted her first book.

The article was not without inaccuracies—it claimed Henning knew nothing of her first book—but from then on, the questions of her identity subsided. The piece carried no by-line, but an editor's note said it was from the pen of a well-known American writer who preferred to remain anonymous. The writer was possibly Poultney Bigelow. The American journalist, who was a friend of Kaiser Wilhelm II, had spent a summer on the Baltic with Mary and Henning some years earlier. The article concluded with the news that the couple planned to visit America early the next year: 'There can be no doubt of the welcome that awaits them.'

Her unveiling and the possibility of an American visit aroused great excitement across the Atlantic, where dozens of papers, including the *Chicago Tribune*, weighed in. 'Elizabeth now known' the paper announced. 'This is mysterious author of "Elizabeth"', ran the headline above a pen-and-ink drawing of her, based on the Snow Queen-like photograph. Her identity might have been revealed, but a contemporary image of her was nowhere to be seen.

At the time the anonymous *Pall Mall* article appeared, Mary had other matters on her mind. She was certainly not about to embark on an American trip. She was eight months pregnant.

A fifth pregnancy took the wind out of her sails. She arrived in England to give birth amid much secrecy. Only her brother Sydney, who was to deliver the child, knew, and she had sworn him to silence. She gave birth on 27 October. A boy. Henning, at last, had his son and heir. The infant was called Henning Berndt, but known to all simply as H.B.

Mary's parents were kept in the dark. They were astonished when Mary arrived at their Bexley home six weeks after the birth. It was not the first time she had come to England without telling her parents, but it was the first time she had produced a baby without their knowledge. Nonetheless, they were delighted. 'Great joy but May, herself, imperturbable, calm and childish as ever. Much flutter amongst our feminines,' Henry wrote.

Henning was overjoyed, he wrote to Henry: 'I am very glad it was at last a son; I think if it was again a female, as we both feared and Dollie firmly expected, the poor being would have been concealed for a long time.' Mary returned to Nassenheide with her son just before Christmas. She placed him under the Christmas tree to present him to his excited sisters. Otherwise, she showed only tepid interest in the newborn.

With five children under the age of twelve, Mary was again smothered in babies. And again she arranged for one of her daughters to stay with her parents. Her youngest daughter Felicitas was about to turn four when she arrived at Henry and Louey's home, in 1903. They adored the curly-haired child, who soon charmed another Beauchamp relative.

New Zealand-born Kathleen Beauchamp had been an occasional visitor to the Beauchamps' Bexley home after she arrived in England with her family in 1903. She spent a couple of Christmases with Louey and Henry, whom she called Granny and Deepa. Henry called her 'the gifted Kathleen'. She had yet to assume the name by which she is known today.

Fifteen-year-old Kathleen was captivated by little Felicitas, who accompanied them to church at Easter in her white embroidered frock, red shoes and straw hat wreathed with daisies. As the hymn 'All Things Bright and Beautiful' began, Kathleen helped the little girl stand on the pew. Felicitas, a musical child, held up her basket of coloured eggs as she joined in. 'Above them all I heard the German baby—exultant—joyful—her cheeks all rosy. [Louey] & I both *cried*—to the Baby's horror and astonishment.' So smitten was Kathleen with 'the blessed German baby' that the fledgling writer penned two stories about her.

When visiting the Beauchamps, Kathleen no doubt heard about her successful writer cousin in Germany. She may have been aware of Mary's latest book, *The Adventures of Elizabeth in Rügen*. Kathleen wrote a short story, which appeared in her school magazine in March 1904, called '*Die Einsame*' ('The Lonely One'). The name was a place on Rügen Island that Mary had referred to in her book.

The Adventures of Elizabeth in Rügen marked the last appearance of the character of Elizabeth. Some critics were perplexed as to whether the book was a travel guide, a novel or a hybrid. *The Spectator* likened the book to a series of watercolours: 'sketches so original, delicate, and beautiful [. . .] as to give their author a high place among the word-painters of today.' But she had the spirit of a landscape poet, rather than of a novelist, *The Spectator* added. *The Times Literary Supplement* found the book delightful. 'A star danced when she was born and gifted her with a spirit of natural gaiety [. . .] This lady travels—as she stays home—with complete originality.'

Mary was delighted when chatty, cheerful Felicitas returned home after sixteen months in England. The girl's sisters fussed over her and she made even her solemn infant brother H.B. smile. But when Mary asked her if she loved her little brother, Felicitas replied: 'I simply hate him.'

For Christmas, Mary gave Henning a copy of H.G. Wells' *The Food of the Gods and How it Came to Earth*. The book was a cautionary sci-fi tale about scientists tampering with nature and inventing a food that produced giants. It was an appropriate—perhaps tongue-in-cheek—gift for Henning, who was then experimenting with potatoes and farm produce. Mary had yet to meet Wells, who would soon loom large in her life. She inscribed her gift to 'Henning from Dolly'. (She varied spellings of names and nicknames.)

Advertisements in the back of the book promoted works by Winston Churchill, Edith Wharton and Rudyard Kipling. A page was devoted to an advert for two of her books, *The Benefactress* and *The Adventures of Elizabeth in Rügen*. Such was her stature and popularity that she took her place alongside some of the era's most prominent authors.

The young man alighted from the train in the dark. He stepped into the middle of a farmyard filled with mounds of manure. There was no dedicated station, no platform, no porter to help with his luggage and no one to meet him. It was 10 p.m. and he had no idea how to get to his final destination.

He abandoned his heavy trunk amid the dung until the following day. A helpful train guard found a farm labourer to guide him part of the way to Nassenheide. There was no footpath marked as he tramped on, the squelch of mud and manure under his feet and the odour of pigs, horses and cows in his nose. Eventually, he reached a potholed carriageway and trudged his way towards the schloss, which was in darkness apart from a solitary light in an upper window.

He rang the bell, a hound bayed and a dishevelled young servant appeared. The young man was ushered into a white-washed hall hung with the trophied heads of animals. At the end of the hall, he noticed an inscription he recorded as: *Idiota, insulsus, turpis, tristis abesto* 'or something of that sort'. (Begone the fool, the insipid, the sad, the foul.) This was likely a reference to Ben Jonson's motto that once adorned the Apollo Club, the London literary dining salon over which he presided.

Edward Morgan Forster certainly felt foul as he stood in the hall with his boots oozing. The new tutor had not been expected until the following day. His bedroom was not ready—the tutor he was to replace was still asleep in it—so he was assigned to a 'nobler' part of the house. He froze throughout the night in the best spare room. The man who would go on to write *A Room with a View*, *Howards End* and *A Passage to India* never forgot his baleful arrival at Nassenheide on 4 April 1905.

E.M. Forster came on the recommendation of Mary's nephew, Sydney Waterlow—Charlotte's son. The two men had become friends while studying together at Cambridge. Forster may have learned from Sydney that his relative in Pomerania was the celebrated writer. But also, Mary's identity was no longer in question: she had entered *Who's Who*. Her listing, as Countess von Arnhim [sic], noted her Sydney birthplace, Beauchamp maiden name and book titles, and first appeared in 1905.

Forster doubted he was right for the position at Nassenheide. He met none of Mary's requirements and had written to tell her so. He couldn't teach mathematics or indeed anything except English and a little Italian, he could not come permanently, nor could he give the position all his time. The more red flags he raised, the more insistent Mary became.

A weary Forster stood before Mary the next day. She was small and vivacious, but her drawling voice grated on him. He soon found her a 'capricious and a merciless tease'. Forster sensed, as Mary spoke to him, that the circumstances of his arrival had lowered his stocks and that he had lost all the ground gained by playing hard to get.

'How d'ye do Mr Forster. We confused you with the new housemaid . . . Can you teach the children do you think? They are very difficult . . . oh yes Mr Forster very difficult, they'll laugh at you, you know. You'll have to be stern or it'll end as it did with [a previous tutor].'

Forster was the latest in a series of tutors to arrive at Nassenheide to help educate the three oldest girls. None had lasted more than a few months. Among those who had beat a hasty retreat were a mild-mannered local schoolmaster, a tyrannical German governess and two ineffectual English ladies, one of whom lasted just two days.

Mary was adept at playing manipulative games with the tutors. She later told Forster she nearly dismissed him the first morning because he had worn an ugly tie. Forster took that with a pinch of salt. He was a match for her games. On one occasion he told her he had met some acquaintances of hers. 'They don't like me,' she told Forster. 'So I saw,' he replied. His quick retort startled her.

Forster was to tutor Evi, fourteen; Liebet, twelve; and Trix, eleven—the April, May and June babies. His employment was hardly onerous; he taught them English composition and Greek history for just an hour a day. He became part of the household staff he called the 'quartette of menials'. They included a new German governess and housekeeper Teppi Backe, whose 'dumb devotion bound her to the Countess'. Teppi would become a lifelong friend to Mary.

The other staff were an elderly French governess with a nutcracker face, grey locks, round shoulders and a childlike soul, and a German tutor Herr Steinweg whose cordial temper and autocratic inclinations made him the natural leader of the menials.

Forster soon picked up some gossip. A quarrel was underway between Mary and an unnamed London acquaintance who believed she had been unfavourably depicted in *Elizabeth and Her German Garden* as a tiresome and demanding houseguest. Mary had insisted she would never do any such thing. But Forster well understood how writers mined those around them for material: 'if she is meditating to turn me into copy, she has every opportunity.'

Forster found little to resemble the abundant German garden of the first two Elizabeth books. The house appeared to be surrounded by paddocks and shrubberies. Although some roses and pansies bloomed as summer arrived, mostly the flowers consisted of lupins, which Henning used for agricultural purposes. The garden merged into sylvan wooded copses.

Forster and the other staff joined the family for lunch and dinner, the latter a formal affair at which evening dress was mandatory. At the sound of a gong, the diners assembled in a drawing room. From there, they were led in silence by Mary and Henning as they filed through the hall, watched by the antlered heads, across to the dining room, where they were waited on by a white-gloved butler and footman dressed in red and black livery with silver buttons.

As Mary and Henning sat at opposite ends of the oak dining table, the stiff formality continued over the meal. The teaching staff were not expected to initiate conversation. At times, Mary could be as silent and brittle as the painted porcelain plates that lined the walls. As the meal ended, Henning would suck up water from his finger bowl and then spit it out. When coffee was served to the count and countess, the teaching staff were not offered any.

Living at Nassenheide was not all rigid decorum and silence. Forster joined in on the musical nights, occasionally dancing the highland fling with Mary, doing the cake walk and playing musical chairs. Teppi had a theatrical streak and would sing when allowed—which wasn't often because she sang out of tune—and would dramatise the tenser moments of Strauss's *Salome*. Forster read Jane Austen's *Emma* and *Northanger Abbey* aloud to Mary. He warmed somewhat to Mary and she to him. Mary suggested that they collaborate on a writing project. He did not relish the idea and was relieved when it fell through.

Henning seemed less impressed with the cultured young Englishman than was Mary. 'The Man of Wrath listens to us with an amused smile as long as we talk literature, but when we come to publishers & prices he objects and says "I never talk of my potatoes, though they are ten times as interesting & valuable",' Forster wrote to his mother.

Henning's voluble complaints about food could reduce Teppi to tears. In other matters he was more accommodating, turning a blind eye to young lovers who entered Nassenheide's grounds by night.

The children shared Mary's inclination to tease, once offering Forster what they insisted was a piece of bread, but he could see was a cake of soap. He took a bite and could see the marks of previous tutors' teeth. All the tutors fell for the jest, the girls told him gleefully. They shared too their mother's haughtiness. Forster found them at times, 'a little unwilling to be mixed with the lower herd'.

Aside from tutoring, Forster played tennis and went on walks and picnics, including a mountain trek to the Oder Berge with the three girls and teaching staff in late May. When Forster later wrote his celebrated novel *Howards End*, he drew on the Oder Berge and the Pomeranian landscape.

Forster was working on his first novel, *Where Angels Fear to Tread*, about an impulsive English widow who travels to Italy and marries a feckless younger local man. When the proofs arrived, Mary read some of them. He awaited the verdict of the bestselling novelist. She kept changing her mind as she read through. The first three chapters she thought clever but they left her wanting a bath. She found chapter four beautiful, but by chapter six, she had reverted to her initial opinion. Little wonder Forster found his confidence susceptible to her shifting opinion. 'I hope that I shall never again be depressed when she thinks me rot—and more difficult—elated when she praises me.'

Rising Anglo–German tensions formed the political backdrop to Forster's time at Nassenheide. These were sufficiently fraught that Forster set an essay question for the children, asking them: 'If there was a war between England and Germany, which would you want to win?' Trix's response was to declare she wouldn't care which side won, she would run away. He found the children intelligent, easy to manage and 'their feeble attempts at naughtiness were crushed without trouble.'

Forster proved well-liked by the children even if, unlike his predecessor, he did not climb trees. When he left Nassenheide in August, Evi and Liebet wrote him poems as a parting gift, while Trix gave him gooseberries. He toured Rügen before he departed Germany, following much of the route of Mary's book. Forster never forgot his time at Nassenheide, recalling it in a BBC radio broadcast in 1958.

Mary turned a summerhouse on the estate into a writing retreat. Her *Treibhaus*, as she called it, was away from the main house and filled with flowers. Above the door, and inscribed in Latin, was a forbidding motto: *Procul este profani.* The words, from Virgil's *Aeneid*, roughly translate as 'keep back, unhallowed ones.'

It was an effective deterrent. Her children were rarely admitted and even Forster entered only once, where she demonstrated for him her typewriter. She had not written for a couple of years, as her five children and their education had absorbed much of her time. But by the spring of 1905, Mary was working on a new book.

The Princess Priscilla's Fortnight tells of a rebellious young German princess who runs away from the suffocating ceremony and etiquette of her father's court. Having spent her first twenty-one years at the top of the social ladder, she wants to spend the next twenty-one at the bottom.

She escapes to rural England where her lack of experience outside of a palace's cosseted confines provides much of the book's farce. A simple peaceful village life eludes her as she unwittingly antagonises most of its inhabitants before a royal suitor arrives and whisks her off to his kingdom. There is a fairytale quality to the story. Yet despite its themes of escape, class and love, it feels a slight work. Nonetheless, it was well-received, with *The Spectator* finding in Priscilla one of fiction's most engaging characters. *The Academy* grudgingly praised it despite its 'ragged plot and occasional heaviness of phrase'. The book 'enchanted us against our reason'.

Henning waved as the carriage took Mary out through the iron gates of Nassenheide. She left behind her silk gowns and pearls. Her bags contained clothes so rough her maid had been shocked when asked to pack garments she considered suitable only for a 'market woman'. Mary was going 'undercover'.

She had secured work with a professor's family at the university town of Jena. Posing as a Miss Armstrong, she told the professor she was an English woman employed as a nanny at Nassenheide. She wanted to use her forthcoming spring holidays learning German from the professor in exchange for assisting his wife around the house.

Mary was hardly any better equipped at the practicalities of housework than her fictional Princess Priscilla. But in the spring of 1906, she spent her days brushing clothes, mending underwear and socks and her nights in a tiny unheated attic room through which the March winds blew. But when the professor's besotted son claimed to have fallen in love with Mary and proposed marriage, she contacted Henning for help. She arranged for him to send a telegram: 'Children sick—return immediately.'

Her research trip was abandoned, but she drew on her experience of life in a professor's house in her next book *Fräulein Schmidt and Mr Anstruther*. It is written as a series of letters from Rose-Marie Schmidt, the unmarried daughter of a German professor, to Roger Anstruther, an upper-class young Englishman. Roger has spent a year boarding with the Schmidts in Jena and, the day before he leaves, he professes love for Rose-Marie, and proposes, but later jilts her. Through her candid, perceptive letters to Roger back in England, Rose-Marie emerges as intelligent, literate and witty. She is a woman neither confined by her humdrum, provincial town nor crushed by an unravelling romance. For the first time, Mary had created a central female character who was neither privileged nor rich. It was also the first time she used the epistolary form.

The book caught the unflinching eye of Virginia Woolf. Not yet a novelist or the intellectual centre of the Bloomsbury set, 25-year-old Woolf was reviewing literature, including for *The Times Literary Supplement*. Woolf believed the book lacked form, was sometimes shallow and slipshod. But the writing was so fresh and happy that Woolf thought asking the author to pay closer attention to these aspects was like asking a thrush to 'whistle a Bach fugue'. Woolf acknowledged the book would be popular and that criticism was beside the point. Indeed, it was. In Australia, *The Sydney Morning Herald* judged the work of such broad appeal that it serialised it daily for nearly two months.

Mary's father wrote approvingly: 'It is decidedly clever [. . .] I greatly admire the way in which the heroine abruptly pays the poor weak thing off in his own coin.' Henry's once-firm confident handwriting was now spidery and shaky, but he signed off with his customary enthusiasm: 'Keep bubbling—Keep bubbling.'

He did not refer to his failing health. But in a letter to a New Zealand relative, he confessed 'I am—alas!—crawling on towards cremation—all my imagination gone together with most of my bodily powers. You must make haste home if you wish to see me in the flesh and not in ashes.' He included a postcard. It was of London's Golder's Green Crematorium.

Hugh Walpole was twenty-two and an aspiring author when he read *Fräulein Schmidt and Mr Anstruther.* He wrote its famous author a fan letter. Mary was intrigued and wrote back to the recent Cambridge graduate. 'Dear Youth,' she began. 'Your letter interested me to the extent of goading me into writing to you.'

Goading her letter certainly was, for what followed was a mix of rebuke and invitation. 'It was nice of you to call me "Miss" Elizabeth. Have you then never heard of the Man of Wrath? I leave for London tomorrow. Would you like to come and see me at my club? I'm looking for a young man to come to us at Easter and talk English to the children [. . .] perhaps you know of somebody. I prefer Cambridge to Oxford, unless it's a Balliol man, and of Cambridge Colleges someone from King's or Trinity. If you want to pour out woes to a person who thinks rather like Rose-Marie [Fräulein Schmidt] on the subject of young men's sorrows write me a line [. . .] Your obliged, amused, and interested "Elizabeth".

The young man who entered Piccadilly's Lyceum Club in March 1907 had indeed experienced his share of woes. The New Zealand-born son of a clergyman had been set to follow in his father's footsteps. When he arrived for his meeting with Mary, he had just spent six unhappy months in Liverpool as a lay missionary at the Mersey Mission to Seamen. Ministering to Merseyside's salty sea dogs was a role for which the sensitive, bookish Walpole was unsuited and one he would later describe as among the greatest failures of his life.

Nonetheless, the experience proved a turning point. A few weeks before he took tea with Mary, he stood by the grimy River Mersey on a winter morning and decided not to enter the church. He resolved instead to become a novelist. The scale of his ambition expressed in his fan letter surprised Mary, who wrote: 'what makes you think you are going to produce a masterpiece. There's no earthly reason why you shouldn't, but it's unusual to be so sure.'

Walpole was at a crossroads when he sat before Mary, who struck him as small, pretty, outspoken and sharp. She asked him to come to Germany to teach her children. It must have seemed a cushy role—educating the pampered daughters of a countess and acclaimed writer at her Pomeranian schloss. Goodbye, Merseyside; hello, Nassenheide.

Walpole arrived in early April, two years after Forster. Like his predecessor, Walpole was soon the object of Mary's teasing, or 'ragging', as he called it. Walpole was mortified when, over the dinner table and surrounded by other guests, she loudly announced: 'Oh, Mr Walpole, I've had such an interesting letter from your father. Do you wear flannel next to your skin?' Every meal was a campaign at which he felt on the defensive.

Mary had three moods, Walpole wrote to a friend: '(1) Charming, like her books only more so (this does not appear often). (2) Ragging.

Now she is unmerciful—attacks you on every side, goes at you until you are reduced to idiocy, and then drops you, limp. (3) Silence. This is the most terrible of all. She sits absolutely mute and if one tries to speak one gets snubbed [. . .] she is not an easy person to live with, but I'm sure there's a key somewhere which I hope to find.'

Mary learned that Walpole kept a diary and asked to see it. She did not expect him to hand it over and was astonished when he did. 'There in it are all his criticisms of each of us—some pleasant and some anything but. I laughed till I cried it was so funny,' Mary wrote to her eldest daughter Evi, then in England.

Mary did more than laugh. She returned his diary annotated with acidic comments. Walpole was dismayed to find himself so cruelly taunted by a woman who regarded him as a crude, ignorant country boy. Years later he recalled: 'I was so miserable, so homesick and so stupid that I used to snivel in the cold dark passages of the Schloss and ache for home.'

Despite this unpromising start, Mary and Walpole would develop an enduring friendship. Walpole became a prolific novelist, best known for his Herries Chronicle series, and dedicated his book *The Golden Scarecrow* to her.

After three months at Nassenheide, Walpole was relieved when he was asked to leave. 'He grows weirder visibly and is the most weird we have yet struck,' was Mary's verdict on Walpole.

Amid tormenting her children's latest tutor, Mary contacted an earlier one. E.M. Forster's semi-autobiographical novel *The Longest Journey* had just been released. It was her turn to write a fan letter. 'I can't tell you how truly beautiful I think it, & if I could it would only make you shrug your shoulders, for what does it matter what the foolish & the illiterate think?'

But the dove could swiftly transform into a serpent. She lashed out at Forster a few months later after he had recommended a friend's school for her daughters. 'I do not know why people think I want to send my innocents to their schools. Lately I have been deluged with letters about it [. . .] From the frost bound calm of Nassenheide you all look like a seething mass of wriggling & struggling & aspiring brains.'

It may well have been such a rebuke he had in mind when he wrote in later years of the power she exerted over him and of her lack of gratitude: 'It does seem odd that one should be so anxious to please such a person, for she isn't distinguished and she's always ungrateful. Yet one *is* anxious, and she will have menials, unpaid and paid, to wait upon her until she dies. To want to be loved does pay.' Forster never warmed to Mary, telling Virginia Woolf in the 1930s: 'No; I don't like her. I think she is unkind and selfish. But she has a wonderful way of making one wish to be nice to her.' He acknowledged, long after her death, that although he appreciated her as a novelist, they were 'almost never' in sympathy.

Forster and Walpole were followed by another Cambridge graduate willing to teach her children. Charles Erskine Stuart was a classics scholar, who helped Mary with her study of Greek and Latin literature. She no doubt teased him as she had his predecessors. With long gaunt features, he resembled a portrait of King Charles I. While the ill-fated English monarch lost his head on the block, Charles the tutor lost his to Mary.

She may have been flattered by his puppy-like devotion. She certainly enjoyed his intellectual company. She was starved of such stimulation in Pomerania. The sequence of smart overqualified young tutors helped fill that void.

Mary was wearying of life at Nassenheide. The simplicity, solitude and wild unbounded freedom that had enchanted her after her stultifying early married years in Berlin had been eroded. The steady drip of increasing responsibilities weighed her down. As the children grew, so too did the size of the household to cater to them. Their tutors in turn needed additional staff to care for their needs. The once-quiet house bustled with activity as servants delivered breakfasts, fed stoves and polished shoes. The twice-daily ritual of stiff, solemn meals—enlivened only by the opportunity to torment the tutors—she found particularly tedious. She made frequent trips alone to England. And she fled the gilded but crushing formality of Nassenheide on trips to Italy and Switzerland with Teppi. Mary's desire for escape—integral to *The Adventures of Elizabeth in Rügen* and *The Princess Priscilla's Fortnight*—continued to grow.

Chapter 7

THE GYPSY QUEEN

Two caravans and a pair of sturdy cart horses were waiting in a damp corner of the Surrey countryside when Mary arrived with her three daughters and Teppi in the summer of 1907.

Horse-drawn caravanning holidays were in vogue with the well-heeled who fancied a taste of bohemian life. Although hardly a bohemian, Mary had several reasons for embarking on a month-long caper through England's home counties. She planned to combine a summer holiday with her girls with gathering material for a new book. Even before Kenneth Grahame's Toad took to the open road in *Wind in the Willows*, she saw the potential for a tale about a horse-drawn caravan trip.

Already assembled on the August day were Mary's niece Margery Waterlow—Charlotte's daughter—with her pony cart, several former tutors from Nassenheide, including the doting Charles Stuart and a later tutor known only as Mr Gaunt, as well as the cart horses' elderly attendant, George, and Gaunt's two dogs.

The trip had barely got underway when Mary took off. She hired a motor car and drove south towards the Kent coast. She pulled up before a large house with a commanding view of the sea. Herbert George Wells had invited her to visit. The man who greeted her was already the successful author of *The Time Machine*, *The Island of Dr Moreau* and *The War of the Worlds*, works that had propelled him out of financial struggle. Spade House, his substantial Arts and Crafts home, was a trophy of his success.

Mary had met Wells at the Lyceum Club a few months earlier. The two authors spoke briefly and she had invited him to lunch, an offer he declined. Fearing she might have taken offence at his rejection, he wrote to invite her to visit. 'I should very *much* like that,' Mary replied. 'I'm caravanning with my three children in Kent & Sussex in August, so if one morning an eager & dusty person appears & you think it's a tramp, you'll know it isn't & let me in.'

Wells was forty, the same age as Mary. But, unlike Mary, Wells had not been born into wealth. His father was a shopkeeper and gardener and Wells had been a draper's apprentice before winning a scholarship, studying biology and becoming a schoolteacher. A socialist, he never forgot his humble roots.

With piercing blue eyes, an abundant moustache and an amused, quizzical expression—the 'Don Juan of the Intelligentsia', as he later called himself—had already had an unusual romantic life. He had married his cousin Isabel Mary in 1891. They parted three years later when he fell in love with one of his students, whom he then married in 1895. He and Jane Wells had two young sons by the time Mary arrived at Spade House. Jane, a keen gardener, admired Mary's books and the two women liked each other.

But it was Wells who commanded Mary's attention. They had much in common. Although known as a science fiction writer, Wells was also an accomplished satirist, including his 1895 novel *The Wonderful Visit*, a copy of which Mary possessed, which ridiculed Victorian England. Mary's visit was brief, but she was taken with the free-thinking Wells.

Mary rejoined her group, where at night the women slept in the vans, the men in tents. The unlikely band of gypsies walked beside the vans during the day. Only occasionally was a footsore traveller allowed to ride inside. But what Mary envisaged as a romantic itinerant summer in sparkling sunshine proved to be a mirage. The August weather was foul, unusually cold and wet, and their progress was slow. By day ten, they had travelled just forty kilometres in almost unceasing rain.

E.M. Forster joined the group around this time. Margery collected him in her pony cart and they bumped their way along country lanes in search of the main party. Eventually, they located the damp group camped in Great Chart, Kent, where Gaunt was cooking a stew.

Weather aside, Forster had other reservations about joining the trip. He was concerned he would not fit in. He was not used to the company of young people or experienced at erecting tents. He may have been wary of Mary after her acidic letter a few months earlier, but she was welcoming. On the first night, Gaunt made up a bed for the new arrival in a farm shed. Forster slept soundly using a pile of straw baskets for a pillow.

As the convoy rolled on, Forster and Gaunt pushed one of the caravans as the regal Mary tossed them biscuits and fruit. Despite the bohemian adventure, she was not one to pitch in. As camp was made and tents erected one sodden evening, she sat reading Jane Austen.

Their route took them near Swinford Manor in Kent, the home of the poet laureate Alfred Austin, whose book *The Garden That I Love* had so impressed Mary and helped inspire her first book.

Mary decided to visit him. Austin had little idea who she was when she and Forster arrived unannounced.

Mary must have put a rosy glow on the trip in an account to her family. Her father Henry noted in his journal that she had so enjoyed 'percolating' around the countryside that she had resolved 'never to live in a house again'.

Her dream of a few simple, wandering weeks—so appealing within Nassenheide's sturdy walls—had turned to mud. The trip was abandoned at the village of Aylesford before the lease of the caravans was up. Perhaps relieved that the cold, wet, uncomfortable ordeal was at an end, Mary kicked up her heels and danced the highland fling with the local parson in his cassock.

Henning arrived in England to meet Mary at the end of her trip. Henning had little to celebrate. The wet summer had not just dampened Mary's caravan trip. In Germany, the foul weather had ruined his crops and put a strain on the estate's finances.

They visited Mary's parents in Bexley in mid-September. Henry's health was poor and he had suffered heart problems. The pain from his 'Angelina', as he called his angina, was unbearable at times. Although his physical health was failing, he was mentally sharp and engaged.

Henry's thoughts turned often to Australia and he noted in his diary the anniversary of his arrival in Sydney in 1850 'to seek my fortune—which I found there—thank God!' He continued to get news from Australia. His son Walter had just speculated on twenty thousand acres of land in rural New South Wales, which he planned to subdivide and sell. The news unnerved Henry. He considered the investment risky, but prayed his son's gamble would prove profitable.

Henry learned of the purchase from Frederic Lassetter, who had returned to Sydney. Frederic occupied Redleaf, one of the city's most splendid harbourside residences. The two-storey Italianate mansion is now Woollahra Council Chambers. On his large waterfront property, he built St Brigid's, now Woollahra Gallery at Redleaf, as a home for his newly married son Arthur, a lawyer. Henry had just had a visit from Arthur. He was two years younger than Mary but had gone fat, grey and bald. Meanwhile, Mary still looked so youthful she could be mistaken for her children's sister, Henry thought.

With his snowy beard and bald head and red silk dressing gown he had brought back long ago from Japan on his round-the-world travels, the elderly Henry reminded Mary of an Old Testament prophet. The once irascible figure had mellowed over the years, she thought. Those who had once worried him were either dead or far away. Henry had become a gentle, benevolent figure, cleansed of the annoyances of his youth, who had arrived 'after much buffeting in untroubled waters'. Mary's visits filled him with joy. 'Dear little May'—as Henry still called her—made a last visit to her father just before she returned to Pomerania.

The beech forests glowed gold as Mary reached Nassenheide in early autumn. After weeks sleeping in a cramped caravan, she was beguiled by the beauty and size of the schloss's rooms.

She had been home just three days when she received the news: her father's heart had failed at his Bexley home on 6 October 1907. The once restless, adventurous Henry Herron Beauchamp had died aged eighty-two. Fractious as he had been as a young husband, among Henry's lifelong possessions was a touching memento of his devotion to his wife: a lock of Louey's once blonde hair, tied in pink ribbon.

Mary returned to England for Henry's funeral. With the death of her endlessly curious and observant father, she had lost her champion and her most valued critic. Her attitude towards her father had changed over the years. As a girl she feared him, as a young woman she revered him, as a mature woman she had grown to love him.

She was proud to be the daughter of a man so honourable, sincere, kind, philosophical and witty, she wrote to Evi in England. 'He hated lies and everything not quite plainly honest. Well, I am going to try and be more like him.'

The loss of her father was the beginning of a troubling time for Mary. Her youngest daughter Felicitas was experiencing bad dreams. The little girl slept in Mary's bedroom. 'Nothing wakes her, and her agonies while they go on are great.'

She received disturbing news from Evi in England, who was studying at St Paul's and was living at the home of a family friend, Lady Maude Whyte. A man in the household had behaved inappropriately towards Evi. Mary wrote in great distress, telling fifteen-year-old Evi never to be alone with him, go anywhere with him or do anything he asked. Mary began making plans to bring her daughter home for Christmas.

Henning was facing financial ruin. After several disastrous harvests, mounting debts and unsuccessful attempts to get further credit, he could no longer afford Nassenheide. His health, too, was suffering; he had developed diabetes and had heart trouble. The stress and demands of running the property were more than he could cope with. The home that had inspired and nurtured Mary's writing would have to be sold. Henning suggested they move to his estate Schlagenthin, where there was a habitable residence.

Mary had other ideas. She wanted to live in England. She had personal, professional and political reasons for doing so. She wanted all their children, not just the eldest, Evi, to be educated there. She had developed a circle of intellectual and influential friends and associates in London and had established herself as a writer. Political tensions between England and Germany were increasing as Europe was dividing into two hostile blocs, with Germany and Austria-Hungary on one side and France, Russia and Britain lined up on the other. The most immediate threat was financial. The family's future would depend on Mary and the success of her writing.

Removal vans drew up to Nassenheide under cover of darkness at Easter 1908. Late snow was on the ground as furniture, silver, paintings and books were loaded aboard. The operation had to be carried out by stealth. Mary and Henning feared their creditors might arrive and stop the removal. The home where she had lived for more than a decade—longer than she had lived anywhere—was being emptied.

The garden she had planted, the schloss, her summerhouse writing retreat and the sylvan woodlands in which she often wandered all passed from view as she was conveyed beyond Nassenheide's stone gates a few days later. She and the four children were bound for England.

Henning remained behind in the echoing house with just Teppi and the butler. He was to join them in England after Nassenheide was sold. He would make occasional trips back to his Schlagenthin estate. At least, that was the plan Mary outlined to Evi. Whether or not that was truly the intention, it was not what happened. Mary's departure for England meant she and Henning would rarely live under the same roof again.

Blue Hayes was a white-washed Regency country house near the village of Broadclyst, about ten kilometres from the cathedral city of Exeter in Devon. It had seven bedrooms, a tennis court and a manicured lawn, and was set on three acres and surrounded by farmland. Tightened finances didn't mean roughing it.

Mary enrolled her four girls in a nearby school. After more than a decade amid formal Junker society, she struggled to adapt to rural Devon's casual ways, where she felt life got around in its slippers. She expected a gardener to snap his heels to her attention, not lean on his spade. And she was accustomed to indicating to her guests that they had her permission to sit down. Such patrician behaviour in Devon astonished her visitors.

After years with few social obligations in Pomerania, she soon found she had frequent visitors. Their visits had to be returned. The result was, she found herself 'entangled in tea-parties'. Seduced by junkets and clotted cream, she and 'the crabs'—her collective name for her children—all gained weight, to her dismay. Mary, like her father, abhorred fatness. She often recorded her weight and that of her children in her diary.

She was lonely, sad and missed her old life. Even the large black dog that came with the property offered her little in the way of companionship. Prince was furtive, aggressive with a 'red hot eye' and Mary was wary of him. At night, Mary stood in the doorway attempting to sight the black dog wandering in the dark. 'The brooding heaviness that oppressed us all in that place [. . .] a sadness that seemed to be in the very bricks of the solitary house, set among soppy, flat green fields.'

Henning made a couple of trips to visit his family before returning to Nassenheide, which remained unsold. To occupy his time there, he wrote a book about agricultural practices. His health was poor, and the solitude and silence at Nassenheide weighed heavily on him. 'Write if you can to your poor lonely old man,' he lamented to Mary.

Throughout her unhappy time at Blue Hayes, Mary needed to work. She was the main income-earner. Her children rarely saw her as she closeted herself away in a building apart from the main house. She was turning her novel *The Princess Priscilla's Fortnight* into a play as well as completing her book about her caravan trip.

If she had planned a chirpy rural idyll along the lines of *The Adventures of Elizabeth in Rügen* when she embarked on her summer trip, the book that emerged was entirely different. She had previously poked fun at what she saw as the boorish elements of the German character. The new book mercilessly skewered it.

The Caravaners, set mostly in England, follows a trip by Prussian aristocrats Baron and Baroness von Ottringel and several German and English friends. It is told from the perspective of the pompous baron, and is the only book Mary wrote in a male voice. In the baron, Mary creates a comic monster. The baron is militaristic and misogynistic, oblivious to his own oafishness. His feminine ideal is a woman smiling but silent. For him, Germany is rugged and masculine, and England feminine—its men pale, puny and effeminate. Through his eyes, England is a country ripe for conquest.

The baron's antithesis is fellow caravaner Mr Jellaby, an English socialist and Labour member of the House of Commons and a man who enjoys the company of women. Jellaby has more than a passing resemblance to the socialist H.G. Wells. Mary created her two central male figures at a time when she had grown to loathe Prussian chauvinism, was alarmed by growing German militarism and when Wells had made a deep impression on her.

She had encountered Wells again on a visit to London and he invited her to spend a night at Spade House. She could not accept his enticement, she wrote to him. 'The water into which I'd get when my relatives find it out wouldn't merely be hot, it would boil, & my only safety lies in being firm in the face of the most delightful temptations,' she wrote.

The purpose of both Wells' invitation and her lighthearted rejection of it is unclear. But amid her worries and responsibilities, the witty, charming man was a bright spot on her horizon. He was, she told him, 'like opening a window into fresh air!'

The Caravaners polarised the critics when it was published at the end of 1909. She had received poor reviews before, but none so vociferous. Some thought she had gone too far in her malicious portrayal of the Prussian baron. *The Spectator* thought the book liable to aggravate Anglo–German tensions, while *The Standard* slammed it as an exercise in bear-baiting.

But the book was hailed elsewhere. 'Not since Mr Bernard Shaw invented Broadbent has a great national type been ridiculed to so merry a purpose [. . .] It is a mixture of delightful farce and exquisite satire,' according to *The Daily News*. *The World* thought it, 'an achievement to make an arch bore so entertaining', while *Punch* considered the book one of the year's cleverest and most amusing.

When Mary re-read her novel three decades later, she was much amused by her younger self. 'Intensely malicious, I now see.' Among the book's later admirers was the Australian author and Nobel Prize-winner, Patrick White. He thought *The Caravaners* one of the funniest books he had ever read. White's admiration for her writing prompted him in 1936 to take a literary detour to Rügen island while visiting Germany.

Mary's devilish black dog became the catalyst to leave Blue Hayes after just a year. Prince had taken to killing sheep. Mary was hauled before a magistrate and ordered to hand the dog to police to be shot. Although she did not care for Prince, she was horrified at the prospect of the dog being killed.

She soon put Blue Hayes up for sale and left Devon for London, where she took a flat in Whitehall Court, an elegant mansion block between the River Thames and St James's Park. While her flat was being readied she went to stay with her sister Charlotte, who had permanently separated from her husband George Waterlow. Charlotte was living at a substantial country home, Ropes, in Fernhurst, Sussex.

Mary and the children joined Henning for a final Christmas at their Pomeranian estate at the end of 1909. It was a desultory holiday in the near-empty house. Even Teppi had departed to teach in a girls' school in Marburg. Mary remained at Nassenheide with son H.B. through January 1910, after the girls returned to school in England.

She found her seven-year-old son genial company and, despite snow, wind and cold, he joined her as they fastidiously kept up a daily outdoor exercise regime called Ten Times Round. This was a running game she had played with all the children in an attempt to keep their weight in check. Mary saw little of Henning except at meals and in the evenings when they played draughts. She spent days in her summerhouse 'cleaning up my soul, which has got into a great confusion & muddle lately'.

Nassenheide eventually sold but there was no sudden boost to the finances. The estate was to be paid for in instalments over several years. This meant Mary needed to keep earning. Henning's health was declining. On his doctor's orders, he entered a sanatorium in the Italian spa town of Merano.

Mary plunged into a frenzy of engagements when she returned to London in February 1910. She heard social reformer Sidney Webb speak at the Fabian Society and George Bernard Shaw at the Eugenics Education Society. She attended talks on the prevention of destitution and on women's suffrage. She spent nights at the theatre and at music concerts and made frequent visits to St Paul's. She dined with Bernard Shaw and attended his new play *Misalliance*. She also dined with her children's former tutors E.M. Forster and Hugh Walpole, with popular writer Mary Cholmondeley and other London friends. She took Evi to dancing lessons and made holiday arrangements for the other children.

In May, she visited Henning at his sanatorium. His illness made him irritable and anxious, and the afternoons they spent together were solemn. Despite her anxieties over Henning's health and his constant bad humour, Mary still found beauty and solace in her surrounds, where after nightfall 'the glow worms dance about in the air & are a lovely green light till you catch one & then it is just a dull worm,' she wrote to her daughter Liebet. Henning was deeply unhappy at the sanatorium and it was decided to move him to another, in Bad Kissingen, Bavaria. Mary accompanied him to the spa town.

Mary's stage adaptation of her novel *The Princess Priscilla's Fortnight* was due to open in London's Haymarket Theatre. The large West End theatre, where Oscar Wilde premiered *A Woman of No Importance* and *An Ideal Husband*, was a prestigious venue in which to launch her comic play and herself as a playwright.

Mary wondered whether she would be able to dash back from Germany to see it. As Henning's health improved over several weeks in Bavaria, she decided to make a break. She reached London in time for final rehearsals for *Priscilla Runs Away* as the play was known.

As its playwright, she was billed not simply as 'Elizabeth' but as 'Elizabeth Arnim'. The Germanic 'von' was dropped. This may have been a strategic decision at a time of rising Anglo-German tensions. It was the only time in her writing life that she was billed as Elizabeth Arnim.

Shortly before the play opened, Mary gave her first newspaper interview, to the *Daily Mail*. It was one of only two press interviews she ever gave. The paper breathlessly described Countess Arnim, as it called her, as having a girlish figure, expressive face, brown curled hair and a winning smile that added to the 'charm of her conversation'. Seeing her play reach the stage meant more to her than any of her books, she insisted. She knew nothing of the workings of the theatre and had never before attended a rehearsal. 'To go to the theatre and find one's thoughts embodied—that is an experience so strange, for in some instances the living characters I see there are exactly as I had pictured them in my imagination.'

None of the play's characters was based on people she knew. She had done that only in her first two books. 'In *Elizabeth and Her German Garden*, you will see my three little girls, something of my husband and myself, much of our home and garden,' she said. The anodyne article did not refer to the controversy around her identity that had swirled around her a decade earlier, not least in the *Daily Mail*.

Three girls in gloves and white muslin dresses passed beyond the neoclassical façade with its Corinthian columns and into the Haymarket theatre's plush auditorium on 29 June 1910. Evi, Liebet and Trix were accompanied by their Uncle Ralph, Mary's brother.

Mary had instructed her girls on what to wear and how to behave at the premiere. 'You're not to shout author! That is the last thing just you, my own spawn, must do [. . .] apart from the fact that females don't shout, it is as bad as if I myself shouted for myself!'

Mary was nowhere to be seen. It is unclear if she even attended the premiere. Her daughters, whom audience members recognised as the April, May and June babies, received flowers intended for her.

In the title role, the casting of a talented young actress Phyllis Neilson-Terry was fortunate. She was theatrical royalty—her aunt was Ellen Terry and her cousin Sir John Gielgud. Several critics thought the young actress's performance was the production's saving grace. The reviews of the four-act play were tepid. *The Times* likened the play to a cup of literary cocoa. *The Manchester Guardian* thought the play 'pleasantly ordinary, conventionally pretty, and makes no serious demand on the intelligence'. Its critic expected the play would be a popular success anyway. It was. The play ran for six months.

Chapter 8

EMOTIONS AFTER BREAKFAST

Mary returned to Bavaria two weeks after the play opened. Henning was in bed when she arrived but greeted her with a laurel wreath. Throughout their marriage, this is the only indication that he ever celebrated her achievements as a writer.

She sat with Henning most days in the sanatorium garden, and she arranged for their three oldest daughters to join them from England, to spend their summer holidays with their father. Henning's health picked up sufficiently to take a day trip with his daughters to an old church. He seemed so much better that Mary began making plans to take him to his estate Schlagenthin, where he longed to be.

She was so encouraged by his improvement that she took Evi and Trix for a day trip to a nearby market town. It was the first time Mary had left her husband's side in five weeks. But when she returned, Henning was again unwell.

He was agitated when she arrived, as she usually did each day, after breakfast the next morning, 20 August 1910. She had been there only a few minutes when she heard him groan. Then silence. Aged fifty-nine, Henning's heart had failed.

Mary was heartbroken. 'It is very dreadful to see somebody die,' she wrote to Louey. 'I know poor H couldn't ever get well & would only have gone on being miserable, but being with him when he died & knowing how desperately he wanted to live, at any cost, even tormented, makes one feel such unutterable sympathy with him, longing to keep him, & yet he looked so happy and peaceful after he was dead—a little contented smile on his poor thin face.'

On the day she planned to travel to Schlagenthin to ready the house for Henning's arrival, she journeyed there instead to prepare for his funeral. Charlotte and Teppi joined her as Henning was interred in the family mausoleum.

Mary had known widowhood was inevitable, that Henning would never recover. Throughout Henning's protracted illness, she'd had time to contemplate her next move. She may also have sensed freedom, after twenty years of marital and societal obligations as a Prussian countess. She would have been aware that she did not have the temperament to care for an invalid husband for years. But her diary ceased on the day of Henning's interment. Her pattern of silence at traumatic times suggests that whatever relief she may have felt, it was tempered by more complex emotions.

If she was grief-stricken, she was also stoic. She wrote to daughter Liebet on black-edged mourning paper, the custom of the time. Her tone was lighthearted as she related how Evi—who remained with Mary in Germany before starting at Girton College, Cambridge—had been trying to learn a bicycle but had fallen so often she'd crushed the estate's dahlias. Mary instructed Liebet to carry out various tasks and upbraided her for her attitude to school.

Absent in any of the black-edged letters is any mention of Henning. Did she wish to spare her children further distress? Over the previous two disorienting years they had been uprooted from the childhood home in Germany and transplanted to England. Now their much-loved father was gone. Did they wonder if he had been quickly forgotten by a mother about to embark on a holiday around Europe?

Mary wrote of her unorthodox attitude to death years later. 'Whenever I have had to do with death it lifts me up rather than casts me down—right up out of all the small silly pitiful things that our lives are so caught in, into a place where everything is calm & where somehow, till life blurs it all out again, I seem to *see*.'

Mary did not linger at Schlagenthin. She put the estate up for sale and turned her back on Germany. That chapter of her life was over. She made her way through Switzerland and down to the French Riviera. She was accompanied by Teppi, who had quit her teaching job to rejoin Mary's employ. Mary did not tell her children the main purpose of her journey. She was looking for a place to live and work. She wanted somewhere large enough to accommodate all her children during their holidays and far away from the social whirl of London.

By late October she was back in Switzerland, at Sierre, east of Lake Geneva. There, Mary and Teppi spent their days walking through alpine meadows and panting up mountains, returning exhausted each night to the elegant Hotel Château de Bellevue. Mary had returned to the country where, four decades earlier, she had spent part of her happy childhood. Her father had once described Switzerland as paradise on earth. Mary was similarly enraptured: 'it is so good to be here—it really might well be the House of God and the Gates of Heaven.'

Mary wrote to H.G. Wells from the Bellevue on mourning paper to praise his newest book *The New Machiavelli*. The novel tells of a British politician who embarks on an affair with a young graduate. He abandons his wife and career to live with his lover in Italy.

Wells had a scandalous relationship of his own to draw on. He had embarked on an affair with Amber Reeves, a bright Cambridge graduate and Fabian two decades his junior. She had become pregnant to him and they made a brief attempt at domesticity in northern France. By the time their daughter was born in December 1909, Amber was back in England and Wells had returned to his wife Jane.

Mary thought Wells' book was wonderful, writing: 'never did a man understand things as you do.' But what she wanted to read were his reflections on the fictional couple after the intoxicating heat of passion tempered. 'What happened to them as the dreadful ordinary years passed with all their days full of getting up, & walking, & having meals, & going to bed, & no friends anywhere, & just their two selves. Is any one strong enough in love & fine thinking to stand the effect of all the little hours?'

Mary knew all about those 'little hours'. The question she posed to Wells was one she had no doubt asked herself many times. It was one she would soon address in her writing.

She signed her letter not as Mary Arnim, as she had in her previous letters to him, but as Elizabeth. Around the time she became a widow, she shed the outer skin of Mary, the name she had been given at birth. Instead, she took on the name of her fictional creation, publicly and privately. For the rest of her life, she would be known as Elizabeth.

Beyond its gentle sloping meadows, the land had views across the Rhône Valley and of Mont Blanc, the Weisshorn and Simplon. Elizabeth had found what she was looking for. It was one of the driest and sunniest places in Switzerland, a far cry from damp Pomerania. She bought the site, which was near Randogne sur Sierre. The choice of Switzerland was, on the one hand, a return to a distantly familiar country, but there was novelty too. She would build a home of her own. A Swiss chalet.

In the meantime, she returned to England. She spent weekends at her sister's country house. Charlotte was now a grandmother, her daughter Margery having given birth to her first child, a girl. Elizabeth, however, was not inclined to coo over the infant: 'to me a baby has always been a weariness & a dreariness,' she wrote to Liebet.

Elizabeth took a new flat in St James's Court in Westminster. Neither her London flat nor Charlotte's Sussex home was large enough to allow her five children to visit together, so they visited in relays. Between overseeing construction of the chalet and travelling frequently to Germany to sort out Henning's estate, and the lack of a suitable home in which her children could visit her, Elizabeth saw little of her family during this time.

Elizabeth shared her excitement at creating her chalet with her children and expected it would be finished by the autumn of 1911.

> Christmas will see us all re-united in a real home again, which will be a great joy. I look forward to it as the abode of simple joys & hard work—in a climate where the sun shines just as often as in England it rains or is grey. It is to be a little Nassenheide, with many added advantages & beauties—I want you crabs to fill it with your friends whenever you like, for I shall have my Treibhaus to work in so won't in the least be disturbed by your riotings.

In the event, the chalet was not finished by Christmas. Elizabeth ended up spending it at Charlotte's home instead. But the partly built chalet was not commanding all of Elizabeth's attention. Wells and Elizabeth became increasingly close in the wake of her widowhood. Wells' most obvious presence until then had been in her imaginative world, as the sympathetic English socialist Jellaby in *The Caravaners*.

Elizabeth invited Wells to lunch: 'it will give me great pleasure to try and make you vain,' she flattered him. Wells later gave Jane an account of his lunch with the 'bright little Countess von Arnim' but played down any sexual attraction. 'She talks very well, she knows *The New Machiavelli* by heart, and I think she's a nice little friend to have [. . .] Her conversation is free but her morals are strict (sad experience has taught her that if she so much as thinks of anything she has a baby and she never even let her husband be in the same house with her after the birth of the last).' The two successful authors began to see a great deal of each other and she invited Wells and his family to stay when the chalet was finished.

By early 1912, she was seeing Wells several times a week. He was her most frequent London companion. They took walks along the Embankment, through Kew Gardens, visited St Paul's and shared meals and motoring trips. Her friendship encompassed the Wells family. Elizabeth stayed at their new home, Easton Glebe, in Essex. So too did her nine-year-old son, who was about the same age as H.G. and Jane's two sons.

Elizabeth's creative network expanded to include Somerset Maugham, Henry James, composer Ralph Vaughan Williams, traveller Gertrude Bell, Liberal grandee Augustine Birrell, and artists Philip Burne-Jones and Thomas James Cobden-Sanderson. She also saw former Nassenheide tutors Hugh Walpole and, especially, Charles Stuart.

Elizabeth's nephew Sydney Waterlow, Charlotte's son, was also among her regular visitors. Dubbed 'Monarch', perhaps for his imposing figure and grand manners, he was on the fringes of the Bloomsbury set. An associate of Vanessa and Clive Bell, Henry James and Rupert Brooke, Monarch had proposed marriage to Virginia Woolf (then Stephen) in late 1911. She declined and soon married Leonard Woolf. Monarch was disparaging of his family's colonial roots, telling Virginia Woolf that his grandmother Louey—Elizabeth's mother—was a rat catcher's daughter.

Louey had recently been left an allowance from her wealthy brother Frederic Lassetter in Sydney. Frederic had died the previous year at his Redleaf home and been buried in Sydney's South Head cemetery. He left an estate of £230,000 and provided Louey with £100 a year for life.

Elizabeth made several trips to Europe, including to see her daughter Trix, who was studying in Berlin. On the anniversary of Henning's birth in April, she laid flowers at his mausoleum at Schlagenthin. She visited Switzerland to check on the chalet's progress and her youngest daughter joined her there. Felicitas was about to start school in Lausanne. Elizabeth was proud of her little girl, impressed with her dignity and good behaviour.

Wells was invariably Elizabeth's first caller when she returned to London from her travels. Watching from the wings, Teppi observed that Elizabeth's emotional world appeared to be ruled by him. Elizabeth was certainly drawn to the intelligent, free-spirited Wells. 'Never had she conversed with anyone endowed with so agile a brain, so nimble a tongue,' according to her daughter Liebet.

Wells found Elizabeth, a 'bright and original little lady indeed'. She was shrewd, witty and wise. 'She mingled adventurousness with extreme conventionality in a very piquant manner.' But he considered her 'incapable of philosophical thought or political ideas'.

He claimed their affair ignited while Elizabeth was staying at Charlotte's country home, and he was lodging nearby at Cotchet Farm. 'We went for walks over the heathery hillside, conversing upon life very cheerfully, and came to an easy understanding,' he recalled.

Whether Elizabeth and Wells were lovers is contested. Wells leaves no doubt they were, romping across Europe and carrying on a liaison so energetic that twice they broke a bed. 'It was a cheerful thing to hear Little e [. . .] explaining in pretty but perfect German why her bed had gone to pieces under her in the night,' Wells wrote.

Elizabeth had found lovemaking with Henning a serious, disagreeable business but was aware it might be otherwise, according to Wells. 'I attracted her,' he boasted. He and Elizabeth made love al fresco under pine needles on Swiss mountains. One such day, after reading aloud a purse-lipped letter in *The Times* from novelist Mrs Humphry Ward, denouncing the moral tone of younger writers, they stripped off under a tree and 'made love all over Mrs Humphrey [sic] Ward'.

Behind a wardrobe in Elizabeth's chalet was a secret door, Wells claimed. Its well-oiled castors prevented nocturnal creaking that might alert other guests. Wells portrayed his relationship with Elizabeth as being physically vigorous, but for him it lacked a vital element: 'I cannot imagine a relationship more free from passion than ours. Its practical convenience was undeniable.'

But Wells' kiss-and-tell account did not see daylight until long after he and Elizabeth were dead. 'The Episode of Little e'—a reference to the way she signed her letters to him and his pet name for her—was a chapter in *H.G. Wells in Love*, his candid autobiography about his relationships with various women. Published only in 1984, the book is an intimate exploration of his beliefs in free love and rejection of sexual constraints, beliefs he practised assiduously. Wells made several incorrect claims in it about Elizabeth—including that she was born in Ireland and that she had eloped with Henning against her family's wishes.

Elizabeth's daughter Liebet, in her 1958 biography of her mother penned under the name of Leslie de Charms, suggests there was no affair. Elizabeth, in her witty but opaque memoir *All the Dogs of My Life*, portrayed Wells (thinly disguised and unnamed) as more of an annoyance than a serious amorous contender. Despite the breezy dismissive picture she later painted, Elizabeth's diaries chronicle something different. They suggest a highly charged, turbulent relationship that continued for two years. It is hard to imagine this being simply platonic.

Under a vast starry sky, the snow-capped mountains glittered as Elizabeth contemplated the view from her bedroom. The chalet looked down on a wide valley, with cherry trees and green slopes, and beyond to a small town, where at night its distant lights quivered.

'Our little house hanging [. . .] by its eyelashes half-way up to heaven.' The 'little house' was hardly a humble cottage. The Chalet Soleil, set on twelve acres, had sixteen bedrooms and four bathrooms as well as attic rooms for servants. With low ceilings, exposed beams and oak panelling, the intimate living rooms were filled with books from Nassenheide's library. Doors opened onto a terrace and garden. The panoramic views took advantage of the elevation: 1400 metres above sea level. The chalet was so substantial that tourists at times mistook it for a hotel and wanted to book in.

Curious sightseers might have been deterred by the words written across the chalet. Visible in large letters to all who approached, Elizabeth repeated her Latin motto from Nassenheide, except this time she banned the lazy, not just the merely foolish, along with the sad and foul: *Ignavus insulsus tristis turpis abesto*. Over a porch, she also repeated Nassenheide's welcoming evocation of Greek gods, graces and muses. Down a path from the main house, she built a small chalet to use as a writing retreat.

Construction of her new home was behind schedule and it was not habitable until autumn of 1912. As she readied to leave London in mid-November for an extended stay at the chalet, she saw Wells—whom she called Geak or simply G—almost daily. Wells sat in her train carriage chatting as she was about to depart from Victoria station. She suggested he come with her. 'He didn't want to enough. Saw, in this way, the last of G.' She wrote to him from the chalet a few days later 'bowing myself out. Alas for the end of what was going to be so lovely.'

Far from an end, their tempestuous relationship had barely begun. Wells was not about to take Elizabeth's Dear John letter quietly and was soon on the chalet's doorstep. Five days of 'horrid talks' and rows followed, interspersed with skiing and half-hearted attempts to patch up the relationship. The acrimony reached a crescendo one early December afternoon in which she saw 'a devil in G. of cruelty & horridness' and he departed in the dark a few hours later.

Elizabeth's most faithful and placid companion throughout this time was her enormous Swiss mountain dog. The newly acquired Coco accompanied her on mountain walks, bounded beside her in the snow, and carried parcels and provisions from a nearby village. Each night before bed she took Coco, who came up to her waist, from her firelit living room to the terrace and they stood beneath the starry sky. He became her favourite among her dynasty of dogs. With his giant paw resting on her foot, he sat with her as she worked. He alone had permission to enter her writing retreat.

Elizabeth's children arrived for their first Christmas together at the chalet, along with other guests, including the ever-faithful former tutor Charles Stuart. Elizabeth could, at last, realise her dream of seeing her chalet filled with her children and friends. On New Year's Eve, Elizabeth took her party to the Palace Hotel in the nearby village of Montana-sur-Sierre, where they danced their way into 1913.

As her guests departed after the holiday, Wells arrived at the chalet with his two sons for a brief visit. He returned several times over the next two months. Each time his presence was accompanied by quarrels and reconciliations, until the pair left for London in early March, travelling in separate trains.

Elizabeth entered the Duomo in Florence on a cold, windy May evening. She stood on the stairs she had climbed with Henning, at the top of which he had so clumsily proposed nearly a quarter of a century earlier. Back then, her life, like the city below, lay before her. Now, she was a widow in her mid-forties. Alone in the darkness, Elizabeth offered a prayer for Henning's soul.

It was a sombre end to a day that had begun with 'emotions after breakfast'. Elizabeth had vacillated between anger and dejection since she and Wells had arrived in Florence a few days earlier.

Wells was involved with another woman. Rebecca West was a young journalist and reviewer who had entered Wells' life the previous autumn. She was nineteen when she wrote a provocative review of his novel *Marriage* for the feminist weekly *The Freewoman.* Wells admired her witty, intelligent writing and invited her to lunch at his home. He soon found the brunette as attractive in person as in print.

Whether or not Elizabeth knew of his latest entanglement, harmony was briefly restored back at the chalet—'things all honey again.' Wells worked at the chalet on his futuristic novel *The World Set Free*, which anticipated the development of nuclear weapons. He read sections of it to Elizabeth and she thought it the best he had written. She and Wells posed for a photograph together around this time. In a light summer dress and large hat, she leant back on him as he kissed her hand. It is an image both tender and theatrical.

They explored Italy's northern lakes in August. Teppi, who joined them, had gradually warmed to Wells and was charmed by his humour. Elizabeth asked her opinion of him, and Teppi ventured that he was clever, amusing and egotistical. Elizabeth replied that Teppi's characterisation had forgotten something: Wells was creative like God, and cruel like the devil.

On his return to London, Wells wrote several letters to Elizabeth from which she concluded that he was 'more or less sick of me!!' If she did not yet know about Rebecca West, she likely soon would. Jane Wells arrived at the chalet in September. Wells never kept his many extra-marital affairs from Jane—these were conducted if not with her approval then with her acquiescence. It is inconceivable that Elizabeth and Jane did not discuss Wells' involvement with Rebecca. When Jane departed nearly two weeks later, Elizabeth noted simply: 'Great catastrophes etc.'

Wells made his final appearance at the chalet in late October. It was a visit characterised by tears, penitent evenings and his bad moods. Their relationship was in its death throes. When he departed on 5 November, Elizabeth noted with relief that he was 'out of my life. Thank God—Restored to Freedom—He unkind & rude all day, then suddenly dear & wonderful at end. His last remark as he left the chalet & I bade him farewell in the porch was, crying "It's all because I'm so common". Poor Gh [Wells]. So it was RIP.'

This time, it was. He visited her once at her flat when she returned to London at the end of the year, by which time Rebecca West was pregnant to him. Wells gave his version of his parting from Elizabeth: 'It was your fault,' she told him. 'You were only half a lover.'

'It was your fault,' he retorted. 'You didn't really love.'

Chapter 9

THE WICKED EARL

He slithered his way up the frozen path to the chalet. His trousers were tucked into galoshes, he wore a starched white collar and had a gold watch chain across his waistcoat. As he stood mopping his brow, he did not look like a man meant for mountains.

'If he stayed, it was even then plain that he would stay indoors [. . .] And I would sit with him. And together, in a sitting position, though neither of us yet knew it, we would advance towards both our Dooms.' That is how Elizabeth, years later, recalled the arrival at Chalet Soleil of John Francis Stanley Russell, 2nd Earl Russell.

But at the close of 1913, Elizabeth was smarting after the end of her affair with Wells a few weeks earlier. She was ripe for an antidote. It came in the shape of the large, unshakeably confident, forty-eight-year-old aristocrat. The earl was, at least in social class, the antithesis of Wells.

Frank, as he was always called, was Liberal aristocracy. The grandson of a former British prime minister, Lord John Russell, and the son of unconventional, agnostic blue blood parents, Viscount Amberley and Kate Stanley. The young Frank had run wild, ridden bareback, stolen apples and learned to swear and curse from Walter Scott's novels, all of which he had read by the age of eight. He was 'an unwashed, ill-bred, impertinent little child,' according to his maternal grandmother.

He had bullied his brother Bertrand, who was seven years younger. As an adult, Bertrand thought Frank was such a bully that he could never retain anyone's love; he recalled his brother's suffocating, overbearing personality: 'after I had been with him some time I began to feel as if I could not breathe.' Throughout his life, Bertrand's affection for Frank was mixed with fear. Bertrand would become one of the twentieth century's greatest minds—a Nobel laureate, philosopher and pacifist. Frank had a talent for scandal.

Both his parents were dead before Frank reached his teens: his mother of diphtheria and his father two years later of bronchitis. Frank and Bertrand were despatched to their elderly paternal grandparents, where puritan piety and austerity ruled. Frank loathed the restrictive atmosphere, while the Russell family regarded him as 'a limb of Satan.'

Frank left Oxford amid a whiff of scandal concerning a fellow student before becoming a member of the House of Lords at twenty-two. He served on the boards of various companies including insurance, gold miners and car manufacturers, as well as on local councils. He developed a fondness for women, cars and gambling, and he dabbled with cocaine. He was dubbed the Wicked Earl.

How and when Elizabeth met Frank is unclear. One account says they met at a Sarah Bernhardt performance in London in 1894 and continued to see each other. But confirmation that their paths had even crossed back then has never surfaced. It is more likely Elizabeth met Frank nearly two decades later, around the time she became involved with Wells.

They had certainly met by 1911 when Frank invited Elizabeth as well as Wells to spend Easter with him and his wife Mollie at their Sussex home. It is possible they stayed there more than once. Wells recalled staying with the Russells at the height of his affair with Elizabeth, during which he felt his way in the dark along a passage to her room, attempting not to wake Mollie, who slept with her bedroom door open.

Newly widowed, Elizabeth occasionally called on Frank and Mollie, whose country home was close to Charlotte's. In London, Elizabeth had dined with Mollie a week before Frank arrived at the snow-bound chalet.

Elizabeth could not have been unaware of Frank's turbulent marital history. His infamous court battles had been widely reported, reaching as far as Brisbane's *The Telegraph* and Western Australia's *The Kalgoorlie Miner*.

Frank had married his first wife, Mabel Scott, in 1890. She left him just three months later and petitioned for a judicial separation. So began a decade of litigation. He accused her of cruelty; she accused him of sodomy, of threatening her with a pistol and shaking her like a rat.

He was still married to Mabel, who took to the music hall stage, when he met Mollie Somerville. She was an Irish-born, twice-married shoemaker's daughter, a feminist and several years older than Frank. The couple travelled to the US, where Frank obtained a divorce from Mabel in April 1900, and they married in Reno, Nevada. But the American divorce was not recognised in England. Frank was arrested at Waterloo Station in June 1901 and charged with bigamy.

As a peer, Frank was entitled to a trial by the House of Lords instead of with a mere jury of commoners. The ancient privilege was generally reserved for serious charges, such as treason—Anne Boleyn's trial being the most famous case. Only one peer had ever previously been tried for bigamy and Frank was the first peer in sixty years to be tried for a felony.

Tickets were issued for this rare, highly theatrical pageant held in the imposing Royal Gallery at the Palace of Westminster, amid portraits and gilt statues of monarchs, wood panelling, stained glass windows, and artist Daniel Maclise's monumental depiction of *The Death of Nelson*. The public took their seats as peers peeped into the gallery, like the performers in amateur theatricals pulling aside the curtain before the performance has begun. Frank, with his perennially wandering eye, noted the galaxy of smartly dressed women who lined the walls.

Scarlet-robed peers filed in—dukes, barons, earls and archbishops—and were presided over by the Lord Chancellor, with his white wand of office, who was seated in front of a throne. Frank, in gold spectacles, grey frock coat and a bright red tie, delivered a passionate speech about his troubled life and misapprehension of the law—a surprising admission given he was a barrister. 'Oedipus when he married Jocasta was not more innocent than Lord Russell, if you were to believe him,' observed *The Manchester Guardian*'s sketchwriter.

Frank was sentenced to three months in Holloway prison. It was hardly onerous. As a first-class prisoner—convicted for a misdemeanour—Frank was entitled to have his own clothes and furniture, so he installed in his cell his writing desk, bed and armchair. He found little fault with his treatment, declaring it restful and agreeable. He enjoyed a bath in a large stone tub, and had his breakfast delivered with his morning papers. He complained only about a three-week delay obtaining his watch and nail scissors.

Those close to Frank failed to see the appeal of the woman he had been prepared to go to jail for. His friend, the philosopher and writer

George Santayana, called her an old frump, a 'fat, florid, coarse Irish-woman' who smoked, gardened, and drank whisky with and between meals. She was nonetheless a good soul, who mollified the servants Frank had exasperated. In her loose tea gowns surrounded by a pack of white lapdogs, she was 'as happy as an exacting husband and a dwindling income could allow her to be'.

Mollie wrote several books, including *Five Women and a Caravan* under the name Countess Russell. Published in 1911—two years after Elizabeth's *The Caravaners*—it was a lighthearted first-person account of a trip with women friends, in which she refers to her husband as 'my owner'. It should have served as a warning. Mollie gave Elizabeth a copy, inscribing it 'from her most devoted admirer'.

Frank was among more than a dozen guests in a Christmas and New Year crowd at the chalet that included Elizabeth's children as well as their friends, and her own friends including Thomas James 'Cobbie' Cobden-Sanderson, who had been Frank's boyhood guardian, Hugh Walpole and her nephew Sydney Waterlow. The atmosphere was exuberant as the guests tobogganed, played music and one young woman danced in the manner of Isadora Duncan.

Frank remained behind when Elizabeth took her guests once again to the Palace Hotel on New Year's Eve for a fancy-dress ball. When he welcomed her return from the party with *Glühwein* and pancakes, he must have seemed a model of care and attention. She was sad to see him leave as the new year began.

Back in London, amid the Italianate columns of the Reform Club, the Pall Mall club where Liberal grandees and bankers mingled, Frank wrote to Elizabeth a letter of breathless ardour and eroticism.

His love for her throbbed in his veins: 'I am volcanic inside my best beloved: to me this is no idle sport, no casual aside, but an upheaval, a bursting, a flow of red hot lava. Are you frightened? Do you want to be loved so much?' he wrote.

Elizabeth was elated by his words, she 'wondered if it wouldn't shine through me visibly & give me away' to her remaining guests. Her remaining guests included Cobbie, who watched Elizabeth on her sledge in the snow, flying down the slopes, and sat beside her at dinner but detected nothing unusual. As he prepared to leave the chalet Cobbie noted: 'Elizabeth will be alone, her own world to create.'

That world quickly became consumed by Frank. Elizabeth replied to his passionate letter, presumably offering encouragement since he responded with another of equal fervour. 'I lay in bed panting with my heart all fluttering with anxiety,' he wrote. She was his twin soul, he was filled with joy and pride at her love, he worshipped at her feet. Elizabeth was too distracted to work. She found herself thinking of 'F. & happiness instead'.

Frank returned briefly to the chalet in early February after Elizabeth's guests had gone and they sat together for four days bathed in the winter sun. 'Perfect sunshine inside as well as out,' Elizabeth wrote in her journal.

Elizabeth cast their early courtship in a considerably less sunny light years later, observing how her behaviour changed in his presence:

> Gradually it became my chief concern that he shouldn't slip, that he should be safe and comfortable out of doors as well as in, that he should have the chair he liked, that the meals should be according to his wishes, which turned out to be chiefly legs of

> mutton. I can't account for my behaviour. I had never before felt any desire to serve, to obey, to stand with bowed head and hands folded, to be, as it were, the handmaid of the lord.

Their whirlwind romance took a dramatic turn two weeks after Frank returned to England. He left Mollie and intended to divorce her. Elizabeth was stunned, and not just because Frank had not consulted her about his plans.

Elizabeth had not been seeking another husband. Part of Frank's appeal was that he was safely married. When she saw him in England in March, he gave her a ring. She did not stay around long to celebrate. When Frank waved her off to Italy the next day, she put considerable time and distance between them.

Elizabeth incubated what became *The Pastor's Wife* for years, making notes for the book more than a decade earlier. But only with Henning's death could she fully give shape to a work that, more than any of her previous books, appears grounded in her own bleak experience. The novel was about the soul-destroying nature of matrimony and the misery of endless pregnancies.

She arrived in Florence—the city in which Henning had proposed to her—to work on the book, away from her still snow-bound chalet, and settled into Villa Le Fontanelle, which had once belonged to the Medici family.

She was joined by her youngest daughter Felicitas, who was fourteen and at boarding school in Lausanne. Felicitas was musical like her mother, and they also shared a love of nature. Elizabeth noticed how the girl gazed in awe at an orange tree in the villa's garden. Felicitas had never seen one before. Sensitive and artistic, Felicitas was the daughter with whom Elizabeth may have felt the strongest spiritual kinship.

As an infant, Felicitas had enchanted Katherine Mansfield. Now, Elizabeth delighted in the girl's company. Felicitas was 'so extremely & delightfully & intelligently *interested*—which is of course the measure of intelligence,' Elizabeth rhapsodised to Liebet. Teppi took Felicitas sightseeing most days as Elizabeth worked.

But within a couple of weeks, Felicitas aroused Elizabeth's ire. Felicitas had been 'rude & horrid to Teppi & devilish in fact.' What lay behind this is not known. An exasperated Elizabeth was still cross with her daughter the next day and declared her a 'surprising nuisance.' Felicitas soon returned to her boarding school and peace was restored. It was the first inkling of a shadow falling between Elizabeth and her youngest daughter.

During her two months in Florence, working on her book that questioned women's role as wives and mothers, Elizabeth encountered a group of women who had taken vastly less conventional paths. There she met the British writer Vernon Lee. Born Violet Paget, Vernon was a feminist and lesbian who dressed in male attire. Elizabeth found her delightful, amusing, caustic company and formed a long friendship with her.

Vernon had made her home in Florence, which had a significant lesbian ex-pat community at that time. At its apex were a Balkan princess called Jeanne Ghyka and her artist lover Florence Blood, a petite but aggressive woman dubbed Baby Blood. Their home was Villa Gamberaia, near Settignano, a seventeenth-century villa with a formal garden overlooking the Arno Valley. Vernon was a regular visitor to Villa Gamberaia and took Elizabeth to tea there, where Baby Blood expounded to her on the 'homosexuelle liebe.'

Elizabeth's relationship with Frank soon commanded attention. He was being harried by well-meaning friends, he told her in a letter. Among those warning him against divorcing Mollie was George Santayana.

Santayana had written to Frank, likening him to Henry VIII, who wanted to marry all his lady-loves only to wish later that he could cut off their heads. Having found domestic peace with sensible Mollie, who was accustomed to Frank's ways, Santayana considered it folly for his friend to end his marriage. Santayana felt sorry for Mollie, who had made many sacrifices for the sake of her marriage.

Santayana had private doubts, too. He had yet to meet Elizabeth, but was aware she had maturing daughters. He feared Frank might elope with one of them. Santayana promptly read several of Elizabeth's books. He was astounded, given the horror of domestic tyranny so evident in her writing, that Elizabeth would even consider marrying Frank.

Elizabeth returned to her chalet at the end of May 1914, where she received a bombshell. Her daughter Felicitas had been accused of stealing money. It was not the first time, according to the principal of the girls' boarding school, Château des Apennins. Elizabeth was ordered to remove her daughter.

Elizabeth travelled to Lausanne. By the time she arrived, she learned the school had sent Felicitas to a sanatorium above Montreux. Elizabeth consulted doctors about her daughter and frantically tried to find a more suitable place in Lausanne for her.

After two unsuccessful weeks, in which a better place for the girl could not be found, Felicitas was removed from the sanatorium and brought to the chalet. Felicitas protested her innocence of the theft but her mother refused to accept her denials. Elizabeth had a 'horrid & degrading evening' at the chalet with Felicitas. No doubt, Felicitas had been told her fate. She was to be banished to Germany, to the girls' school in Marburg where Teppi had previously taught. This was a more rigid institution than the carefree lakeside château.

It was also a long way from her mother and most of her siblings. Only her sister Trix was in Germany, studying piano in Berlin, but she was far from Marburg. When Felicitas left the chalet in tears the next morning, escorted by Teppi, the implacable Elizabeth did not even bid her daughter goodbye.

Elizabeth did not speak of what had unfolded to Liebet when she arrived at the chalet a few hours after Felicitas's departure. Elizabeth remained silent on the matter, and she and Liebet left for a hiking holiday in the Italian Alps a week later. Elizabeth could be unpredictable, inconsistent and harsh towards those close to her. If she intended Felicitas's exile to be brief, events would soon make that impossible.

Elizabeth and Liebet were walking near Lake Orta in late June when they paused to talk with an Italian man. He told them Archduke Franz Ferdinand, heir presumptive to the Austria–Hungarian throne, had been assassinated—shot by a Serb nationalist in Sarajevo, Bosnia, the previous day. The ramifications would soon be felt across Europe and beyond. The events in the Balkans quickly consumed Europe, where the continent's greatest powers split into two armed camps. Britain, France and Russia faced off against Germany and Austria–Hungary and Italy.

But when she returned to the chalet, the escalating tensions seemed remote as Elizabeth's summer guests came and went, including Vernon Lee and her children's former tutor Charles Stuart. Games of badminton were played and daughter Evi arrived. In late July, Elizabeth read with alarm English newspaper reports of the unfolding crisis. Within days, Austria-Hungary was at war with Serbia. Then, on 4 August, Britain declared war on Germany.

Many in Britain assumed the war would end quickly. Had not Britain won the Second Boer War, the Second Opium War and put down the Indian Mutiny over the past half-century? And Britain still ruled the waves with its superior naval power. But Germany's military might had grown in the wake of the country's unification.

Elizabeth did not attempt to get Trix and Felicitas out of Germany and to the chalet. Elizabeth, too, may have assumed the war would be brief. Some days she found it hard to believe war was even underway. Mail was still getting through, including proofs of *The Pastor's Wife* which she worked on as she decided whether or not to remain at the chalet.

Elizabeth's first concerns were practical. She stocked up on extra food. Fearing her money held in Germany may be frozen, Elizabeth travelled to the nearby town of Sierre to withdraw what she could from Deutsche Bank. When Teppi returned from Germany after taking Felicitas to Marburg, she told how Germany was mobilising, and that Deutsche Bank was shut.

Although Switzerland was neutral, the impact was immediate and dramatic. Food soon became so scarce that not even maize could be obtained for Elizabeth's dog Coco. Sierre filled with Swiss soldiers guarding the railway station. Hotels began closing and Elizabeth sheltered several stranded Englishmen. Rumours spread of lawlessness and Elizabeth feared her chalet might be looted. With Britain and Germany at war, Teppi returned to her homeland.

The month of August was as volatile as the political landscape. Sunshine was punctuated by violent thunderstorms—which always made Elizabeth uneasy—and her most pressing fear was that Chalet Soleil would be struck by lightning.

She decided to flee to England. This would not be easy. Although she had been raised in England and considered herself British, legally she was German by marriage. The name von Arnim would not be welcome on British soil. She risked being refused entry or even being interned as an enemy alien.

She desperately needed another identity. She obtained a passport in the name of Arnold. The name sounded similar to Arnim and might help avoid any slips of the tongue. Some say the passport was arranged by her doctor brother Sydney Beauchamp in England, who borrowed it from a patient. Elizabeth's diary notes only that a mysterious Mr Dobbs, who visited the chalet throughout August, had secured a passport for her.

She needed cash. Although Deutsche Bank had agreed to release her money, she visited banks in two different towns before she could get her hands on any. Elizabeth settled her bills, burned some of her papers and buried others. She was ready to go.

Shortly after breakfast on 28 August, Elizabeth, Evi and Liebet made their way down from the chalet. Elizabeth took only a knapsack and a handbag. Coco, her mountain dog, carried her handbag by its strap, reluctant to release it when the time came to part. Coco was left with her caretaker.

The three women headed first to Bern, where they hoped to be assisted by an English official. He proved unhelpful and they travelled on to Geneva, where the 'Arnolds' went early to bed, anxious and depressed.

Elizabeth's anxiety was not helped the next day when she and her daughters caught the wrong train. They wanted to go to Paris, but onboard they discovered their train was headed to Lyon. As their train crossed into France, they saw the toll the war had already taken on that country, where 27,000 soldiers had been killed on 22 August alone—one of the deadliest single days in the entire war. As they passed through the station at Ambérieu-en-Bugey, the wounded were lined up on the platform, awaiting transfer to hospitals.

Their mistake cost them a day, and time was critical. They had to overnight in Lyon and spend the day in the city. They caught a night train to Paris, sitting up all night. Bleary-eyed, they reached Paris early the next morning. Chaos confronted them. Frightened citizens were attempting to flee the city ahead of the German advance.

By a 'miracle'—and possibly the judicious application of francs—Elizabeth and her daughters reached the port of Le Havre, where they boarded a crowded steamer heading across the channel. She instructed her daughters, who spoke English with German accents, to keep silent. With no room below, they slept on the deck, resting their heads on coils of rope.

Five anxious and exhausting days after fleeing the chalet, Elizabeth and her daughters were at last on English soil. But Elizabeth could not rest. She needed to shed her German nationality. Her first port of call when she reached London was to the Foreign Office and her lawyers to arrange her naturalisation. This was approved by the end of September. After more than two decades with German nationality, she was English once again: 'So am free,' she wrote in her journal. She was a refugee, but not an alien. She had been 'readmitted to that blessed British fold which I ought never to have left', she wrote to Walpole.

Elizabeth's daughters obtained work as trainee nurses in two large London teaching hospitals, Evi at St Thomas' and Liebet at the Middlesex in Fitzrovia. With their German accents, however, the two young women were viewed with suspicion, despite their education at English schools and Girton College, Cambridge. As foreigners, Evi and Liebet had to report regularly to a local police station and seek permission to travel beyond a small radius. But Elizabeth could at least spend time with the girls on their rare days off.

She took a flat in Albemarle Court in central London and was happy to be reunited with Frank. She visited him at his country house. Frank was all sunshine and solicitousness as, surrounded by his pack of little white dogs, he showered her with flowers.

The couple went on motoring outings in the country; he was an early enthusiast. There were occasional squalls. On a trip to the Peak District, Frank became 'tiresome & cross' when he was unable to get breakfast in their hotel. His continued dark mood threw a cloud over the journey. No sooner had they returned than Elizabeth wrote to Frank about the 'hopelessness of marriage'. But they were back in each other's arms days later sharing a 'heavenly evening of happiness'.

Although Elizabeth's friends were aware of her romance with Frank, she did not want it known that marriage was on the cards. However, rumours were spreading. She was convinced the source was her nephew Sydney Waterlow; she went to see him and told him to stop his gossiping.

Some friends were quietly warning her about Frank, including one man who knew him well, his former guardian Cobbie. Elizabeth was not ready to listen. She dismissed his comments as 'very extreme & unfair about F'. Frank had captured her heart. She found herself awaiting his visits like a love-struck teenager: 'Watched for him all morning with nose against window. Queer.'

Chapter 10

A FAMILY FRACTURED

The book Elizabeth mulled over longer than any of her career, *The Pastor's Wife*, was released in October 1914. She was at the height of her genius when she wrote it. That was the verdict of her friend, the British philosopher George Moore, years later. He considered it a work of truth and beauty. Today, the book is regarded as one of her finest.

It was not the consensus at the time. Miserable, sad and bitter, were among the words aimed at it by some critics. Those who had been beguiled by the charm and froth of her earlier books were shocked at the dark turn she had taken in her most ambitious novel so far.

The Pastor's Wife tells of a naïve young Englishwoman who lives with her controlling father, a bishop, and who can't see much ahead of her other than life as a frostbitten virgin. Ingeborg (English, despite her name) departs on a whim to Europe, where she meets a Prussian pastor, Robert Dremmel, who courts her. Too unassertive to reject him, she stumbles into marriage. Ingeborg takes refuge in nature and for a while is happy with her provincial life in Prussia with her dull, older husband who, like Henning, studies agricultural developments.

Ingeborg is soon pregnant and terrified of the prospect of childbirth. She wants chloroform to dull the pain. Her request is refused and she endures an agonising birth. Five more painful pregnancies quickly follow before an English artist enters her stultifying life. Edward Ingram is a painter, not a writer, but there is much of H.G. Wells in Elizabeth's portrait of this cultured, talented, married artist. Ingram holds the promise of a bigger life and convinces her to join him in Italy.

Ingeborg's disillusionment with marriage and motherhood, the description of childbirth and her inability to bond with her child are frank and harrowing. Despite this, *The Pastor's Wife* is told with Elizabeth's trademark wit and, in her descriptions of nature, lyrical elegance.

Elizabeth satirises Germans but, in contrast to *The Caravaners*, she does not simply champion British characters. Male behaviour is her primary target. Dremmel is neglectful and Ingram is a charming rascal, but it is the potentially violent and tyrannical behaviour of Ingeborg's father that is particularly unsettling.

The Times Literary Supplement and *Punch* were among the papers shocked by her 'odious' portrayal of the English bishop, with the latter's critic protesting that Elizabeth was 'hitting below the gaiters'. *The Daily News*, however, praised the novel, venturing that the book removed forever a complaint that no woman had ever written an account of the psychological state of motherhood.

Yet the book's questioning of male dominance, and of matrimony and motherhood as the goals for women—which today makes *The Pastor's Wife* seem ahead of its time—was overshadowed by the book's timing. Its release within weeks of the outbreak of World War I meant many reviews overlooked her critique of male–female relationships and focused instead on what could be gleaned from the novel about the German temperament. *The Spectator*, which considered the book Elizabeth's most notable, saw in Pastor Dremmel's relentless pursuit of the improvement of East Prussian soil a reminder that the goal of Germany was the wholesale destruction of England.

The war soon ripped Elizabeth's family apart. German-born Evi and Liebet were in England under suspicion while English-born Trix and Felicitas were stuck in Germany. Elizabeth managed to get letters to and from the two girls in Germany.

These were sent via Switzerland and forwarded by the chalet's caretaker.

But the tone of the girls' letters distressed her. Trix was beginning to believe the 'furious ravings' of German newspapers about the 'wicked' English. Felicitas's letters were so full of wild political assertions and invective—perhaps fuelled by her fury at being banished—that Elizabeth told her to stop writing. Having physically exiled her daughter for stealing, Elizabeth then cut communication with her over the girl's political views. And so Elizabeth gave herself another cause for deep regret.

Elizabeth was desperate to prevent the deportation of her two daughters in England as enemy aliens. She instructed Liebet and Evi on how to answer questions from the authorities. They should say their German father was dead, their mother was English and lived in England. They should say that they had no home in Germany and no one to whom they could go; they were half-English by birth and wholly English in sympathies.

Elizabeth's rage at Germany grew. She wrote to Walpole: 'I wish I were a man—wouldn't I be off to the front! I have a wholly barbarous desire to kill at least one German before I die!'

Telegraph House sat on a hilltop, surrounded by two hundred and thirty acres of land, most of it virgin forest of beech and yews. Frank's West Sussex house had a square corner tower with four large windows with views in each direction over fields and woodland and down to the horizon.

It had once been the site of a semaphore station that signalled messages between nearby Portsmouth and London. News of the battle of Trafalgar may have reached London that way, Bertrand Russell wrote. Despite its commanding position, the house itself was ugly and inefficient. But Frank adored it.

Elizabeth joined him there for Christmas. She always put great effort into the festive season. At Nassenheide especially, she had often spent weeks in preparations: decorating trees, planning fun activities for her children. Elizabeth was without her children for the first time. Her only relative to join her at Telegraph House was Charlotte, who arrived on Christmas Eve to stay the night. Her sister had no sooner returned home when a 'misunderstanding' between the lovers cast a pall over Christmas Day.

But any reservations Elizabeth had were quickly set aside. Such was her devotion to Frank at this time that she was content to sit with him as he read aloud to her—from chemistry books. He had an enduring interest in science and was particularly absorbed by chemistry and engineering.

Despite a year that included banishing Felicitas, the outbreak of war, fleeing her chalet and her family divided, Elizabeth was upbeat as it ended. Frank had brought immense joy into her life: 'what happiness I've had this whole year because of him.' As the New Year dawned, Elizabeth declared that 1914 had been the happiest year of her life. 'Now let's see what this one's got in it.'

The new year soon brought increased volatility in her relationship with Frank. The couple seemed incapable of being together for more than a couple of days at a time without conflict. Yet whenever Frank was absent, Elizabeth was filled with benevolent thoughts about him and longed for his return. A diary entry in late January is typical: 'F & I very happy. He went to Luton after breakfast till tea. Was happy all day thinking of him. [He] Came back in a tiresome absorbed mood which gradually chilled me. We fell out.'

Her need for Frank was like an addiction. Its passion brought great highs and lows. She found his boyish moods appealing; he could make her laugh. At his best, Frank could be entertaining, engaging and charming. But his shifting moods could leave her emotionally drained, beset by depression, loneliness and tiredness.

She rented a house in Radlett, Hertfordshire, for a few months so she could work on a second play for the Haymarket theatre. But some days she was so paralysed by sadness she could not write. Elizabeth chronicled the minutiae of her shifting moods—and Frank's. Since fleeing to England, her journal had become less a record of appointments and weather reports and more a log of vacillating emotions.

She was a divided soul, deeply conflicted about her involvement with Frank. Her competing inner tensions were not confined to her relationship with Frank. These were evident in every aspect of her life. When she was in company, she wanted to be alone. When alone, she needed company. In the city, she wanted to be in the country; in the country she missed the stimulation of the city. Her wealth and success as a writer allowed her to satisfy these competing sides. She could move between London and the country, between company and solitude. But nowhere are Elizabeth's psychic divisions more apparent and more torturous than in her relationship with Frank.

Their attempts to celebrate the first anniversary of their relationship—when he'd returned to her chalet—were as damp as the February weather. They both had influenza. Frank appeared to have contracted a virulent strain, which made him particularly pitiful. But he rallied enough to read to Elizabeth from a chemistry book, which was mercifully diluted with small doses of Keats.

Elizabeth's first full spring back in England after so many years brought joy in the natural world. On her frequent walks, she saw early crocuses raising their colourful heads before ceding to daffodils, primroses and fragrant hyacinths. Music was another refuge. She was often drawn to St Paul's to listen to Allegri's *Miserere* with its transcendent a cappella voices. At a country church, she saw a boy practising the organ and asked if she could play. She sat down and performed some Bach, and the accomplished musician in her found it heavenly to play again.

She gave up her house at Radlett in spring. It had served its purpose. She had written her play in the four months there, although it was never produced. She stayed frequently with her sister Charlotte. They took a walk one day near Cotchet Farm where H.G. Wells had stayed during the early heady days of his romance with Elizabeth. The sight revived for her 'quaint memories'.

There was always much laughter and silliness with Charlotte, but at times her sister was anxious about the war. The early months of 1915 saw the first Zeppelin raid on the English coast and, across the channel in Belgium, Germany had unleashed lethal chlorine gas on allied soldiers. Charlotte was fearful for her two sons in uniform. John was in the navy and Cecil, known as Puddle, was in the army and stationed in France.

When Puddle returned on a week's leave, Elizabeth and Charlotte proudly walked on each side of the young man in khaki as they paraded him through the village. Elizabeth felt as happy as she had once been parading her little daughters in their Sunday hats to villagers at Nassenheide.

Elizabeth took a new London flat at Queen's Gate, Knightsbridge. There she dropped the Germanic 'von' from her name. She told Liebet to write to her simply as Mrs Arnim and that, when she visited, she should also ask for Mrs Arnim.

Elizabeth caught a London taxi with a woman behind the wheel. As the war continued, women began moving into activities traditionally performed by men, but female drivers were still relatively rare. Elizabeth may have sensed the freedom the ability to drive would bring, just as she did as a young woman when she learned to ride a bicycle. A few weeks later, Frank gave Elizabeth her first driving lesson.

She found the lesson unnerving, but she was determined to master it and she persisted with frequent instruction. She had a few minor mishaps, including knocking down a hedge at her sister's home. But in April she was involved in a crash at Notting Hill. She was panic-stricken, fearing the accident would have 'horrid consequences' if it was reported in the press. To prevent this, she went to see her friend Augustine Birrell, an influential Liberal Party politician. Her reaction appears extreme, but it was not embarrassment that prompted her alarm.

Elizabeth did not want any news reaching Germany that she was living in England, or that she had become British. She had taken pains to conceal this from Trix, Felicitas, Teppi and others in Germany. Elizabeth feared the impact public knowledge of her whereabouts would have on her two daughters stranded there, and on her money still held in Deutsche Bank. Birrell sent her to the Home Office, which sent her to Scotland Yard, where she spoke to the assistant commissioner. He assured her the incident would not get into the newspapers.

The war made everyone jittery and fearful. Walking near her sister's home, Elizabeth used her binoculars to look at a pretty cottage and surrounding fields. A group of children shouted at her that she was spying. 'So have the disgusting ways of the Germans dragged us down to all sorts of ugly behaviour.'

Even in the educated, literary circles in which she moved, she encountered hostility. At a lunch, she was introduced to actor Norman Forbes-Robertson, a prominent member of the Garrick Club. He asked archly if her husband was 'fighting against us'. She answered simply that he wasn't.

As the war raged, she found lighter moments. She met the war correspondent and author Alexander Filson Young at a lunch. He had recently written the first book about the sinking of the *Titanic*. But it was another maritime incident he told her about that impressed her. He had been aboard HMS *Lion* when it came under German attack. At the time, he had a copy of her book *The Pastor's Wife* in his cabin. A shell hit the book, leaving it charred.

Elizabeth enjoyed the company of Frank's young brother Bertrand, whom she came to know at this time. Bertie, as his friends called him, reminded her of H.G. Wells. Bertrand was then a lecturer at Trinity College, Cambridge, and a noted mathematician. He credited his lifelong love of mathematics to Frank, who gave him his first lesson in Euclid when Bertrand was eleven years old. The brothers were vastly different in temperament and appearance. Frank was a tempestuous bear of a man, his younger brother was measured, slender and birdlike.

Bertrand was politically engaged, supporting a range of liberal causes, including women's suffrage, and was a proponent of free love. He was also a pacifist. He thought the war and Britain's entry into it a mistake. He had argued for Britain's neutrality and organised a petition to that effect among Cambridge's dons.

He held vastly different views from Elizabeth on the war and on Germany itself. Nonetheless, she attended in May a peace meeting organised by politician and pacifist E.D. Morel, whose political courage Bertrand admired. She was not impressed, noting spikily: 'Found it such rot I left.' Bertrand, meanwhile, found Elizabeth's bellicose attitudes hard to take.

As spring turned to summer, a couple of incidents with Frank unsettled Elizabeth. She drove to Telegraph House with Liebet and Charlotte to pay him a surprise visit in late May. She knew Frank disliked being taken unawares, and she felt uneasy at arriving unannounced. Although he seemed pleased to see her, what should have been a joyful visit was tainted by her fears beforehand.

She also knew Frank was a gambler. Although he'd promised her he would curb his ways, he had not. When he confessed he had lost about £40 in a late-night game of bridge in London, she was filled with anxieties. She wrote in her journal: 'I greatly disappointed he should have broken his promise to me & full of doubts about future if I were ever to marry him.'

Frank was testing her faith in him and her patience. Even her willingness to listen as he read chemistry books to her was wearing thin, as she noted a few days later: 'Gott strafe chemistry' (May God punish chemistry).

Amid her doubts about Frank, she had a sudden urge to see H.G. Wells. She called to see him and Jane Wells. By then Wells' young lover Rebecca West had given birth to their son Anthony West. Wells was spending time between both households, a situation Jane again tolerated. Wells had found his erotic love for Rebecca tested by the arrival of a baby. Perhaps the strain showed. Elizabeth was stunned by the change in his appearance since she had last seen him. Her reaction to the man who had left her for another and younger mistress was mixed with a generous dose of schadenfreude. She found him 'much motheaten & run to seed—was greatly amused'.

Elizabeth went straight to St Thomas' Hospital as soon as she heard the news. Evi had been sacked as a trainee nurse. Elizabeth wanted to know why. Her daughter's dismissal had nothing to do with her being German, matron told her. The girl was scatterbrained, unreliable and would not carry out orders.

Evi was not the only daughter Elizabeth had concerns for in the summer of 1915. She learned that Trix, previously studying piano in Germany, was working as a nurse and had been sent to Lille in German-occupied France, a city close to the battlefields. Trix had expected to nurse the wounded; instead she was treating men with venereal diseases. She was deeply unhappy with the work and with the harassment she had encountered. She and other German nurses in the town were verbally abused in the street by the French locals.

Elizabeth confided to Liebet: 'I fear if the French get back into Lille they'll make short work of any German women.'

Elizabeth typically penned her letters on notepaper printed with the address of where she was staying or living at the time. But a note to Teppi in Germany was written on Chalet Soleil letterhead. Elizabeth did not want Teppi—or any officials who might open the letter—knowing she was in England. The letter maintained the fiction Elizabeth was at the chalet as she expressed the hope that she and Teppi would meet again 'here in Switzerland'.

In July, Frank sailed off on a three-month business trip to South Africa, where he served on the board of a gold mine in Rhodesia. His decree nisi, a provisional step towards his divorce from Mollie, was granted soon after he departed.

Elizabeth spent much of the summer staying with Charlotte at her Sussex home near Haslemere. H.B. also came for his school holiday. When the fickle English summer weather allowed, Elizabeth spent it outdoors, walking or in a garden. Elizabeth found refuge in the garden of her niece Margery after one long afternoon conversation about the war: 'the snapdragons didn't care what the Germs & Russians were doing.'

For months, the war news had been bleak. A German U-boat had sunk the *Lusitania* off the coast of Ireland with the loss of nearly 1200 lives in May. Two members of Elizabeth's extended family were among the survivors on the liner bound from New York to Liverpool. Frederic M. Lassetter, a grandson of her uncle Frederic, had been returning with his mother from convalescing in the US after being wounded fighting in Flanders. When the vessel was torpedoed, Frederic and his mother jumped into the sea, where they clung to a box until they were rescued.

Hopes of a short war had faded; the war had escalated. By August,

German troops had captured Warsaw from the Russians. Elizabeth tried to shield herself from news of the war. She resolved not to look at the morning newspapers until lunchtime, so she could write without distraction. She tried to remain positive. Charlotte, with two sons in uniform, was increasingly anxious. Elizabeth was too, but she more obstinately clung to rays of light.

Throughout Frank's three-month absence, Elizabeth was remarkably buoyant. But as his return drew closer, along with his divorce from Mollie, her anxiety increased. Bertrand visited her for a couple of days, during which she confided in him about her relationship with Frank.

She told him she had initially been unguarded with Frank because he was safely married and therefore suitable as a lover. She had not anticipated that he would suddenly divorce Mollie. 'It took her breath away, and rather flattered her,' Bertrand confided to his own mistress Lady Ottoline Morrell, the influential, aristocratic society hostess. 'She [Elizabeth] drifted, said nothing definite, but allowed him tacitly to assume everything. Now she is feeling very worried, because the inexorable moment is coming when his divorce will be absolute and she will have to decide.'

Elizabeth's objections to Frank included that he slept with seven dogs on the bed, read Kipling aloud and loved Telegraph House, which was hideous. Bertrand did not believe these were her only reasons.

'She is a flatterer, and has evidently set herself the task of getting me to be not against her if she breaks with him. But it is an impossible task. I am too fond of my brother, and shall mind his suffering too much, to forgive her inwardly even if she has a perfectly good case. She says she is still in great uncertainty, but I don't think she will marry him.'

In contrast, Cobbie worried that she would. Frank was their main topic of conversation when he visited Elizabeth a couple of days after Bertrand left. Cobbie wrote candidly in his diary: 'She loves to be loved, and is gradually, and despite the motes in the beams of his affection, being absorbed into the system of his devotion—I might perhaps more accurately say, into the atmosphere of his egotism. And perhaps, despite the motes, she may be happy there; but it will be an atmosphere of his creation, and her own liberty will be lost.'

Elizabeth's reservations about her love affair were swept aside when she and Frank were reunited in mid-September. She was overjoyed: 'Great & infinite bliss to be together again.' Frank visited her almost daily at Charlotte's. They went for picnics in the woods, wandered in heather and took turns driving through the countryside. Elizabeth thought him an angel.

But within a couple of weeks of Frank's return, she was feeling the strain of his presence and moods. She took off alone to Lyndhurst, near the New Forest in Hampshire, ostensibly to write for a week. Although she did little writing, she walked in the forest and enjoyed the solitude at her hotel. 'I never speak except to order more coals. My tongue is having a greatly needed rest.' She found herself, for once, simply frittering away her time, and typically ambivalent about the experience: 'Enjoyed being idle. Deplored enjoying it.'

In early November, a week-long episode in her relationship with Frank unfolded that suggests her emotional vulnerability and rapidly eroding self-confidence. She telegrammed Frank to say she was in London and could stay on to see him. She received no answer and returned crestfallen to her sister's home at Hatch. In distress, she telegrammed him again. And again. Still he did not reply. When he eventually turned up, he seemed unaware of and indifferent to her efforts to contact him. She knew her behaviour was out of character.

By mid-November, she had 'difficulty remembering that I have a separate spirit'.

Meanwhile, the future of her daughters in England increasingly worried her. The threat of deportation hung over them; they were viewed with suspicion and their movements restricted. She wanted to get them out of Britain until the war ended. She made plans to send Evi and Liebet to still-neutral America. She asked Bertrand Russell for help. Did he know a respectable, loving American family who might provide shelter?

In the end, her own American friends, her publisher Frank N. Doubleday and writer Poultney Bigelow, offered to assist. To her daughter Liebet, Elizabeth attempted to put a positive spin on the American plan. 'A cheerful jolly girl, ready for anything, would fall on her feet at once & have a heavenly time. She *must* however be willing to lend a cheerful hand at anything. I *know* you will. I have doubts whether Evi will.' Elizabeth hoped Liebet might instil in the more reckless Evi the need to make a success of the opportunity being offered.

Elizabeth spent a second Christmas at Telegraph House with Frank, where Charlotte and Bertrand also joined them. She enjoyed the company of Bertrand, who read aloud a lecture he had written, and they went on a long walk together, returning late for tea. Frank was sweet and tender—in the mood she loved best—over Christmas. But after the guests had gone, his mood changed, as it often did when they were alone, particularly when they were alone on his terrain, Telegraph House. 'I full of doubts about the future in consequence.'

On New Year's Eve, she penned a more tempered summary of the year in her journal than she had a year earlier: '1915 was not nearly so happy a year for me as 1914 but yet with many happinesses in it, all, I think, owing to my dear F. (Also pains).'

Elizabeth tossed and turned all night. Liebet was to sail to America the next day. Elizabeth wasn't sure how she could bear letting her go. She had spent the weeks leading up to Liebet's departure arranging a new wardrobe for her, taking her to concerts and to say goodbye to her Beauchamp relatives. She reassured her daughter, and herself, that it would be for just a short time. Liebet sailed on 22 January.

Elizabeth had such concerns about how Evi would fare in America, she tried to secure work for her in London. None could be found, and so Evi sailed to America two weeks after her sister.

Between Liebet's departure and Evi's, Elizabeth learned that Frank's divorce was about to be finalised. He was overjoyed. Elizabeth set aside her reservations and on a crisp, frosty morning, she walked alone along the Embankment and into St Paul's to 'render thanks for my great happiness'. The divorce came through on 24 January and Elizabeth and Frank spent a subdued evening together 'quaking at the possibilities before us'.

Chapter 11

THE DREGS OF MISERY

In pouring rain and yellow fog, Elizabeth and Frank emerged from a Covent Garden registry office on 11 February 1916. Elizabeth had again wed in the most miserable month of the year. This time, there was neither a lavish ceremony nor family celebration. Charlotte and Bertrand were the only witnesses.

Elizabeth's mother was incredulous when they visited her a few hours afterwards. Louey continued to be so unhappy about the marriage that Elizabeth resolved—briefly—not to visit her again. Whatever their private reservations, Elizabeth's friends offered congratulations to the new Countess Russell, including H.G. Wells and Cobbie. The latter thought Elizabeth appeared tremulous with controlled emotion while Frank beamed like the sun when they broke the news to him a few days after the ceremony.

News of their marriage was kept out of the papers for fear of complications for her daughters in Germany. Elizabeth wrote to Liebet of her marriage: '[Frank] spoils me so completely that I'm certain I shall lose any faculties I ever had & simply become just a round ball of purring contentment.' She swore Liebet and Evi to secrecy. She did not want Trix in Germany to know she had married.

On the day Elizabeth shared her news with Liebet in America, Frank's ex-wife Mollie Russell made headlines there. Ironically, Mollie was dispensing marriage advice. She warned young American women to beware of attempts to marry Britain's Prince of Wales to one of them. He was not up to American standards. The heir to the British throne was puny, intellectually weak and inbred, Mollie asserted in a widely syndicated article. No mention was made of Mollie's recent divorce in the piece in which Mollie was referred to as the Countess Russell.

Elizabeth and Frank's first weeks of married life were mostly amicable. Frank's London home at 57 Gordon Square was being redecorated so they stayed nearby at the Palace Hotel, Bloomsbury. But she felt deserted and hurt when he suddenly left her one evening to go to his club. His evenings playing bridge at his club soon became more frequent.

At Telegraph House she oversaw the renovation of what she called her hut. She planned to use it to write in. Frank nursed her through a bout of flu at Telegraph House in early March. As she was recovering in bed one morning, she heard his raised voice, angry with one of the servants. She was appalled at this behaviour that reminded her of Henning's tempers with staff. She was barely back on her feet when Frank's fury turned on her. He accused her of touching items in his office. She vowed never to go near his office again.

Elizabeth's disillusion with Frank so soon after her wedding raises the question: what possessed her to marry him? Elizabeth did not need his British nationality. She had already acquired that. She did not need his name or his title. She was already a countess. She knew there were risks for her daughters in Germany if word got out of her marriage. She married him despite this.

Elizabeth was not blind to his tempers and his insensitivity. Her journals are full of these. But so too are her declarations of love. She was willing to overlook his faults, at least for a while. She seemed convinced that underneath his moody surface was a loving human being. He exerted a magnetic pull. She may have believed that she could change him and that after his two unhappy marriages she was the woman who could restore his happiness. Bertrand had suggested that she had let the relationship drift along. If so, her novel *The Pastor's Wife* had proved prophetic. Elizabeth had simply offered no resistance.

Her anger towards her mother dissipated and she took flowers to the still sprightly Louey on her eightieth birthday. Elizabeth, who had resolved to cut contact with her mother, may have realised by then that Louey's reservations about Frank were justified. Just six weeks after her wedding, Elizabeth was contemplating leaving him. She saw no hope in their future together.

Frank was prone to sudden mood swings and erratic behaviour. These may have been exacerbated by his use of cocaine. Elizabeth refers to collecting medicine for him that contained cocaine. Although Elizabeth fought with Frank over his cocaine prescription, this appears to have been triggered by the high-handed manner in which he ordered her to get it rather than over the drug itself.

At that time, cocaine use would not necessarily cause concern. Cocaine was used in literary and other circles and regarded as a drug for intelligent people in need of stimulation rather than an indication of moral depravity. Even Queen Victoria was said to have indulged, while Arthur Conan Doyle's Sherlock Holmes was its most famous fictional recreational user. When World War I broke out, cocaine was still legal in Britain and its use by soldiers was encouraged, not least by Harrods department store, which sold 'A Welcome Present for Friends at the Front'. The present contained cocaine, morphine, syringes and needles.

The extent of Frank's cocaine use is unclear. But his continued high-stakes gambling, despite mounting debts and promises to quit, suggests an addictive personality.

Elizabeth was at home at Gordon Square in April when the phone rang. A journalist from the *Evening News* informed her that American newspapers were about to publish news of her marriage. The reporter wanted to know if the rumour was correct.

Her marriage was front-page news in the US the next morning. *The Washington Post* called it the 'remarkable secret marriage of one of England's most-talked-of couples'. Elizabeth, it reported, had been prominent in society, but since the war had been in a difficult position because of her German connections. The paper was well-informed about the fate of her two eldest daughters. It reported that because of their German name and accent, Elizabeth had sent them to America. Elizabeth hoped Evi had not let the secret out. She feared what might befall her two English-born daughters Trix and Felicitas, cut off from her in Germany.

Elizabeth was unaware that news of her marriage had already leaked. In Australia, *The Age*, Melbourne, published a lengthy report in late March, more than a week before *The Washington Post*. It noted Earl Russell's scandalous previous marriages, and bigamy trial, as well as his authorship of a book entitled *Divorce*, 'on which subject he may be considered an authority'. It described Elizabeth as a writer and the daughter of H.H. Beauchamp, but made no mention of her Australian birth.

In England, *The Times* gave just two sentences to the marriage, while the *Tatler* claimed the marriage was an open secret. But public knowledge of her marriage deepened her unhappiness, as did Frank's behaviour. 'Have made up my mind not to take anything to heart but sedulously cultivate not caring. It means letting great love for F. go & has been a terrible decision to arrive at but only so, by being indifferent can I live with him. If I love him I'm too hurt & wounded too often & would not be able to go on living. But oh oh oh. He is specially intolerable & quarrelsome at T.H. [Telegraph House] I hate & dread T.H.'

In London at least, Elizabeth had distractions, including overseeing changes at Gordon Square, hiring staff, arranging the move of her furniture there and giving up her old flat. She saw Charles Stuart and was happy to learn he had just become engaged. She farewelled him before he left for the Front.

She saw a more impressive side of Frank as she went to hear him speak in the House of Lords, in which he argued for better treatment of conscientious objectors. He spoke often in debates, and although Elizabeth did not always agree with his arguments, she appreciated his eloquence.

She missed her daughters and longed to embrace them. When Elizabeth walked past the Middlesex Hospital, she looked up longingly at Liebet's old ward window. She thought back too to their brief time at the chalet together. She had taken their happiness there for granted. Elizabeth was gratified that Evi seemed happy with the Bigelows. In Germany, Trix had taken responsibility for Felicitas.

Fearing funds for her schooling were about to be frozen, Trix had arranged for Felicitas to work in a hospital in Bremen. But letters from Trix had become scarce and Elizabeth feared Germany had blocked mail to Switzerland.

Her sister remained a source of happiness, and when Charlotte's son Johnnie came home on a month's leave at Easter, having hired a Rolls-Royce for the duration, Elizabeth enjoyed motoring with him and listening to him read aloud from his war diary.

Elizabeth read *The Times* with horror on 3 June 1916. The *Black Prince* had gone down in the Battle of Jutland in the North Sea. Her nephew Johnnie, who had just returned from leave, was aboard. She drove immediately to see Charlotte. Margery was with her mother when Elizabeth arrived. The young woman clung to the hope that her brother had survived. Early reports said sailors involved in the massive battle, in which an estimated six British cruisers were sunk, were being picked up by rescue trawlers. Charlotte did not share her daughter's hope.

Elizabeth returned to her sister's the next day. She was met at the door by Margery and nephew Monarch. There were no survivors of the *Black Prince*. Johnnie—Commander John Beauchamp Waterlow—was among the 857 men dead.

As Elizabeth absorbed the tragic news, she was handed a telegram that had arrived for her from Teppi. It was brief but devastating. Felicitas was dead. There were no details of the circumstances in which her youngest daughter, who she had long ago dubbed "Martin", had died in Bremen.

Elizabeth knew only that she would never again see the daughter whose childhood nightmares she had once tried to soothe, who was once transfixed by the sight of an orange tree but whom Elizabeth had banished after she'd been accused of theft. Elizabeth drove back to Telegraph House in a gale 'tasting the depth of desolation'. She was desperate for news of what had happened. 'My little Martin! The pitifulness of it all alone there without her Mummy & only sixteen—& I don't know why she died—not a word.'

Elizabeth urged Liebet and Evi to show courage in the face of the terrible news. 'I can't bear it—& yet I'm going to bear it [. . .] Liebet darling don't fret—try not to—if you crabs will only hold out & set your teeth & look forward to the happy times that certainly will come, then so can I. But if you aren't able to then I feel that neither shall I [. . .] Sixteen Liebet! Just think of it. Such a sad, tortuous little life she had.'

Elizabeth was consumed not just with her own grief but with anguish for daughter Trix in Germany, who had taken responsibility for Felicitas, and she longed to comfort her. Elizabeth contemplated whether she could get Trix to America to join her sisters. She could not bear to tell her son, H.B.

She advised Liebet and Evi to keep news of Felicitas's death to themselves, so they were not forced into wearing mourning, and the questions this might prompt. If the sisters were quiet and wished to explain their behaviour, they could say they were mourning the death of their cousin Johnnie. Elizabeth's advice suggests the difficulty in grieving the loss on enemy soil of Felicitas.

Even before she knew any details of how her daughter died, Elizabeth had no doubts about where responsibility lay for her daughter's death: 'Martin's death is just as directly the result of the war as Johnnie's.'

It was two weeks before Elizabeth learned from Teppi that Felicitas died of double pneumonia. Teppi had been contacted on 1 June; she was told that Felicitas was ill and had been taken to hospital in Bremen. Teppi rushed to the hospital and found the girl too ill to speak. The doctor assured Teppi that Felicitas was strong and would pull through and told her she did not need to contact Trix. But early the next morning, Teppi received a phone call. Felicitas had died in the early hours.

Full of remorse at her actions, Elizabeth wrote back to Teppi:

> No one knows better than you how shattered I must be about everything that happened, about the thoughts of the last time I saw Martin, leaving me forever and ever, without a kiss, without love, after the sad scenes of the last days at the chalet. If only I had held her in my arms once again! To tell her how deeply I loved her, and that it was just *because* I loved her so deeply that I suffered so much about what she did in the past [. . .] Teppi, how can anyone bear such things? I don't know. My heart bleeds for Trix. She has suffered and battled enough.

Elizabeth begged Teppi for details of Martin's last days. Had she started work in Bremen? How had she contracted such a terrible illness? And seeking, perhaps, a sliver of hope to allay her guilt, Elizabeth asked: 'Did she say something about her mother that could console me?'

The war meant Elizabeth could not travel to Germany for the funeral. She conveyed to German relatives her wish that Felicitas be laid to rest with Henning at the family mausoleum at Schlagenthin. '[I] feel she *must* go to Papa who loved her so,' she wrote to Liebet. But her message arrived too late. Felicitas was buried among von Arnim family graves elsewhere in Germany, at Criewen.

Elizabeth and Charlotte attempted to comfort each other. 'I can't look at her little face without wanting to howl like a dog,' Elizabeth wrote. The two sisters had each lost a child just hours apart. Yet the circumstances were so different.

Charlotte's son had died serving his country in the largest naval battle of World War I. Many shared Charlotte's loss, for the Battle of Jutland cost more than 6000 British lives alone. Johnnie's death could be publicly acknowledged and grieved as public memorials were held.

Elizabeth's grief was private and complex. Although friends, including Jane and H.G. Wells, conveyed their sympathy, Elizabeth could not even attend Felicitas's burial. Her daughter had died, psychologically and physically, on the other side of a war. And she had died after Elizabeth's cruel exile of her, accused of a theft Felicitas always maintained she had not committed.

If Elizabeth hoped for emotional support from Frank, this was in vain. He became increasingly controlling, moody and angry. Bereft at the loss of her daughter and nephew, Elizabeth was horrified as Frank berated a servant who had forgotten to put a towel in his room. 'I got down to the very dregs today of hopeless misery,' she wrote in her journal.

Frank soon turned his anger on Elizabeth, reeling off her faults, calling her brutal, vicious and sulky. He abused her in front of her sister and before the staff at Telegraph House. He admonished her on a cold wet day in Oxford for not waiting for him in the street rather than at the hotel where they were to have lunch. Nonetheless, she still clung to a glimmer of hope. 'I'm so eager to be happy with him that I'd do anything for him if he'd be decent & kind.'

Frank's behaviour invariably improved in the presence of outsiders, including when his friend George Santayana came to stay at Telegraph House in June. It was the first time Elizabeth had met Santayana, who had been so opposed to Frank's remarriage. Santayana's first impression of the diminutive figure who waved to him from behind the wheel of a car, as Elizabeth collected him from a railway station, was of a little girl. Even up close she seemed to him childlike, with a tiny nose, eyes and a small, innocent mouth. He found her pretty, slim and more intelligent than her predecessors.

Elizabeth knew of Santayana's reservations about their marriage. Frank had shown her Santayana's letter, in which he likened his friend to Henry VIII. She was eager to convince Santayana that she was the woman to take Frank in hand—that she had the character, intellect, charm and youth to make a new man of him, or at least return him to his true good self. Santayana was not convinced. A string of women, including Frank's two previous wives, had also thought themselves capable of redeeming him. Santayana did not think the new marriage would last.

'The marvel was that so many women, by no means fools, thought they could manage him, and that each in her turn believed herself predestined to redeem him and anchor him to the safe haven of her arms [. . .] now Elizabeth thought so: the simplest, the most battered, the most intelligent of women were alike in their infatuation and blindness.' What soon unfolded was a realisation of Santayana's most famous aphorism: 'Those who cannot remember the past are condemned to repeat it.'

Santayana found the atmosphere at Telegraph House charged with matrimonial thunder. Frank was jealous of the closeness that developed between his wife and his friend. Elizabeth confided to Santayana that Frank as a husband was vastly different from Frank as a lover. And she told Santayana that Frank was sexually sadistic. 'Love-making for him was no laughing matter, no playfulness of a mad moment. It was a loving wife's sworn duty to be obedient; and if she rebelled and fled from her husband, he said she was cruel,' Santayana wrote in his autobiography.

Santayana harboured few illusions about Frank. He knew Frank was self-obsessed, domineering, full of petty habits and rules. As he was Frank's friend, the rules did not impact him; they were simply character quirks. But Santayana came to realise that towards women he was a tyrant. 'His wives and his cats were his prisoners, condemned to be petted at pleasure.'

Elizabeth wrote a letter to Liebet, and the domestic tyranny she describes is shocking. 'I'm practically in prison. Within the limits of the wire fencing I can go & come if I have first asked if I may go for a walk, but to get outside it means almost every time bad blood.'

To her journal, she confided how submissive she had become in her attempts to appease him. 'In order to get him to be so [amiable] I have to be incredibly slavish—never move without asking permission—constantly begging his pardon if I have done anything contrary to his wishes.' The independent, determined Elizabeth had all but vanished. She felt 'kicked to death by life'.

Mythical birds stretched their wings atop the clocktowers of the Royal Liver Building overlooking the River Mersey. Aboard RMS *Adriatic* Elizabeth too was ready for flight. Her destination was New York.

Elizabeth had planned her escape all summer. She kept Frank in the dark and bided her time. Her son had come to stay at Telegraph

House for the school holidays, having just finished at prep school. She had enrolled him at Eton and wanted to see him settled in his new school in autumn. That was all that kept her under the same roof as Frank. She drove her son to Windsor and spoke to his tutors before she left him at the exclusive school as the term began.

She was ready to make her move. She knew Frank would soon leave Telegraph House for one of his frequent trips to London. He drove away in pouring rain, blissfully unaware of what she was about to do. She visited Charlotte to say farewell. Elizabeth took a morning train to Liverpool and boarded the ship, which sailed out of the northern port city in the early evening of 27 September.

For the second time in two years, Elizabeth was fleeing her home. She would not sleep on the deck with her head on a coil of rope this time, but in a cabin aboard the elegant White Star passenger liner. The ship was chased by a submarine the day after departure, but otherwise the eight-day journey passed without incident.

Liebet was waiting when Elizabeth arrived in New York. Also waiting was an American friend, Jane Whitehead. Jane was a painter and musician, and her wealthy English husband Ralph Whitehead had recently founded a utopian art colony called Byrdcliffe, above Woodstock in New York state's Catskill Mountains. Influenced by William Morris, Ralph built a series of Arts and Craft style buildings and chalets there. (Byrdcliffe has since been a refuge for many artists, including a youthful Bob Dylan.)

Elizabeth stayed two weeks at Byrdcliffe and visited Evi, who had taken a teaching job in nearby Connecticut. But with winter approaching, Elizabeth did not plan to spend it freezing on the east coast. She had fantasised for months about sitting out the war in a wooden house in California drinking iced coconut water beneath a cloudless sky. 'Don't ever be surprised if you see a dusty little Mummy with a battered knapsack walk up to your front door one day en route for California,' Elizabeth had written to Liebet in the wake of her daughter's arrival in America.

Accompanied by Liebet, Elizabeth took a train across the country and after a week's travel was transfixed by her first blinding glimpse of California. Late autumn was suddenly left behind as the light and landscape transformed near San Bernardino. 'Suddenly the door opened and in came summer,' is how she expressed it in her novel *Christopher and Columbus*, which drew on her American experience. 'Here was summer without sultriness, without gnats, mosquitoes, threatening thunderstorms, or anything to spoil it; it was summer as it might be in the Elysian fields, perfectly clear, and calm, and radiant.'

Elizabeth's feckless, impoverished grandfather had come to California in his youth and tried unsuccessfully to make his fortune. As a girl, she may have heard from him tales of those adventures. But for her, the gold was not in the hills but in the enchanting sunset sky.

They stayed near Santa Barbara in the Montecito foothills at a cottage hotel at San Ysidro from where Elizabeth wrote to Frank telling him where she was. She worked on a new novel, *Christine*, one that may have palliated some of the grief and remorse she felt over her daughter's death. It is arguably her most controversial book.

The eponymous Christine is a talented young English violinist studying in Berlin in the months leading up to World War I and here she falls in love with a Prussian Junker. The book is written as a series of affectionate, sentimental letters from Christine to her adored widowed mother in England. At one level, the book presents an idealised version of a deeply devoted and musical daughter—the daughter Elizabeth may have wished Felicitas to have become. But Christine's letters describe the anti-British hostility she encounters and the increasing German bloodlust as the country moves towards war.

The book's preface is ostensibly written by Christine's mother, Alice Cholmondeley, three years after her daughter died of double pneumonia in a Stuttgart hospital in August 1914. Alice claims she initially kept her daughter's letters private, not wanting to rush to harsh judgement of the German people about whom, like most people in England at the time, she knew little.

'Now, as the years have passed, and each has been more full of actions on Germany's part difficult to explain except in one way and impossible to excuse, I feel that these letters, giving a picture of the state of mind of the German public immediately before the War, and written by someone who went there enthusiastically ready to like everything and everybody, may have a certain value in helping to put together a small corner of the great picture of Germany which it will be necessary to keep clear and naked before us in the future if the world is to be saved.' The preface concludes in words that echoed Elizabeth's response to the death of Felicitas: 'The war killed Christine, just as surely as if she had been a soldier in the trenches.'

Christmas Day at San Ysidro was subdued. Elizabeth and Liebet, who was sick with a cold, played chess. Elizabeth thought of happier Christmases past and found herself in tears. She summarised the year in her diary: 'This year (1916) was the most wretched of my life. I have never been so unhappy as from February to September.'

The new year had barely begun when, without warning, Frank arrived at San Ysidro. The peaceful atmosphere changed as suddenly and dramatically as the arrival of the Santa Ana devil wind that blows through Southern California. As in previous times of distress, Elizabeth stopped writing in her diary. But Liebet watched in dismay as her mother bowed to Frank's demands, however outrageous, anxious to pour balm on the situation. Their activities were 'now strictly ordered by a heavy hand, and there was instant retribution in the form of prolonged ill-humour at the slightest, even accidental deviation,' Liebet later recalled. Rows ensued between Liebet and Frank.

In early spring, Elizabeth and Frank left by train to New York, and from there he sailed back to England. Liebet remained in California with friends while Elizabeth stayed on the east coast, determined to finish *Christine* before she left America.

Elizabeth had also turned her novel *The Benefactress* into a play, entitled *Ellen in Germany*, and in New York she sounded out a theatrical agent, hoping to secure a production. But America had just entered the war; the public had no appetite for a play in which its heroine loved a German. The unpublished, unproduced *Ellen in Germany* was written under a pseudonym—as K. Casaubon, a name redolent of George Eliot's *Middlemarch.*

While staying with friends in rural Virginia, Elizabeth received news that Charles Stuart had been killed in the war. She had often laughed at his dog-like devotion to her, but she was devastated by his death. Charles had married just two weeks before he left for the front and died unaware that his young bride had conceived. After the loss of her daughter and her nephew, Charles's death took with it any faith Elizabeth might have had in a Christian eternity. 'Life is getting very much whittled away of all that one has had [. . .] death is a most dreadful thing—it behoves one to live in the utmost possible peace & love with each other while we've got each other—however tiresome & difficult we are sometimes we're still *alive*—that awful, cold, endless death, that wiping out forever of love & dearness is intolerable to think of,' she wrote to Liebet.

Back in California, Liebet had become engaged to a young man called Corwin Butterworth. Elizabeth gave them her blessing, telling Liebet that there was nothing in the world like one's own lover and husband. 'All other happinesses are as pale compared to that.' Elizabeth dashed across to California for the wedding before returning to New York and then boarding a ship to England in late summer. She had loved America and Americans, but she was eager to get back to Frank. She was convinced the old Frank had been replaced by a new improved version.

Chapter 12

'ALICE' IN PROPAGANDA-LAND

The advertisement in *The New York Times* trumpeted *Christine* as 'A New Novel by a New Author'. Elizabeth was hardly a new author. But alone among her books, *Christine* was published under a different name entirely: Alice Cholmondeley. The book's conceit is that Alice Cholmondeley has published her daughter's letters. This soon became a source of controversy.

The book's stridently anti-German tone found a receptive readership in an America that had just entered the war when *Christine* was released in the US in July 1917. Reviewed on the cover of *The New York Times Review of Books*, it was described as 'true in essentials though it wears the garb of fiction—so real is it that one is tempted to doubt whether it is fiction at all'. The book's lucid analysis of the German state of mind just before and at the beginning of the war provided a lesson that easygoing America needed to learn, the review argued.

Other reviewers were confounded as to whether the book was fiction or non-fiction. *The Nation* thought that if Christine's letters were genuine, the book demonstrated beyond doubt that the German middle class had wanted war even before the Sarajevo assassination. But if the letters were not real, the reviewer deplored 'the wretched taste of an author who just at this time would dare to confirm our worst suspicions of Germany by an elaborate fiction parading as [. . .] fact'. It demanded the book's US publisher Macmillan ferret out its authorship and ascertain the conditions under which it was written.

Macmillan claimed not to know. It offered *The New York Times* a brief explanation. The manuscript had come to the publishing house not from the author but a lawyer acting as her agent. All dealings had been with this agent.

But the newspaper soon raised a quizzical eyebrow, reporting that Alice Cholmondeley was rumoured to be a pen-name of an otherwise well-known English writer. A correspondent to the paper, signed simply AOL of Baltimore, weighed in and pointed to Elizabeth von Arnim as the likely author.

Macmillan rejected arguments that the book should not have been published because the author wished to remain unknown and because there was no proof the work was genuine. The book was offered to them by a reputable lawyer and merited publication whether fact or fiction, the publisher countered. It could not confirm nor deny that Elizabeth von Arnim was the author, but saw nothing conclusive to indicate it was.

Other names were soon raised as likely authors, including American writers Gertrude Atherton, Owen Wister and James Lane Allen. Anti-German Atherton was furious. She was not the author of this 'obvious fake, and ingenious (if laudable) bit of anti-German propaganda', she wrote to *The New York Times*. *Christine*'s publisher and author had treated the public as a 'pack of silly children', she said. Atherton did not believe Elizabeth was the author and leapt to her defence. 'Poor Countess Arnim! [. . .] the most poignantly funny writer living' had been accused of writing it merely because it contained dabs of humour. Atherton considered the book a poor addition to the 'overflowing cup of hate which we are all hoping will choke Germany before long'.

Macmillan again defended publication, stating: 'Having no positive proof in their hands, and being unable to communicate with the author, who is unknown to them [. . .] they have adopted the only honourable course that was open to them. It is their conviction that *Christine* is fact—but they cannot prove it, and they say so quite openly.' As the controversy continued, *Christine* became America's sixth bestselling book for the year.

In the smoke and mirrors surrounding the book, Elizabeth continued to deny authorship. But fear of putting her daughter Trix in Germany in danger may not have been the only reason for writing under a nom de plume. At the time Macmillan published the book in the US, Elizabeth had a contract with rival publisher Doubleday, which had published her two previous books in the US.

While Macmillan publicly claimed ignorance of *Christine*'s authorship, Frank Doubleday was in no doubt. He recognised Elizabeth's style. She cheekily told him she hoped her style was not so 'unbuttoned' as Cholmondeley's. But when he quizzed her on why she had gone back on their agreement she toughed it out. She claimed she had not even heard of the book until he brought it to her attention. 'But nobody believed her, least of all ourselves,' Frank Doubleday wrote in his *The Memoirs of a Publisher*. She later admitted to him that Macmillan had initiated the book and therefore she did not feel she could then give it to Doubleday.

Elizabeth claimed that not even her husband knew she had written *Christine*. It's likely he did not, since Frank demonstrated no interest in her writing.

But Elizabeth even denied having penned the book to her daughter Liebet, who had been with her in San Ysidro when she was writing it. Elizabeth dissembled to Liebet: 'I have indignantly repudiated such a charge—how tiresome people are once they get an idea into their heads—well, there's nothing to do but to continue to deny. I expect it was written by *you*! For I do see a certain family likeness about it, but I've had lots of imitating women first & last, & this is probably one of them.' But her other daughter in America, Evi, was convinced Elizabeth was the author.

Why Elizabeth chose the nom de plume Alice Cholmondeley is curious. It was simply capricious, one newspaper correspondent suggested, because Cholmondeley (pronounced Chum-lee) was every bit as unrecognisable when pronounced in English as her birth name Beauchamp (Beecham). This seems improbable. Authors put much thought into naming characters, and so a nom de plume would likely be every bit as carefully chosen. Her choice may reflect Elizabeth's fondness for some literary mischief in a book she wrote against the backdrop of her marriage to Frank.

Elizabeth knew popular English novelist Mary Cholmondeley. The two women had dined together and were guests of honour at an annual Author's Club banquet in 1911. Like Elizabeth (with whom she shared a birth name of Mary), Cholmondeley wrote her first books anonymously, including *Sir Charles Danvers*. That novel hinges on an Englishman seeking a divorce from his American wife. When he returns to his homeland, he learns the divorce granted in the US is not recognised in England.

There was another link between Elizabeth's nom de plume and

her husband's troubled marital history. The tickets to her husband's infamous bigamy trial in the House of Lords were issued by the Lord Great Chamberlain, the Marquess of Cholmondeley.

Elizabeth was back in England by the time *Christine* was released in September. *The Times Literary Supplement* could not make up its mind if *Christine* was fact or fiction, but decided this was irrelevant. The book was full of truth, told by someone who knew the Germans well and so vividly 'it is hard to believe it was written by any but an eye-witness'. *The Daily Telegraph* said Alice Cholmondeley ought to be an asset to the Allies. 'As propaganda for the outside world, [the book] should prove remarkably effective.'

With its anti-German rhetoric, the question of the book's propaganda purpose is a moot one. Liebet years later described *Christine* as 'Elizabeth's contribution to the war effort'. At the time *Christine* was published, the British government was involved in a covert effort to use writers and publishers to further its war effort and influence opinion, particularly in America. This began within weeks of Britain's entry into the war when, on 2 September 1914—just as Elizabeth had arrived in London after escaping the chalet—twenty-five prominent authors met in secret to discuss how they could assist the war effort. Those present included Arthur Conan Doyle, Thomas Hardy, G.K. Chesterton, J.M. Barrie and two of Elizabeth's associates, Arnold Bennett and H.G. Wells.

The meeting was convened by a cabinet minister, Charles Masterman. He had recently been appointed chief of Britain's War Propaganda Bureau, headquartered at Wellington House, Buckingham Gate. One result of that meeting was the so-called Authors' Manifesto published in *The New York Times* and London's *The Times* on September 18. It was signed by all those at the Wellington House meeting. In addition, Rudyard Kipling, popular novelist H. Rider Haggard and poet Laurence Binyon—remembered for his World War I poem *For the Fallen*—added their names to the list of more than fifty authors and intellectuals. (Noticeably absent were the names of members of the Bloomsbury group, plus George Bernard Shaw and Bertrand Russell.) The manifesto ran again a month later in *The New York Times*, this time as a full-page item with facsimiles of the authors' signatures.

The manifesto proclaimed the authors' unambiguous support for the war, which Britain had to join or face dishonour. Some authors had previously been champions of goodwill towards Germany and even advocated for peace, it noted. But all were now agreed of the righteousness of the Allied effort. The seemingly spontaneous show of author solidarity was drafted by Masterman. It was one of the bureau's first efforts to harness intellectual backing for Britain's entry into the war.

Much of Wellington House's effort was aimed at influencing neutral countries, especially America. The bureau also secretly arranged the production of books or pamphlets through mainstream publishers. It believed works and opinions had greater credibility if appearing independent of the British government. More than twenty publishers were involved, including Macmillan, publisher of *Christine*.

So, it is hard to imagine Elizabeth wasn't aware of the efforts underway to use prominent writers to influence opinion towards the war and Germany. Although there is nothing to link her directly to the work of Wellington House, she was certainly sympathetic to its covert aims. Curiously, shortly after the war ended *The New York Times* made a gnomic comment that Elizabeth worked for the British government during the First World War.

At Telegraph House, Elizabeth was wallowing in a 'bath of love'. She was overjoyed to be reunited with Frank, who 'envelops me to the exclusion of the world'. But rather than feeling smothered and controlled, she was content. 'I like being with male creatures.'

The only family member she saw in the days after her return was her rapidly maturing son, H.B. He was tall, slim, moustachioed, and had acquired Eton manners and voice in the year since she'd deposited him at this new school.

At Gordon Square, Bertrand had moved in with Elizabeth and Frank. Bertrand brought with him his books, and pictures of philosophers Spinoza and Leibniz, and the house was full of signs of intelligence as it had never been before. Elizabeth was fascinated by Bertrand, an elf-like figure she described as 'a Christ & a devil, angelically saint-like & thoroughly malignant—the weirdest of human beings'. The brothers were such a contrast to each other that living under the same roof would create 'volcanic interest'.

Bertrand was likely living under Frank's roof out of financial need. He had paid a high price for his anti-war stance. Convicted and fined for making anti-conscription statements in a leaflet in 1916, he had been dismissed from his position at Trinity College. He had given away most of his money after learning it was invested in an engineering firm doing war work.

Frank had no such qualms. He ran munitions factories and during the war proudly escorted King George V around one of them. The monarch was the first of the newly minted House of Windsor, having changed the name from the House of Saxe-Coburg a few months earlier because of anti-German feeling.

Elizabeth and Frank moved between Gordon Square and Telegraph House. George Santayana visited but, far from the matrimonial thunder he had previously encountered, he found the middle-aged second honeymoon Elizabeth was having with her wicked earl embarrassing to observe.

Writer Frank Swinnerton telephoned one day during this time. He was struck by Elizabeth's languid voice as she invited him to tea. He was familiar with her literary voice from her 'arch, acid, charming self-portraits'. Like Santayana, his first impression of the small, fair figure before him was that she was like a child. 'Then one observed that the child was precocious. And then that she was terrifying. She was so terrifying to some men that they trembled under the gaze of her rather prominent merciless pale blue eyes, and collapsed altogether before the demurely drawling boldness of her tongue.' At one point in their first meeting, Swinnerton told Elizabeth that he trusted her. 'Oh, but you mustn't do that!' she replied.

Elizabeth was about to become a grandmother. She longed to be with Liebet in America for the birth of her daughter's first child. Elizabeth jested about how she would need to acquire white hair and granny glasses to fit her new role. She advised her daughter to use chloroform and to stay in bed as long as possible after the birth.

Elizabeth was dismayed when she learned Liebet had given birth to a daughter without chloroform and endured unnecessary pain. History was repeating. 'It is exactly like what happened to me till I took to producing my young in England.' Elizabeth noted there was one difference in their experience of childbirth. 'You have a proper decent husband, who won't force you, as I was forced instantly, before I had even bodily recovered, let alone spiritually, to have another.' She advised Liebet not to have any more 'spawn' for a long time and recommended she neglect her domestic duties rather than sacrifice herself.

With her diary still silent and her letters to Liebet mainly about babies, Elizabeth gave only an occasional glimpse of the state of her relationship with Frank. 'Dad's very loving & overwhelming—I'm engulfed—but it's nice to be loved, even if it has to be overwhelming.' Elizabeth's wit remained sharp as she delivered the odd barbed reference to Frank. She found the notepaper she used for her letters difficult to write on, likening it to Frank—slippery, thick and dear. She dubbed isolated Telegraph House 'Wuthering Heights', with Frank as its brooding Heathcliff.

She had little time for her writing, as Frank commanded her attention. So too did his lapdogs. The size of his pack had increased to eighteen with the arrival of a litter of puppies. Elizabeth wondered if she would ever write again.

Elizabeth's attention was also taken with Bertrand, who had once again angered the authorities. He had written an article for a pacifist journal attacking America's use of troops to break strikes. The article, considered likely to cause bad relations between England and America, saw him hauled before the courts. Elizabeth took her seat in Bow Street Court on 9 February 1918 as the court was told that Bertrand had lost all sense of decency and had gone out of his way to insult a great nation and ally. The magistrate described Bertrand's offence as despicable and sentenced him to six months' imprisonment.

Initially, Bertrand faced the prospect of spending his days employed sewing mailbags while being forbidden access to his books and writing material. His conditions were changed on appeal and, although he was still forbidden his tobacco, he was allowed to write. Within two weeks he had written twenty thousand words of his *Introduction to Mathematical Philosophy*.

Elizabeth was among his regular visitors in Brixton prison and the pair exchanged letters. Bertrand found a way of smuggling letters from prison by enclosing them in the uncut pages of books. Theirs was an affectionate, at times lighthearted exchange. 'One doesn't have a relation in prison every day!' she wrote. She told him that her doctor brother Sydney Beauchamp, whom Bertrand had consulted, had asked after his former patient and 'especially after that portion of you over which he had brief control'. Sydney had once joked to Bertrand that his treatment (for piles) would cure his celebrated patient of his pacifism. From jail, Bertrand asked Elizabeth to inform her brother that the predicted change of views had not yet taken place.

Bertrand was aware of Elizabeth and Frank's marital problems. He could hardly have avoided them at Gordon Square. But even in jail he could not escape being drawn in. He liked Elizabeth. He found her kind, and his affection for her had grown as he got to know her. But he had to tread warily because of Frank's temper, Bertrand confided to Ottoline Morrell. 'I am very fond of her, but embarrassed by the necessity of not arousing my brother's jealousy, which is quite oriental.' But their quarrels, he said, might require him to take Elizabeth's side. Yet if he did so, he would starve and he did not wish poverty to stop his work. Bertrand hoped Elizabeth would not leave Frank while he remained in prison. But if she did, he wanted them to stay in touch, as she would always have his affection.

At times Elizabeth visited with Ottoline Morrell, who remained friends with Bertrand although their affair was by then over. She was a striking, aristocratic and eccentric figure, in billowing gowns and enormous hats, and later the basis for D.H. Lawrence's Hermione Roddice in *Women in Love.* At 182 centimetres, Lady Ottoline was as tall as Elizabeth was diminutive, with a mane of auburn hair and long face that reminded Bertrand of a horse. She presided over Garsington Manor, her Tudor home in Oxford that became a focal point for the Bloomsbury group and a refuge for pacifists during World War I.

Bertrand had met Elizabeth's cousin Katherine Mansfield at Garsington Manor and had become smitten with the young New Zealander. Elizabeth arranged for books to be sent to Bertrand, including Katherine Mansfield's new short story, *Prelude.* It was one of the first published by Leonard and Virginia Woolf's Hogarth Press, founded in their Richmond living room. Although Elizabeth was aware of her young cousin's writing, they were not in contact.

Elizabeth and Ottoline did not warm to each other. Ottoline found Elizabeth patronising towards her. Over tea together one afternoon during this period, an insensitive—or mischievous—Elizabeth told Ottoline how devoted Bertrand was to his new young mistress, Lady Constance Malleson, and lavished praise on her. Ottoline resolved to avoid Elizabeth in future.

Elizabeth also visited Brixton with Constance. She was an actress, who performed under the stage name Colette O'Niel. As Bertrand, prepared to leave prison, he asked Constance and Elizabeth to bring his dispatch case, pipes and tobacco, so he could leave prison in style. On his release in September, he spent several days with Elizabeth and Frank at Telegraph House.

The long bloody war was over. Elizabeth watched as London's streets filled with its war-weary citizens on the day the Armistice was signed, on 11 November 1918. 'London was mad with joy, but there was a tremendous sort of solemnity about it, for every single person had suffered in some way & most of them in many ways,' she wrote to Liebet.

Relieved as Elizabeth was that the war was over, she was anxious about Trix in Germany and the conditions she might confront. Elizabeth feared that food shortages there would result in anarchism.

Frank was a Fabian—he had joined the British reforming socialist organisation before the war—and Elizabeth attended Fabian Society lectures, on the one hand, and high society dinners, on the other. And she hosted glittering soirees attended by the likes of American socialite 'Emerald' Lady Maud Cunard, who had been dubbed 'a most dangerous woman' by British Prime Minister David Lloyd George because of her beguiling influence on politicians. Nancy Astor, poised to become the first woman to sit in the House of Commons, was also among those seated around Elizabeth's dining table as the year ended.

Elizabeth began collaborating with Bertrand on a writing project with the working title *Ellen and Arbuthnot*. This was envisioned as a series of fictional letters between an effusive, naïve young woman called Ellen Wemyss to an older, sophisticated but jaded writer, Mr Arbuthnot. (She would recycle the names Wemyss and Arbuthnot in two later novels, *Vera* and *The Enchanted April*.) The plan was that Elizabeth would write the Ellen letters and Bertrand would reply as Arbuthnot.

But the collaboration did not advance much further before Elizabeth called a halt. She felt paralysed by the project, which had proved harder than she had anticipated. She wrote to Bertrand: 'You will think me a great shilly shallyer, especially after my original confidence [. . .] I was overcome by a dreadful feeling of *you*, and so could not burble out in the natural way which would be essential.'

Frank was having an affair with his young secretary. He had taken a new office in an attempt to hide his dalliance, but Elizabeth had learned of it. She had also learned of other affairs and betrayals.

Yet even as she contemplated leaving him, she vacillated. 'I think I'm going to have to leave Dad definitely—it's impossible to live with him I find—he does too many secret things that are entirely incompatible with marriage,' she wrote to Liebet. 'I may struggle on a bit longer, but doubt it, for it is making me ill & will finish me if I don't get away.'

The gloss Elizabeth had put on her marriage since reuniting with Frank—convincing herself and others that he had transformed—was a sham. The new improved Frank had been an illusion. 'You know what he was like at San Ysidro—well now add to that & worse than that of tempers rudeness, secret plottings, everlasting gambling for high stakes at bridge, & adultery. I caught him *at that* last spring & forgave it but said I wouldn't again forgive. Now I've discovered other times & I'm sick to death.' Yet her resolve wavered. She still hoped to redeem the marriage, despite all evidence to the contrary.

Amid her despair over her marriage in early 1919, Elizabeth's 82-year-old mother caught flu, which then became pneumonia. Louey, who had travelled far from her hard-scrabble Tasmanian birthplace, died peacefully on 18 February. Louey had never approved of Frank but had loved her daughter unconditionally.

In the wake of her mother's death, Elizabeth found the courage to leave Frank. The final straw came in late March when she was confronted at Gordon Square by what she called 'behaviour of a secret nature that made it impossible for a decent woman to stay'. What that behaviour was she did not say. She already knew of his adultery and high stakes gambling. She left Frank a note telling him what she had discovered and fled. The shard of hope she'd maintained in his better nature was finally shattered. 'I now so thoroughly know how utterly *bad* he is—& last time I still believed he was good & straight but cursed with an ungovernable temper.'

She took refuge in the Knightsbridge home of her brother Sydney. Few, apart from Charlotte, knew where she was. She did not want Frank to know her whereabouts. She suspected he would soon plot how to punish her.

❧

As she ran from her marriage, Elizabeth's latest novel was released. Its upbeat tone was a sharp contrast not just to *Christine*, which preceded it, but the circumstances in which she now found herself.

Christopher and Columbus is a lighthearted tale of the adventures of seventeen-year-old twins shipped off to America during the war. Anna-Rose and Anna-Felicitas are the orphaned offspring of a Junker father and an English mother, unwanted and viewed with suspicion in England. The tale drew on her daughters' combined experience as enemy aliens in England and Elizabeth's voyage to America and travels to California.

Elizabeth had been full of misgivings about the book. At five hundred pages she considered it too long. Most reviewers agreed, although that did not prevent the book from becoming among the year's ten bestsellers in America.

The Sunday Times considered the book full of gaiety and sunshine, but *The Spectator* missed the 'sub-acidic' flavour of her earlier works. Among the many reviews, a favourable one in *The Athenaeum* drew Elizabeth's attention. It was penned by Elizabeth's cousin, Katherine Mansfield, who wrote: 'In a world where there are so many furies with warning fingers it is good to know of some one who goes on her way finding a gay garland, and not forgetting to add a sharp-scented spray or two and a bitter herb that its sweetness may not cloy.' Katherine ventured that amid a glut of tales about young women fleeing the family nest only to encounter torments and disasters, Elizabeth's book stood out.

The review is the first significant crossing of Elizabeth and Katherine's literary paths. In its wake, Elizabeth decided to visit Katherine at her Hampstead home, where she lived with her husband John Middleton Murry, then editor of *The Athenaeum.*

Elizabeth approached the tall, grey building—dubbed The Elephant, because of its bulk and colour—on a wet June afternoon. Wrapped in furs and feathers, she stepped out of the rain and into Katherine Mansfield's life.

Katherine, thirty-one, was small with dark eyes and hair, a severe fringe and unsmiling mouth. Elizabeth had not seen her cousin for about a decade. At that time, Katherine had been a music student whose London guardian was Harry Beauchamp, Elizabeth's musical brother who was professor of singing at the Royal Academy of Music. Katherine had brought her then-fiancé and singing teacher George Bowden to meet her London Beauchamp relatives.

Bowden was besotted with Katherine, but her unruly heart was elsewhere. She was in love with, and pregnant to, a young violinist. Harry was so concerned at his young charge's planned nuptials that the tea was barely cold before he wrote to her family back in New Zealand. Nonetheless, Katherine's marriage to Bowden went ahead. The bride wore black. Katherine abandoned her husband within twenty-four hours and, after travelling to Bavaria, lost the baby.

Katherine's first collection of short stories, *In a German Pension*, drew on her time there. Published in 1911, its title was redolent of Elizabeth's bestselling first book, and it was a modest success. Katherine continued to write short stories as well as reviews.

Katherine mixed with the Bloomsbury set and was more bohemian than Elizabeth. She was often at Garsington Manor and counted

Virginia Woolf, and Frieda and D.H. Lawrence, among her friends. Katherine was close to Bertrand Russell. Although he admired her passionately, he could be repelled by her envy and dark hatreds.

The Antipodean-born cousins who sat over tea in Hampstead had much in common, besides their Beauchamp birth name. They shared the restless Beauchamp spirit—they were constant travellers, shifting countries and continents. They were outsiders, women born into middle-class families whose fortunes had been made on the other side of the word. Elizabeth had married outside her social class, into Prussian and then English aristocracy. Katherine was the 'little savage from New Zealand', as her Queen's College principal had called her.

Both women were musically gifted: Elizabeth as an organist, Katherine a cellist. They had each suffered devastating losses during the war. Elizabeth, her daughter Felicitas—the little girl Katherine had once adored—while Katherine had lost her beloved only brother Leslie 'Chummie' Beauchamp.

But there was much that divided them. Elizabeth was a generation older than Katherine. Elizabeth had robust good health; she was impatient with illness and considered there was little a dose of castor oil couldn't fix. Katherine's health was poor. She had contracted tuberculosis and also suffered what she called 'rheumatiz'. This was likely arthritic pain from untreated gonorrhoea acquired about a decade earlier.

Elizabeth was successful, famous, titled and her writing had made her extremely wealthy. Katherine struggled for money and notice. Elizabeth's books were widely reviewed internationally, Katherine's most recent work *Prelude* had barely made a ripple.

Elizabeth's success, so apparent in her prosperous appearance, may have rubbed salt into Katherine's easily wounded confidence. Their meeting was hardly a resounding success. Katherine penned a withering description of her cousin, who resembled a bejewelled leech: 'I keep thinking of Elizabeth's hands. [. . .] Tiny and white covered with large pointed rings. Little pale parasites, creeping towards the thin bread and butter as if it were their natural food,' Katherine wrote to her friend Ottoline Morrell—herself no admirer of Elizabeth's. Yet Katherine saw something of herself reflected back at her as they sat 'saying very much the same things in very much the same way'.

Chapter 13

MOUNTAIN SOLACE

Elizabeth needed to retrieve the possessions she'd abandoned when she fled her marriage from Gordon Square and Telegraph House. She contacted her former housekeeper and ascertained when Frank would be away. She arranged for a removal company to collect her belongings and deliver them to Whitehall Court, where she had leased a flat for three years. Among them were sentimental items: furniture that had once belonged to Henning, a bookshelf her son had made as a birthday present and a cushion her daughter had used at Cambridge.

Frank was furious. When he discovered items had been removed in his absence, he contacted his lawyers. He resolved to sue the removalists for damages and trespass. Bertrand attempted to dissuade his brother from embarking on action he considered cruel and vindictive. He hoped Frank would reconsider and find an amicable solution.

Frank turned on his brother, whom he accused of belittling him, and was aggrieved that Bertrand had not used his influence with

Elizabeth to persuade her to return. Frank wanted Bertrand to cease contact with Elizabeth.

Although nothing indicates Elizabeth had second thoughts about leaving her marriage, Bertrand countered to Frank that she had been inclined to reconcile until she received the writ, and then her mood had changed. Bertrand was unhappy at being caught between them. 'I have done my best with both of you, but the quarrel over the furniture is beyond my powers. It is no pleasure to me to act the go-between, since I necessarily incur the ill-will of both of you. But I am surprised that you wish her to see no more of the only person at all likely to soften her towards you,' Bertrand wrote.

The litigious lord was not for turning. London's High Court spent two July days considering who owned everything, from a tea table to curtains, electric lamps, tennis balls (new and used) and a hammock. Especially the hammock. Elizabeth stood her ground and retained her wit when questioned about it by Frank's unfortunately named counsel, Mr Mould. He wanted to know if Elizabeth had allowed her husband to use it.

Elizabeth: Certainly not. It was entirely for me. It would not have held him.

Q: The hammock, I take it, was for general use at Telegraph House?

Elizabeth: No it was solely for me. I used to allow small visitors to sit in it.

She added a dash more levity when her counsel Sir Edward Marshall-Hall quizzed her about the hammock.

Q: Did you ever give it to him?

Elizabeth: Never.

Q: You have more regard for life?

Elizabeth: And for the hammock.

Frank acknowledged he did not actually want any of the items he claimed had been wrongly removed. He told the court he had been 'perfectly willing to let her [Elizabeth] have the whole lot'. Rather, he was furious because the items had been taken, as he saw it, from behind his back. In the end, the judge found in Elizabeth's favour. Including ownership of the hammock.

Now in her mid-fifties, Elizabeth's most pressing task was how to rebuild her life. She was no longer young, but for the first time in adulthood she was not defined by her relationship to a man. She had shed the mantle of widowhood; now she cast off the role of wife.

But she did not divorce Frank. Divorce was still rare in Britain in the early twentieth century, and for women it carried stigma and a whiff of scandal. A divorce between a famous writer and a peer would inevitably have attracted wide attention. And Elizabeth loathed publicity. It is also likely she enjoyed the prestige and trappings that being a countess brought. So, while she shed her husband, she retained her title. For the rest of her life, she was known as the Countess Russell.

Bertrand Russell remained sympathetic to her, and she saw him frequently. In the aftermath of the court case, he wrote to her: 'It is quite hateful to think of your being so tormented & battered [. . .] Now I hope you have done with F. Remember how gay & delicious things there are in the world—don't forget that you have won liberty, which is worth a price—& that you can build up friendships with people who will appreciate you without wanting to destroy you.'

Her first instinct was to return to familiar physical terrain, to the home she had created from scratch. Within weeks of the court case, she rented out her London flat and travelled to her Swiss chalet. Her mountain home was full of ghosts and bittersweet memories. In the five years since she'd fled, her youngest daughter Felicitas, her mother, her nephew Johnnie, and Charles Stuart had died; her family was scattered; and the grand passion for Frank, first ignited at the chalet, had been reduced to a public squabble over a hammock. She had not known 'wretchedness could be packed so tight', she later wrote. She needed to draw on all her reserves just to keep going. But she resolved to turn her back on her sorrows and her face to the future.

One non-ghostly presence remained at the chalet. Coco. The huge dog became her energetic companion on mountain walks. And even as she revisited places that brought reminders of H.G. Wells and Frank, Coco's boisterous, uncomplicated nature was an unmixed joy. 'He at least is simple & kind.'

Elizabeth learned that her daughter Trix was poised to marry a German officer, Anton von Hirschberg. Elizabeth wished her daughter was marrying an American instead. Her distrust and dislike of Germans endured and she feared Trix would be lost to her. In the event, Trix was not cut off, at least not physically. She arrived at the chalet a few weeks after her August marriage. But Elizabeth's hopes of a happy reunion with the daughter she had not seen for more than five years were soon dashed. Trix had become what Elizabeth most feared: thoroughly German. She also found Trix scatterbrained, a poor listener and so indiscreet Elizabeth felt unable to confide in her. She decided not to tell her that her marriage to Frank was over. Nonetheless, Elizabeth sent Trix back to Germany loaded with goods to begin married life.

Finances were tight. Much of Elizabeth's money was in Germany and had been frozen during the war. She attempted to extract it, but the value of the mark was falling. Legal bills needed paying. She also needed money to help support her four remaining children. Her oldest daughter Evi was single—Elizabeth wished she too would marry an American, preferably rich, elderly and kind. Liebet was expecting another child. H.B. was soon to finish at Eton.

Although H.B. was English-born, his German background remained problematic and his prospects in England seemed dim as a result. She considered H.B. easily influenced, innately obedient, in need of a firm hand and clear direction. She grudgingly acknowledged that Frank, with his unceasing stream of orders, had been good for the boy. She asked whether Liebet and her husband Corwin would take him to help them on their Californian ranch. Elizabeth hoped the boy would eventually make an independent future for himself in America, but worried he showed little initiative or ability to seize opportunities.

But there was an obstacle to her wish to send him to America. H.B. had become romantically entangled with a forty-year-old married woman. Elizabeth was furious and feared the woman's husband would horsewhip him. The woman had convinced the musical H.B. that he had the makings of a great singer and was pressing him to remain in England.

Elizabeth began another book. Thinking it would help her finances, the book that emerged would also help restore her soul. It would be her most autobiographical. *In the Mountains* opens as an unnamed English woman, exhausted by unspecified personal troubles, returns alone after World War I to the chalet she has not seen for five years. She arrives, lonely and fearful, in abject despair:

'I'm afraid of loneliness; shiveringly, terribly afraid. I don't mean the ordinary physical loneliness [. . .] I mean that awful loneliness of spirit that is the ultimate tragedy of life. [. . .] I feel ridiculous as well as wretched; as if somebody had taken my face and rubbed it in dust.'

As the writer licks her wounds, amid the honey-scented grass and clear mountain air she hopes will restore her, two Englishwomen named Kitty and Dolly appear on her doorstep. Dolly has been ostracised by her family after twice marrying Germans and cannot return to England.

Over three months, the narrator gives the sisters shelter, her sadness lifts, wit and joy return, and the chalet itself becomes a place of transformation: 'It invariably conquers. Nobody can resist it. Nobody can go away from here quite as they arrived.'

Written as a journal, it is a return to the form of Elizabeth's first book, although its introspective, melancholy opening is a far cry from the lighthearted woman who skipped through her German Garden. The book was published anonymously—not even the name Elizabeth appeared on its cover. *The Times Literary Supplement* detected a practised hand behind the book. Other reviewers speculated that it was the work of Elizabeth von Arnim.

The book had just appeared, in August 1920, and its authorship the subject of much speculation when writer and composer Beverley Nichols met Elizabeth at a lunch. He recalled she floated in late and in French-accented English begged 'Du forgive me, will yiu?' He thought she did not so much talk as croon, 'like a dove that has become slightly demoralized by perching too long on a French hat.' Nichols quizzed her about whether she had written the book. He was convinced she had. She vehemently denied it. 'It sounds like a Bliu [sic] Guide,' she told him. Anyway, she had just published a book the previous year and she wrote terribly slowly. Elizabeth, like her mother before her, was adept at dissembling and deploying her 'sweet, twining ways.'

Nichols was fascinated by Elizabeth's combination of fragile appearance and explosive wit. 'When one meets her, inevitably she suggests Dresden China, with her tiny voice, tiny hands, tiny manners. And then suddenly, with a shock, you realise that the Dresden China is hollow, and is filled with gunpowder.'

Elizabeth took to heart Bertrand Russell's advice to forge new friendships. Her social network expanded after her marriage ended. On her frequent trips from the chalet back to London, she was rarely alone. Lady Randolph Churchill, the mother of Winston Churchill, and writer Marie Belloc Lowndes—Hilaire Belloc's sister—were among those with whom she socialised. She also renewed her friendship with Jane and H.G. Wells. She went to the opera and dined with Lady Cunard. Elizabeth's charm and wit enlivened many high-society dinner tables. Dullness for her was a cardinal sin. When one dinner party bore talked at length about a much-decorated military man who had been wounded in sixteen places, Elizabeth retorted: 'I didn't know men *had* so many places.'

Conversation, not food, was her forte. Her culinary tastes were basic. Left to her own devices, her staple was bacon and eggs. She was overjoyed when she acquired a cook who made perfect Yorkshire pudding. She didn't blink when offered sherry and sausage rolls at one social gathering, but she preferred to starve rather than eat melon and lobster at another.

Elizabeth needed to attend to her son's future. She arranged with her brother Sydney to send the seventeen-year-old to the countryside out of the reach of his married lover—and no more was heard of his paramour. Back in London, Elizabeth secured his ticket and passport, outfitted him for the trip, and spent time with him—taking him to Hampton Court and to Wagner's *Die Meistersinger von*

Nürnberg—before he sailed to America in May. She sent H.B. off with £20 in his pocket—any more and she feared he would lose it or have it stolen—and she arranged to pay Liebet and Corwin £250 a year for his keep on their ranch.

Elizabeth went to stay with Charlotte. One late spring day they drove near the rear of Telegraph House and paused. Elizabeth looked through her field glasses at the monolith on the hill. Her response in her diary was succinct: 'oh the horror!'

Frank meanwhile was brooding, marinating his hurt—he never ceased to see himself as the wronged party. Having lost the court case, he was not about to accept the umpire's verdict and move on with his life. He simply attempted a new strategy to exact revenge. He tried to poison Elizabeth's friends against her. He vilified her around London, circulating written allegations about her behaviour.

Cobbie likely received a copy, since he wrote to Elizabeth asking her if she had seen Frank's 'Manifesto'. Elizabeth didn't know what Cobbie was referring to. She soon found out. Frank had dictated 'intimate insults' about her to his secretary and sent typed copies to her friends and associates.

Frank accused Elizabeth of wanton cruelty, of being incapable of loving anyone, not even her children. He also circulated, according to Wells, a crude parody of *In the Mountains*. Frank insisted he still loved and worshipped her, that her departure had blighted his life. He tried to force those around him to take sides. Frank had long been jealous of Santayana's friendship with Elizabeth. He accused Santayana, who continued to see Elizabeth, of disloyalty and demanded he break with her. Santayana refused.

Frank's wrath reached Bertrand, who was travelling in China. 'I had a savage letter from Frank saying I was writing to you & seeing you & behaviour, as always, disloyal to him.' Bertrand informed

Elizabeth he had seen the typed letters and thought them 'unspeakably horrible'.

Elizabeth herself received two letters full of 'wicked lying abuse' from Frank. She sent a conciliatory reply to the first one and ignored the second. Despite the pain he had caused her, she confided to her diary: 'How I wish we could at least be friends.'

Elizabeth paid another visit to Katherine Mansfield at The Elephant in May 1920. Katherine had had dealings with other members of their extended family in the year since they had first taken tea. Katherine had consulted Sydney Beauchamp about her health. He was so concerned he told Katherine that if she didn't get herself to a sanatorium, she didn't stand a dog's chance.

Katherine had spent part of the winter in the warmer climate of Menton in the South of France, in a house owned by relative Connie Beauchamp. In Katherine's absence, Elizabeth's nephew Sydney Waterlow had moved into The Elephant with John Middleton Murry. But Katherine had taken a dislike to Sydney and insisted he move out by the time she returned.

Katherine was not looking forward to meeting Elizabeth again: 'a thousand devils are sending Elizabeth without her German Garden to tea here tomorrow [. . .] I expect she will stay, at longest half an hour. She will be Oh, such a bundle of artificialities—but I can't put her off,' Katherine wrote to a friend.

Katherine found Elizabeth less artificial than anticipated. Katherine acknowledged feeling great tenderness for her cousin in the wake of her second visit. She also found Elizabeth remarkably candid. 'She has no use for a physical lover. I mean to go to bed with [. . .] That she can't stand—she'd be frightened of. Her very life, her very being, her gift, her vitality, all that makes her depends upon her *not surrendering*,' Katherine wrote to her husband.

The Roaring Twenties had begun, summer had arrived and, back at the chalet, Elizabeth had a plan. This would be no solitary summer. She had invited to stay those whose company she most enjoyed. A lively and literary stream of guests made their way up to the wooden chalet in the middle of 1920.

Cobbie and his socialist suffragette wife Anne were first to arrive, making an undignified entrance in a bullock cart. Frank Swinnerton staggered in on foot late at night having missed his connecting train. They were joined by Henry Festing Jones, biographer of the novelist Samuel Butler; Liberal politician and literary biographer Augustine Birrell and his writer son Francis; poet Robert Trevelyan; explorer Harry Johnston; and pacifist Clifford Allen. Elizabeth's friend Maud Ritchie and niece Margery Waterlow also joined the party.

They danced; they dressed up and down. They shared dinners and musical evenings, played cards, charades and chess. Poetry was read aloud—from Browning to Matthew Arnold—and Elizabeth thought Trevelyan a particularly good reader. On fine days, there were mountain walks. The chalet that summer certainly realised the spirit of the mottos inscribed on its walls.

Many who gathered around the fire or, on warmer moonlit evenings, on the terrace, had crossed paths in London. But unknown to the gathering was a deferential young man who had not been in Elizabeth's company before.

His name was Alexander Stuart Frere Reeves. In time he would become an influential international publisher known as A.S. Frere and credited with fostering the careers of J.B. Priestley, Anthony Powell, Nevil Shute, John Steinbeck and Graham Greene. But when he arrived at the chalet—and long before he dropped Reeves from his name—he was a naïve but ambitious Cambridge student come to work temporarily for Elizabeth during his summer vacation. Elizabeth had responded to his advertisement in *The Times*, offering the young man a role cataloguing and arranging her books. He gratefully accepted—and asked if he should bring dress clothes.

Frere was a man of great charm and wit. Despite the many myths that have swirled around his early life, he was not born out of wedlock, the illegitimate son of a colonel. Nor was he abandoned by his mother and raised in an orphanage. In truth, Frere had been born in Dulwich, London, in 1892, a year after the marriage of his parents Mary Stewart Frere and auctioneer Alexander Wilfred Reeves. But Frere's father soon deserted his family, leaving Mary to raise her young son in grinding poverty.

It could—and according to Frere should—have been otherwise. On his mother's side, there had once been great wealth. The family had owned large sugar plantations in Barbados. But by the time Frere was born, the fortune had been lost and his mother swindled out of her inheritance by a relative. Frere resented the loss of his birthright and the privation in which he was raised. He was determined to ascend the social ladder to where he felt he belonged.

As a young pilot during the war, his service ended when his plane crashed. Invalided out, he had gone to university to study economics, where he also became an editor of the journal *Granta*.

Dark, handsome, if not particularly tall, 27-year-old Frere was soon embraced by the literary, and mostly much older, circle at the chalet. He joined walks and dinners and read Keats and Wordsworth to Elizabeth. He helped paste Elizabeth's bookplate into her books.

With its motto *Chanterai Ma Chanson* (I Will Sing My Song) her bookplate expressed her independent spirit. So indispensable did Frere become that by summer's end Elizabeth dubbed him 'Lieber Gott' (Dear God).

When he became briefly unwell, Frere's reappearance at dinner—still too ill for formal dress—was celebrated by the entire party, who wore dressing gowns in solidarity. The gregarious Cobbie cut an eccentric sight, in a flowing white nightgown and on his head a comb bag with roses attached.

Elizabeth continued to work throughout her sociable summer. She was disciplined in her writing, isolating herself from her visitors. 'I take no notice of my guests & work just the same, and I think they like this—I know I would if I stayed a long time in a house—beautiful never to see one's hostess!'

Elizabeth kept her birthday, her fifty-fourth, a secret. Margery was the only one aware of it, and she was sworn to silence. Margery quietly presented Elizabeth with a box of liqueur chocolates in the little chalet. They gorged on so many they made their tipsy way back up to the main house.

As her guests partied, Elizabeth learned that her daughter Trix had given birth to a daughter, and that Evi planned to marry. But Evi's fiancé was hardly the wealthy, elderly American she had hoped for. She knew only that Eustace Graves was poor and uneducated. Elizabeth feared he might be a plumber who spent his days among lavatories. She worried her daughter was marrying beneath her class and would be unsuited to life as the wife of a working man. But Elizabeth eventually concluded that if the pair were happy nothing else mattered.

After her chalet guests had departed, Elizabeth decided she wanted to visit the Pomeranian home and garden she had not seen for nearly a decade. She was also curious to see Germany for the first time since the great war. But the country filled her with cold horror and she was anxious about how she would be received. 'I wanted to, yet I hated to.'

She was accompanied by her American friend and publisher Frank N. Doubleday—Effendi as he was known, for his initials FND—and his wife Florence. Elizabeth had convinced them to join her and promised Frank a book about the trip. Although she made detailed notes and drafted an essay, the book never materialised.

As their train crossed Germany, Elizabeth saw well-ploughed fields and rows of neat prosperous houses. The sight was a stark contrast to France, through which she had recently travelled, and where the evidence of its blood-soaked soil was so apparent.

Aboard the train, conditions were wretched. The carriage was filthy and so overcrowded they sat upright all night. During the sleepless night, Frank noticed a little bottle hanging from Elizabeth's waist. She told him it was chloroform, and that it might come in handy if the Doubledays got into any trouble in Germany. Frank was horrified, but thankful the bottle had not smashed and suffocated them. When the weary travellers reached Berlin, no hotel accommodation could be found, so they stayed their first night in a hospital.

The ancient beech forests glowed gold when Elizabeth drove through Pomerania from Berlin that autumn. She was delighted to see the familiar forests and countryside as they approached Nassenheide. The land and the villages looked prosperous and unaltered. The gates to Nassenheide were open and the car turned down a winding path to approach the old schloss.

Elizabeth's heart sank. Her once abundant garden, the place that had first inspired her writing, was forlorn. The schloss she had rescued from dereliction no longer looked as she remembered it, having undergone unsympathetic alterations. But digging near the house was one of her old staff, Herman. He was now fat as a tub with a thick white moustache. He was pleased to see the *Gräfin*.

Elizabeth stepped into the hall and looked around. Her old Latin motto that wished fools and others away was still visible. The dining room, where she had so mercilessly teased the tutors over meals, was unchanged. But other rooms had been partitioned. She sat for a while in one of the old tutor's rooms, now Herman's.

Two families now lived in the house and she met some of the prosperous occupants, as well as a truculent Prussian officer who twirled his moustache and insisted Germany had not been beaten in the war. She had seen enough. She gave Herman a hundred-mark note, all the money she had with her, as she readied to leave. She drove away along a road lined with poplars and yellow lupins.

Elizabeth was reflective as winter set in. There was more to life than the trappings of wealth, she wrote to Liebet. 'Look at the lines on the faces of the rich. They get them, not because they own Rolls Royces but because Rolls Royces own *them*. One acquires possessions only to find [. . .] that the possessions have acquired one.' She thought it a thousand times lovelier to be young and struggling than old in a Rolls.

She saw the poverty and hunger afflicting post-war Britain. And she saw her sister frail and in pain from a broken collarbone. It was an intimation of mortality, and underscored that for both women, more life was behind them than ahead. Elizabeth was 'determined that my sunset shall be calm'. She planned a solemn Christmas sitting by the fire with Charlotte, where they would talk about the past 'of which there is much, & of the future, of which there is steadily less & less, & I daresay we shall laugh, & I shouldn't be surprised if we also cried'.

Charlotte was not her only companion on Christmas Day. Frere joined her for lunch and games of chess. She had seen the young man frequently since she returned to London, where they had dined and danced. Frere sent her a stream of warm, chatty letters after she returned to the chalet in the new year. He addressed her, formally, as Lady Russell, but signed himself Lieber Gott or L.G., the initials of the affectionate nickname she had given him.

He updated her on literary news. He had met H.G. Wells and Beverley Nichols and told her how he felt awed in their presence. Occasionally he hinted at deeper feelings towards Elizabeth. He wished he could paint her portrait, since she had an expression in her eyes no camera could capture. He had been listening to Wagner's *Liebestod*, the composer's erotically charged composition. He had become fascinated by John Donne and quoted to her lines from his love poem 'The Dream'. She could hardly not have been touched—and flattered—to receive such delightful letters from a man twenty-six years her junior. She may also have wondered where encouraging such dreams might lead.

Chapter 14

DO NOT MARRY A NOVELIST

Waking at the snow-bound chalet on sunny, pearly, winter mornings filled Elizabeth with joy. On such fine days she walked miles in the mountains amid glittering alpine trees. On her silent strolls, the only sound was Coco's heavy paws crunching into fresh snow. Her long walks were a break from hours in her little chalet working on a new novel. The book she worked on in early 1921 has been hailed as her masterpiece. And an act of literary revenge.

Based on her marriage to Frank, *Vera* is a terrifying portrait of domestic tyranny. Elizabeth's thirteenth book doesn't begin as a marital horror story. The book's first third is vintage Elizabeth, with much wit and satire.

When middle-aged Everard Wemyss appears at the Cornish cottage of twenty-two-year-old Lucy Entwhistle, he is a figure of fun. He could almost be the British cousin of *The Caravaners* boorish Prussian baron or *The Pastor's Wife*'s dull cleric. Wemyss is a businessman with a 'Stock Exchange eye' who speaks 'with the practised fluency of a leading article'. Most of his ideas are recycled from that morning's *The Times*. Lucy, naïve and unassertive, is reminiscent of *The Pastor's Wife*'s Ingeborg.

Vera takes a dark, gothic turn when the bookish Lucy and Wemyss marry and he takes his 'little girl' to live at his country house. The Willows, based on Telegraph House, is isolated, windswept and its red bricks are 'like blood'. It is where Wemyss's first wife, Vera, died under mysterious circumstances. Vera's presence looms large in the house—and has prompted comparisons with Daphne du Maurier's later gothic thriller *Rebecca*.

Lucy quickly learns that reading is not encouraged at The Willows, where books are kept in a locked case to which Wemyss has the sole key. Only the books in Vera's top-floor sitting room, from where she fell to her death, have not been jailed.

The man who seemed initially so kind and protective steadily reveals himself as cruel and tyrannical, and bent on Lucy's total submission. He is prone to moods and vile tempers, and abuses his servants. He controls Lucy's movements and isolates her from her kindly Aunt Dot. As Lucy's despair grows, she wonders whether Vera's fall from her sitting-room window was really an accident. The book ends inconclusively, leaving lingering unease.

Elizabeth was as unflinching in her depiction of a troubled and troubling marriage in *Vera* as she had been about motherhood with *The Pastor's Wife*. Both addressed taboo subjects, but *Vera* is more psychologically complex. With its insight into an escalating pattern of manipulation and intimate abuse, *Vera* remains a startling depiction of what today we would call coercive control.

On a hill above Portofino, a grey stone castle with a circular tower looks down on the Ligurian fishing village below. Called the Castello Brown, its odd Anglo–Italian name is a legacy of its nineteenth-century owner, Montague-Yeats Brown. His descendants still owned the castle when Elizabeth climbed up from the town square to meet one of the owners. She wanted to rent the romantic *castello* for April.

Elizabeth had no sooner finished writing *Vera* than she left her snow-bound chalet for Italy. She already had an idea for her next novel. The *castello* would provide the setting for her most romantic book, *The Enchanted April.*

She was joined at the *castello* by two friends, Emily Strutt and Marie Mallet, a former lady-in-waiting to Queen Victoria and a keen watercolourist. For Elizabeth, the month would be part holiday, part research. Her decision to go to Portofino was also driven by other reasons. Industrial unrest prevented her from going to England as she often did in spring. In addition, Frere's increasingly adoring letters kept arriving. She was unsure what to do about her ardent young admirer. A few months in Italy might keep him at bay.

She walked amid flowering mimosa, wisteria, irises, peach and pear blossom. She entertained her visitors and played chess after dinner most nights. She attended an evening service at the little Catholic church of San Giorgio, down the hill from the castle, which impressed her with its candle-filled interior and piercing singing. She read new works—Lytton Strachey's biography of Queen Victoria—and revisited old—poems by Keats.

Max Beerbohm, the celebrated Edwardian caricaturist and essayist, lived a few kilometres away at Rapallo and Elizabeth went to visit him. She drank honey wine on his terrace and he showed her sketches for a planned London exhibition. And she made a pilgrimage to Percy Shelley's former house at San Terenzo. Its owner was away, but she bribed her way in. She was struck by the wonderful ghostliness of its rooms, unaltered since the young poet drowned a century earlier in the nearby bay.

She remained in Italy after her month at the *castello*, stopping at Lake Orta. She needed to proofread her novel *Vera*. But on fine May days, she walked amid rye fields, picked narcissus and watched fireflies flit like jewels. She struggled to stay inside and work on such days.

In Milan, she was filled with memories of her early womanhood. At the cathedral, she thought of Henning. He had once told her how he had visited it just after their engagement and stood inside the cathedral thinking of his young fiancée. Elizabeth drove to see Leonardo's *The Last Supper*. She had last seen it with her father on the life-changing European trip during which she'd met Henning. Her husband and her father were long dead. Her thoughts soon turned to the living.

John Middleton Murry appeared at the Chalet Soleil on a June morning shortly after Elizabeth returned from Italy. He and Katherine Mansfield were staying at a hotel nearby. They were poised to move into a chalet of their own at Montana, which was about a half-hour's scramble up the mountain from Elizabeth. They planned to rent the three-storey Chalet des Sapins for two years. Katherine's health had deteriorated and she pinned her hopes of improvement on Switzerland's fresh mountain air.

At her chalet, Katherine rested and wrote. She sat on her balcony where, surrounded by pots of coloured plants and the tinkle of cowbells, she looked out at the mountains and surrounding pine forest, and watched the birds come to feed on coconut put out for them. She rarely left her room at the top of the chalet. Sometimes she lacked the strength even to walk down the two flights of stairs to the ground floor bathroom. Her companion Ida Baker, a friend since they'd first met at Queen's College School, bathed her and shopped for food. She depended on Ida far more than on her husband John. Ida was also part-housekeeper and nurse to Katherine. Theirs was a close and fraught friendship, even by Katherine's standards. Katherine dubbed the doggedly devoted Ida both 'The Faithful One' and 'The Albatross'.

Katherine wanted to get to know her older cousin and during the summer of 1921, they developed a deep bond. Their first rocky encounter in Hampstead was replaced by genuine love and admiration. But their blossoming friendship was not without thorns.

At least once a week Elizabeth, accompanied at times by Coco, made the trip up to Chalet des Sapins: '[We have] occasional long talks which are rather like what talks in the afterlife will be like, I imagine ... ruminative, and reminiscent,' Katherine wrote to Ottoline Morrell.

Elizabeth invariably arrived with baskets of flowers, which Katherine adored. 'Breathes there the man, do you think?—who understands a woman's love of flowers?' she wrote to Elizabeth. Katherine described one flower-filled visit from her cousin. 'She appeared today behind a bouquet—never smaller woman carried bigger bouquet. She looks like a garden walking—of asters, late sweet peas, stocks & always petunias. She herself wore a frock like a spider's web, a hat like a berry and gloves that reminded me of thistles in seed [. . .] And then when she smiles a ravishing wrinkle appears on her nose—and never have I seen more exquisite hands.' Katherine had seemingly set aside her former withering description of Elizabeth's fingers as resembling pale parasites. 'She is certainly the most fascinating small human being I have ever known—a real enchantress—and she is so lovely to look upon as well as to hear.'

To the ailing Katherine, Elizabeth appeared a picture of youthful energy and exuberance: 'She looks about 35—not a day more, runs up hills, climbs, laughs just like a girl. I don't think she will ever be older.' Katherine longed, just once, to be able to run down the hill and shout Elizabeth's name beneath her windows. She would never have the strength for that.

Katherine's observations of Elizabeth do, however, retain the odd barb. When Katherine told her she was writing a story about an old man, Elizabeth commented that she didn't care for old men: 'They *exude* so.' Katherine was appalled.

The cousins exchanged books, and Elizabeth loaned copies of Jane Austen's novels. Katherine's husband John was well-supplied with new releases sent to him for review. Among those that arrived over summer was D.H. Lawrence's *Women in Love*. Katherine and John had had a long, complex and fractious relationship with the Lawrences, which had reached its nadir about a year earlier when Lawrence had informed Katherine: 'You are a loathsome reptile—I hope you will die.' Now Katherine and John were the basis of two characters, Gudrun and Gerald in *Women in Love*. The other couple in the novel, Ursula and Rupert, drew on himself and Frieda.

It is hard to imagine the cousins did not discuss the sexually charged novel with its depiction of the destructive relationship between the painter Gudrun and her lover Gerald or the circumstance of the book's creation. Lawrence wrote the book when he and Frieda lived on the Cornish coast, where he had persuaded Katherine and John to also live. In their many talks at Katherine's chalet over summer, the cousins may also have pondered the close-knit literary world in which John reviewed a novel in which he and Katherine appeared as fictionalised versions.

Another book arrived for John around this time, to which Katherine would develop a fatal attraction, *Cosmic Anatomy and the Structure of the Ego* by M.B. Oxon. Katherine became fascinated by the book's mystical, consciousness-expanding contents. It would prompt her to eventually seek a spiritual cure for her physical ills.

At times Katherine was too ill to receive visitors. Bedridden, she was unable to see Elizabeth when she arrived one day. Katherine wrote to apologise: 'I was horribly ungracious to you the other afternoon [. . .] I would have telephoned you and asked you to forgive me but my breath fails me at [the] telephone & I pant like the hart.'

John frequently visited Elizabeth and took back news to Katherine of the Chalet Soleil, which again filled with guests throughout the summer. 'I have drunk in new life in hearing "what happens at the Chalet". I could write a whole book about it,' Katherine wrote to Elizabeth. If she had, Katherine might have observed how a young man had captured her cousin's attention. Katherine was not the only figure who began to play an increasingly important role in Elizabeth's life that summer.

Elizabeth had invited Frere back to the chalet to join her guests, among whom was her sister Charlotte, Hugh Walpole, Maud Ritchie and, briefly, Jane Wells and her boys. Frere played chess with Elizabeth in the evenings, read to her as she lay in her hammock and joined her on long mountain walks. She enjoyed their quiet, shared pursuits. She became infuriated when he abandoned such sedate pursuits to join noisy games of charades with other visitors. She may have resented not being the centre of his undivided attention. At the Chalet Soleil, she was the sun queen around which her guests orbited. As Hugh Walpole noted: 'there *is* something of the boss about her that we all feel and want to escape from.'

As her guests departed at summer's end, Frere remained. Elizabeth set aside what reservations she had about a romantic involvement with a younger man. By the time he returned to England, Frere's letters to her no longer began with a formal 'Dear Countess Russell' but 'My dear Elizabeth'.

Vera was published in September 1921 and Elizabeth marked its release by walking to Katherine and John's chalet. They devoured their copy overnight and telephoned her full of praise.

But the first reviews left Elizabeth dispirited. She was crushed by *The Times Literary Supplement*, whose reviewer argued that if Lucy had fallen for Wemyss's 'slimy blandishments' she got what she deserved. *The Daily Telegraph* suspected feminist propaganda.

But *The New Statesman* considered the book 'one of the most successful attempts at the macabre in English'. Elizabeth had overturned literary convention by creating a book that was as tragic as it was comic. The review was not uncritical—describing her early works full of tiresome women 'smirking coyly about their gardens as if they were having a remarkably satisfying affair with their delphiniums'. The review was written by Rebecca West, whose affair with Wells had prompted the rupture between him and Elizabeth.

Over tea on her porch, John consoled Elizabeth over the negative reviews: 'Of course, my dear, when the critics are faced with a *Wuthering Heights* written by Jane Austen, they don't know what to say,' he recalled telling her. His comment 'raised me to my feet at a moment when I was beaten down on all fours', Elizabeth wrote to him.

Meanwhile, Katherine urged her artist friend Dorothy Brett, who was associated with the Bloomsbury group, to read *Vera*. 'Have you ever known a Wemyss? Oh my dear, they are *very* plentiful! Few men are without a touch [. . .] Not that I can stand the Wemyss "brand". No. But I can perfectly understand Lucy standing it.'

Katherine was taken aback when she learned her sisters had sent a copy to their businessman father Harold Beauchamp, with whom she had a difficult relationship. 'I expect he will admire [Wemyss] tremendously and agree with every thought and every feeling and shut the book with an extraordinary sense of satisfaction before climbing the stairs to my stepmother,' Katherine wrote to Elizabeth.

The critical approval of her relatives meant a great deal to Elizabeth. She was delighted when her nephew Sydney Waterlow wrote, admiring the book, and she shared her joy with Katherine and John. 'On the crest of *Vera* he brackets me with [Katherine], but I shan't last long up there I know. Meanwhile it's very pleasant, and I sun myself and give myself airs.'

Writer Beverley Nichols likely had *Vera* in mind when he described the power and violence that flowed from Elizabeth's pen:

> It is as though she dwelt in an early Victorian drawing room, listening to some passionate dialogue of life that was being carried on outside the window. The voices rise and fall, the rain splashes against the bright panes, the wind moans and whistles round the stoutly built walls. Then, there is a lull, and in the silence may be heard the scratching of her little quill pen, transcribing the violent things she has heard in a tiny, spidery handwriting, catching the thunder in a polished phrase. And when she has finished writing, there, on the paper, is a story as full of tension, fierce and frightening as any that dwells in the broken, passionate sentences of Emily Brontë.

Elizabeth believed *Vera* was her high watermark, but it had taken a toll. 'It was extracted from me by torment, so that I don't want to write so well again—not at such a price.'

Vera landed like a grenade among Frank's circle, and in the London clubs and salons he frequented. The volcanic Frank bailed up associates in the Reform Club, including H.G. Wells, demanding to know if they recognised him or Telegraph House in the book. Wells thought the book displayed entertaining malice and demonstrated Frank's temperamental defects and eccentricities. 'The description of his freaks of temper and tyranny and his house are absurdly true,' Wells wrote.

Bertrand Russell was shocked by the book. He found it 'intolerably cruel' and later advised his children emphatically: 'Do not marry a novelist.' Society hostess Mrs Belloc Lowndes was horrified. She thought the book unmistakeably directed at Frank.

Frank insisted he'd been libelled and threatened to sue. His lawyers wrote to Elizabeth's publishers. Frank had been caricatured and brought into contempt, they argued. The book was a covert and scurrilous attack upon him. The letter concluded with a surprising and incriminating postscript: the identification of Frank was so convincing that several of his friends had asked him what he intended to do. Macmillan replied they were satisfied Wemyss was fictitious and Elizabeth had confirmed this. She would hardly say otherwise.

This time, Frank dropped his legal action. Most likely his lawyers had convinced him that he would not only lose the case but make a public fool of himself in the process. Certainly, that was what Elizabeth thought. 'He was going to get up in a public court & before the whole world put the cap on his own head!' she wrote to Liebet.

Although Elizabeth knew the publicity would have boosted *Vera*'s sales, she did not want to face Frank in court again. She did, however, allow herself a little theatrical relish, imagining how her diminutive figure in the witness box would have elicited sympathy. '*Poor* little thing, wouldn't I have been, with only my little eyes & the tip of my nose appearing over the top of the box!'

Katherine missed Elizabeth when she left the chalet in autumn. Katherine had grown to love the cousin who had been her intellectual and social lifeline all summer, and upon whose company she had become increasingly reliant. 'No doubt Elizabeth is far more important to me than I am to her. Shes [sic] surrounded, lapped in lovely friends [. . .] Except for her we are lost in our forest,' Katherine wrote to Dorothy Brett.

Back in London, Elizabeth's thoughts turned to Katherine and John at their chalet. Elizabeth saw them as if through the wrong end of opera glasses, tiny remote figures, pickled in poetry, while she was furiously busy doing things she could not even remember the next day. 'A sort of awful innocence surrounds you like a halo, viewed from here [. . .] Have you any idea of what a beautiful life you two are leading?' This may have come as scant consolation to the desperately ill Katherine, isolated on a Swiss mountain as winter approached.

Katherine responded with a moving and gracious letter, and was round-eyed at every snippet of news. 'I think of you often. Especially in the evenings, when I am on my balcony and it's too dark to write or to do anything but wait for the stars. A time I love.' London seemed so far away. 'I see you stepping into carriages driving to the play, dining among mirrors and branched candlesticks and faraway sweet sounds . . . I open your door to illustrious strangers, Mighty Ones, who take off their coats in the large hall and are conducted into your special room where the books are . . . Do not forget us.'

Elizabeth did not. She wrote to Katherine and John frequently during this period. Elizabeth told how she had met Katherine's Russian-born translator friend Samuel Koteliansky and invited him to tea. Koteliansky associated with the Bloomsbury group and his early translations of Dostoevsky and Chekhov would help bring the writers into prominence in the English-speaking world. But Elizabeth worried that she might be out of her intellectual depth. 'Doesn't he belong to the intelligentsia? And I don't feel happy with them, any more than they do with me.'

Elizabeth shared with Katherine her anxieties about what Frank might do next. Although he had dropped his libel action, he was preparing to sue for desertion. 'I seem always to be at my solicitor's telling him of new attacks.' She was trying hard not to let anything Frank did touch her.

She was disappointed in *Vera's* simmering sales so far—'more discussed and less bought than any book of mine'. But she was warmed when Arnold Bennett, whom she had recently met, told her he considered it a great book. She was amused when she overheard at a party a furious woman telling her husband: 'Don't you get Wemyssing me.'

She had read a delightful article about Katherine's short story 'Bliss' in a London paper. Katherine, meanwhile, recognised a certain literary kinship between herself and Elizabeth. Katherine wrote to Dorothy Brett: 'Only one thing, my hand on heart I could swear to. Never *could* Elizabeth be influenced by me. If you knew how she would scorn the notion, how impossible it would be for her. There is a kind of turn in our sentences which is alike but that is because we are worms of the same family. But that is all.'

The most talked-about play of 1921 was *A Bill of Divorcement*. Its subject matter caused a sensation, dealing with a woman who has divorced her insane husband. It was set a few years in the future, when such a right had become possible.

Written by Clemence Dane (Winifred Ashton) it was staged against a backdrop of agitation for fairer divorce laws and women's rights, issues that had gathered pace after World War I. At the time, it was much harder for women than men to seek a divorce. While a husband could seek a divorce on the grounds that his wife had committed adultery, a woman had to prove other offences had also been committed, such as incest, cruelty or bigamy.

As she contemplated what Frank might do next, Elizabeth attended the controversial play and also met the playwright. When she wasn't visiting her lawyers, Elizabeth was frequently at the theatre, ballet or especially music concerts. Her musical tastes were broad, embracing Gilbert and Sullivan's operettas as well as concerts of Bach and Liszt.

But her greatest passion was for Wagner's operas and she spent many nights at Covent Garden, where she had a box which she shared with friends and family, including her brother Sydney who joined her for *Das Rheingold*. He was now Sir Sydney, having been knighted the previous year for his service as physician to the British Delegation at the Paris Peace Conference. She saw Sydney again a few days later, on a day when she also visited Sydney's former patient Bertrand Russell, whose wife Dora had just given birth to their first son. Elizabeth travelled to Cambridge a few days later to hear Hugh Walpole take part in a debate.

Next morning, she called on Frere, now an editor of the literary magazine *Granta*, at Christ College, to wish her young lover a happy twenty-ninth birthday. Unlike Elizabeth, Frere had read over breakfast a brief item in *The Times*. Sydney Beauchamp was dead. Elizabeth's sixty-year-old brother had been run over by a bus in London the previous evening. He had been walking in Pall Mall when he was hit and he died soon after at Charing Cross Hospital.

Frere did not say a word about it to Elizabeth. He later wrote to her, explaining that he had not wanted to break the news to her when she was about to take the train home alone. Hugh Walpole had agreed he should remain silent. Frere hoped she wasn't angry with him and that she understood he had acted from the soundest of motives.

When she reached London and learned the news, she was devastated. To Elizabeth, 'Sinner', as she always called him, was a saint, a source of lifelong support. He was the brother she had been closest to. Sydney, who had become a respected obstetrician, had rescued her from painful childbirth to deliver three of her babies. He had comforted her after Henning's death, helped her daughters get work as nurses during the war, and sheltered her when she left Frank. 'He was composed *only* of love,' Elizabeth wrote to Liebet. 'I can see no flaw at all in his character, & I have never known him ever impatient. He was a child of light [. . .] I know of no man so good.'

Elizabeth sat beside Charlotte and Margery at Sydney's funeral at the Holy Trinity, Sloane Street, where she was also joined by her brothers, Harry and Ralph, and other family members. The dean of St Paul's officiated at the service attended by a large and titled congregation, after which Elizabeth went alone to St Paul's to 'bless God for Sinner'.

Katherine learned of Sydney's death from the newspaper a few days later. 'Cruel, terrible Death! There is nothing more to say [. . .] Dear precious Elizabeth, would this had not happened to you!' Katherine, whose own brother had been killed, well knew the pain of such a loss.

By the time Elizabeth replied a month later, equanimity and steely resolve were the dominant notes. Her unadulterated love for Sydney had made his death bearable. 'There's none of that awful feeling one must have of "Why did I. How could I?" when someone dies whom one loved and yet got angry with at intervals.' They were questions she must have asked herself in the wake of the death of her daughter Felicitas.

Elizabeth resolved to behave better to her siblings. 'You should see me now being carefully angelic to Charlotte! I shall never be able to sniff impatiently at Rally [Ralph] again. Yes I will; I'm sure I will, for that is quite different and always has been. Charlotte though will need the most watchful treatment, for I do love her and do sometimes get irritable. She is a pathetic little figure. We both felt so *safe* while Sinner was there, and now we don't. But I'm tougher than she is and can bear not being safe better. He was our only man, us having unanimously shed our husbands.'

Chapter 15
COUSIN KATHERINE

Coco was lying across the chalet's doorstep when Elizabeth returned from London in late January 1922. The old dog could barely wag his tail in welcome. He neither barked nor raised his giant head as she approached. She sought help to carry the paralysed Coco inside to the warmth and then she telephoned the vet. But it was clear her beloved mountain dog would not recover. Coco was put down a few days later.

Keen to see her cousin, Elizabeth donned stout boots, leggings and breeches to insulate against the bitter cold and took the train up to Montana the day after she arrived at the chalet. Katherine was in bed and they talked for an hour over cups of drinking chocolate. At one point Elizabeth called Katherine's story 'At the Bay', which had just been published in the literary journal *The London Mercury*, a 'pretty little story'. Elizabeth's remark may have been clumsy rather than deliberately patronising. She had slept badly the previous night after discovering Coco in distress.

Elizabeth was born Mary Annette Beauchamp in Sydney, the youngest of six. Her family always called her May. (Ann Hardham family collection)

Kirribilli Point's villa Beulah, where Elizabeth spent her early years, had sweeping views across the harbour to Sydney. (Sketch by Conrad Martens, State Library of NSW)

Elizabeth's older sister Charlotte gave birth to her first child out of wedlock at fourteen. The sisters remained close throughout their lives. (David Norton family collection)

Newly married, Elizabeth moved to Berlin with her husband Count Henning von Arnim in 1891. (Ann Hardham family collection)

After three years of marriage, Elizabeth was the mother of three daughters. She fictionalised them as the April, May and June babies. (Ann Hardham family collection)

Elizabeth's remote home Nassenheide in Pomerania was where she began her writing career while raising her children. (Ann Hardham family collection)

Sunday Examiner Magazine.

A Great Literary Mystery.

Who Really Wrote the Now Famous "Elizabeth and Her German Garden"?

The Princess Henry of Pless? The Countess Von Arnim? or Princess Henry of Prussia?

WHO wrote "Elizabeth and Her German Garden"?

The world of letters is sorely puzzled.

The book is a chronicle of days spent in one of the most delightful gardens known to literature.

Whose is it?

"Elizabeth's" style is charming. Yet its creator remains anonymous.

Critics have tried to fit it to some one already famous in the world of authors, but without success.

It breathes a rare acquaintance with the customs and manners of German aristocracy, told by one who is skilled in the use of English.

No one but a woman could have written it.

What woman?

Two have been named—the Princess Henry of Pless, the beautiful daughter of Mrs. Cornwallis West, and the Countess Von Arnim, whose husband is high in the diplomatic circles of Austria.

Both these women have been alternately accredited and denied the honor of authorship which critics sought to add to those charms already thrust upon them by nature.

A third aspirant has arisen. She is a woman who outranks the other two in birth, if not in brains.

Rumor has finally allotted to Princess Irene, wife of Prince Henry of Prussia, granddaughter of the Queen of England and daughter of the late Princess Alice of Hesse, the authorship of "Elizabeth and Her German Garden."

"The Garden," she says, "was an absolute wilderness. It is all around the house, but the principal part is on the south side, and has evidently always been so. The south front is one-storied, a long series of rooms opening one into the other, and the walls are covered with Virginia creeper. There is a little veranda in the middle, leading by a flight of rickety wooden steps down into what seems to have been the only spot in the whole place that was ever cared for. This is a semi-circle cut into the lawn and edged with privet, and in this semi-circle are seven beds of different sizes, bordered with box, and arranged round a sun dial, and the sun dial is very venerable and moss-grown and greatly beloved by me."

Does any one recognize the garden?

Its lilacs are banked half a mile long right past the west front of the house. It is within driving distance of the shores of the Baltic, which is nine hundred miles long and many miles wide; it is planted with quantities of ipomoea, "the one thing needful to turn the most hideous desert into a paradise."

Whose is the paradise?

By such hints as these thousands of Elizabeth's admirers are trying to fix her identity.

"Elizabeth and Her German Garden" is the diary of a woman who says, "I am always happy (out of doors, be it understood, for indoors there are servants and furniture), but in quite different ways, and my spring happiness bears no resemblance to my summer or autumn happiness, though it is not more intense, and there were days last winter when I danced for sheer joy out in my frost-bound garden, in spite of my years and children."

The book has no plot, not even the suggestion of a romance. Yet it is full of freshness and charm. It is full of the radiance of a garden surrounded by corn fields and meadows. In it Elizabeth finds with her husband, whom she designates variously as "Man of Wrath" and "Sage," and her three babies, April, May and June, called for the months in which they were born, "peace and happiness and a reasonable life."

Before that for five years she had submitted to "weeks of sensible life and the horrors of a flat in town."

What town?

The literary world is guessing. By every evidence the woman speaks English perfectly and writes it as well. She must have spent her life divided between Germany and England.

She is a woman who, though married, loves solitude.

For six weeks she describes herself as blissfully happy alone.

"During those six weeks," she writes, "I lived in a world of dandelions and delights. The dandelions carpeted the three lawns—they used to be lawns, but have long since blossomed out into meadows filled with every sort of pretty weed. * * * My dreams seemed to melt away in a dream of pink and purple peace."

In the old house, that was once a convent, there were no bells.

"I used to take a great dinner bell to bed with me," said the owner of the garden, "so that at least I might be able to make a noise if frightened in the night."

She speaks of this time as "a time of blessedness." In the midst of it in the following fashion she introduces her husband: "Then he appeared suddenly, who has a right to appear when and how he will, and rebuked me for never having written home, and when I told him that I had been literally too happy to think of writing he seemed to take it as a reflection on himself that I could be happy alone."

The Princess Henry of Pless, who is undeniably clever, undeniably well educated, and the wife of a distinguished German nobleman, was first hailed as the author of "Elizabeth."

Facts were brought to bear to prove it.

She had had every opportunity to gather all the atmosphere needed. She might have written about "Elizabeth and Her German Garden" while living on her husband's fine old estate, at Furnstein, in Pomerania, on the shores of the Baltic Sea.

"Elizabeth's" Garden is boldly located in that vicinity. She speaks of a picnic on the shores of the Baltic.

The Princess has been married nine years, but she has not devoted them all to the mastery of flowers and shrubs.

She has given many of them over to the study of nature, but if reports be true it was man nature that interested her chiefly.

The Countess von Arnim, it is believed, might have written of "six blissful weeks alone" in a garden of dandelions and daisies.

Some years ago the Countess, a charming English woman, daughter of Henry Beauchamp, Esq., married the son of that Ambassador who was famous for his encounters with Bismarck. It will be remembered that Count von Arnim was accused by the Chancellor of having made use of State secrets in order to speculate on the Paris Stock Exchange.

The Countess Von Arnim spent all her girlhood in England, some of the ten years of her married life near the Baltic Sea on her husband's estate at Schlosien.

She has had a life of excitement that has not been all pleasurable. She has not a train of suitors that are her slaves in public. She has a reputation for eccentricity and cleverness enough not to use it in ceasing to be womanly.

Excited critics said she might have written of those "six blissful weeks when I lived in a world of dandelions and delights."

The Countess von Arnim might be Elizabeth, who quoted "Two paradises 'twere in one to live in Paradise alone." She might be by the strength of her admirers, but she is not. She has denied the allegation.

Again the great literary world is guessing.

Now a new claimant has risen for them to consider.

The Princess Henry of Prussia has traveled widely. It will be remembered that last year she joined her husband, the brother of the German Emperor, on his memorable visit to China. She is frequently with her sister, the Czarina, at the Court of Russia. She is very intelligent and very thoughtful.

On her husband's estate at Kiel, situated on a bay of the Baltic, she has been much alone.

She might have written in ecstasies of mignonette and pansies.

She might have cried with Elizabeth, "What a happy woman I am, living in a garden with books, babies, birds and flowers and plenty of leisure to enjoy them. * * * Sometimes I feel as if I were blest above all my fellows in being able to find my happiness so easily. I believe I should always be good if the sun always shone, and could enjoy myself very well in Siberia on a fine day. And what can life in town offer in the way of pleasure to equal the delight of any one of the calm evenings I have had this month sitting alone at the foot of the veranda steps, with the perfume of young larches all about, and the May moon hanging low over the beeches, and the beautiful silence made only more profound in its peace by the croaking of distant frogs and hooting of owls."

Elizabeth
and her
German Garden
New York
THE MACMILLAN COMPANY

PRINCESS HENRY OF PLESSE

THE COUNTESS VON ARNIM.

PRINCESS HENRY OF PRUSSIA

"MY garden is surrounded by cornfields and meadows, and beyond are great stretches of sandy heath and pine forests, and where the forests leave off the bare heath begins again; but the forests are beautiful in their lofty, pink-stemmed vastness, far overhead the crowns of softest gray-green, and underfoot a bright green whortleberry carpet, and everywhere the [illegible]

The identity of the mysterious author known only as 'Elizabeth' captivated newspapers on both sides of the Atlantic in 1900, including the *San Francisco Examiner*.

Elizabeth's parents, Louey and Henry Beauchamp, adored their little granddaughter Felicitas. Overcome by the demands of motherhood, Elizabeth left her youngest daughter in their care for more than a year. (Ann Hardham family collection)

Elizabeth dubbed her first husband the 'Man of Wrath'. She caught Henning in an unguarded moment at Nassenheide around 1905. (Ann Hardham family collection)

As a Prussian countess, Elizabeth's life was privileged but ruled by rigid formality. (Ann Hardham family collection)

E.M. Forster joined the 'quartette of menials' at Nassenheide in 1905. Seated clockwise from rear left: Herr Steinweg, E.M. Forster, French governess Mme Auger de Balben and housekeeper Teppi Backe. (King's College Archives Centre, Cambridge, EMF/27/300)

Felicitas was a joyful, musical child. At Nassenheide, she played with the family's enormous, but docile dog Ingulf. (Ann Hardham family collection)

After four daughters, in 1902 Elizabeth finally produced the son her husband longed for. She cradled two-year-old Henning Berndt, known as H.B., in Nassenheide's garden. (Ann Hardham family collection)

LEFT: Author H.G. Wells met Elizabeth in 1907. She was captivated by the free-thinking 'Don Juan of the intelligentsia'. (Alamy) RIGHT: Elizabeth's wit was as her piercing as her pale blue eyes. She was fond of feathers and furs, and wore them for her 1916 passport photo. (Ann Hardham family collection)

Newly widowed, Elizabeth was accompanied by housekeeper and friend Teppi on the search for a home in Switzerland. (The Huntington Library)

Elizabeth built her grand mountain home Chalet Soleil, and a little writing chalet, 'half-way up to heaven' in Switzerland. (Ann Hardham family collection).

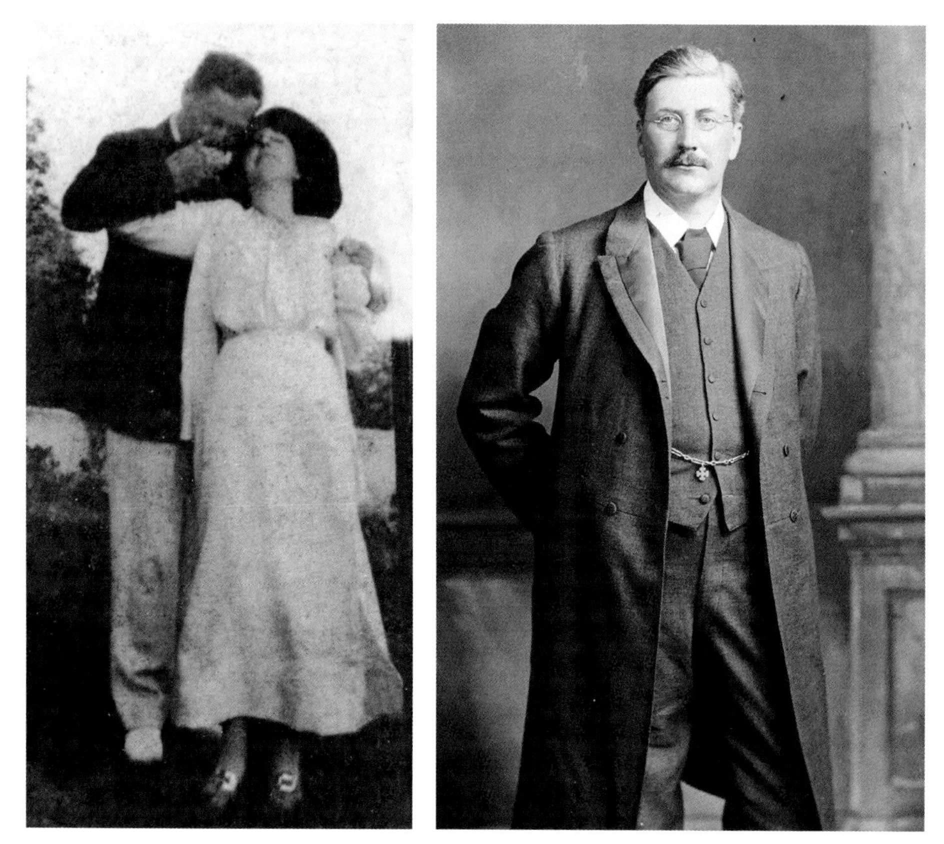

LEFT: Elizabeth and H.G. Wells in a warm embrace at the chalet around 1913. (The Huntington Library) RIGHT: Frank Russell, the Wicked Earl, had a turbulent marital history and had been jailed for bigamy before he became Elizabeth's second husband in 1916. (Maull & Fox/Wikimedia Commons)

Elizabeth loved riding a sledge in winter: 'There is nothing so absolutely bracing for the soul as the frequent turning of one's back on duties.' (Jamie Ritchie family collection)

Summer guests at the chalet in 1920 included, clockwise from rear left: Augustine Birrell, Elizabeth, Francis Birrell, Thomas 'Cobbie' Cobden-Sanderson, explorer Harry Johnston and Alexander Frere. (Jamie Ritchie family collection)

Alexander Frere was a handsome Cambridge student when he came to work for Elizabeth at the chalet in the early 1920s. Twenty-six years younger than Elizabeth, Frere became her lover and literary confidant. (Jamie Ritchie family collection)

Katherine Mansfield and her husband John Middleton Murry moved to live near Elizabeth in Switzerland in 1921. (Alexander Turnbull Library, Wellington, New Zealand).

Elizabeth's brother-in-law Bertrand Russell and his wife Dora were among the summer guests at the chalet in 1922. (Jamie Ritchie family collection)

Elizabeth tormented Hugh Walpole when he tutored her children as a young man, but the pair became life-long friends. (Library of Congress, Bain collection)

Elizabeth rarely sat for a portrait. She did not want the public to know anything about her. She was in her late-fifties when this photograph was taken. (Ann Hardham family collection)

Elizabeth's home Mas des Roses on the French Riviera, where she lived during the 1930s. (Jamie Ritchie family collection)

Alexander Frere remained in contact with Elizabeth after their affair ended. He published her memoir, *All the Dogs of My Life*, and fostered the careers of John Steinbeck and Graham Greene. (Elizabeth Frere Jones family collection)

As political tensions escalated in Europe in 1937, Elizabeth was visited by daughters Liebet and Trix. (Ann Hardham family collection)

Elizabeth missed her family and friends after fleeing Europe for America in 1939. She shifted around hotels, staying for several months at the rambling Gold Eagle Tavern in South Carolina. (Ann Hardham family collection)

Elizabeth, with her cocker spaniel Billy, was photographed for American *Vogue* in 1940. (Ann Hardham family collection)

Oscar-nominated Bette Davis portrayed the aging beauty Fanny Skeffington in the 1944 movie of Elizabeth's final novel *Mr Skeffington*. (Alamy)

Katherine was furious at the comment. She scorned Elizabeth in her diary, describing how her cousin had arrived dressed in black and looking like a cross between a bishop and a fly.

> She spoke of my "pretty little story" in the *Mercury*. All the while she was here I was conscious of a falsity. We said things we meant; we were sincere, but at the back there was nothing but falsity. It was very horrible. I do not want ever to see her or hear from her again. When she said she would not come often, I wanted to cry *Finito!* No, she is not my friend.

Then Katherine took revenge. She picked up her pen and over the next five hours Katherine wrote a story no one would ever call 'pretty'. 'A Cup of Tea' is a brutal caricature of Elizabeth. In it, rich, sophisticated Rosemary Fell takes home a poor, timorous, young woman she meets on a London street. Rosemary plans to shower her with benevolence. Over tea and sandwiches, Rosemary pets and patronises her. But Rosemary's grace and favours suddenly halt when her husband arrives and admires the pretty guest.

Katherine, overshadowed by her famous, wealthy cousin and emotionally dependent on her in her isolated chalet, may well have felt like the poor unnamed woman in her story.

Oblivious to the effect her ill-chosen words had had on Katherine, Elizabeth sent up gifts she had brought from London, including a knitted petticoat and bath salts. Katherine wrote to thank Elizabeth, but remained furious at her cousin's remark about the story and the characters she had so carefully crafted. 'Good God!' Katherine wrote to Elizabeth. 'How I worked at them and tried to express and squeezed and modelled . . . and the result was a *pretty* little story! I sank to the bottom of the ocean after you'd gone and stifled thought by writing another story which wasn't—couldn't be pretty.'

In the stew of conflicting emotions Katherine felt towards Elizabeth, she retained a fascination and even admiration for her older cousin. She found Elizabeth's ability to work unruffled and without distraction courageous. For the highly sensitive Katherine, even the sounds of doors banging, footsteps on the stairs or the smell of cooking disturbed the equilibrium she needed to write.

When Elizabeth sent a conciliatory letter, Katherine found it so generous and sweet she was 'ashamed of what I said or thought the other day.' Katherine offered an olive branch: 'We are solitary creatures *au fonds*. It happens so rarely that one feels another understands. But when one does feel it, it's not only a joy; it is help and comfort in dark moments.'

Katherine appeared uneasy with their conversation when Elizabeth visited again in late January. 'A strange fate overtakes me with her. We seem to be always talking of physical subjects. They bore and disgust me, for I feel it is a waste of time, and yet we always revert to them.'

Elizabeth thought Katherine looked frail and unwell. Katherine's health had deteriorated over the winter. She had decided to pursue a 'miracle cure'. She had learned of a Paris-based Russian doctor, Dr Ivan Manoukhin, who had developed an experimental, albeit expensive, treatment for tuberculosis. Katherine arranged to go to Paris for Manoukhin's treatment. She planned fifteen treatments and would be away for four months, she told Elizabeth. Katherine noted Elizabeth's surprising response: 'She suggested that if I did become cured, I might no longer write.'

Moving to Paris was risky. At her chalet, Katherine was well cared for with Ida Baker tending to her needs; John was present and Elizabeth nearby. Katherine had been prolific despite her illness at Chalet des Sapins; it was where she penned some of her most celebrated stories, including 'At the Bay', 'The Garden Party' and 'The Voyage'.

Elizabeth hoped the cure would work but feared Dr Manoukhin's bold promise was too good to be true. On the day of Katherine's departure at the end of January, Elizabeth made her way in the snow down to Randogne railway station to bid her cousin farewell. Katherine's train was due to pause there en route from Montana.

But as the train halted with Katherine aboard, somehow the two women missed seeing each other. Elizabeth assumed Katherine had taken a different train. Only when Elizabeth bumped into John after the train departed did she realise otherwise. Despite Elizabeth's determined effort to bid farewell to her cousin, it seems both women were so wrapped up against the cold—Elizabeth in a veil—they failed to recognise each other.

Elizabeth waded through snowdrifts down the path to her little writing chalet. The snow was so heavy on its roof she feared the building would collapse. When a path was cleared between the main chalet and her little one, it was a narrow slit between towering walls of snow. She was up to her eyelashes in snow. She put a photograph of brother Sinner in the little chalet to bless her while she worked, and another of him beside her bed to bless her while she slept.

Elizabeth had begun her next book while she was in Italy, and even had a title for it; she now set aside two months to concentrate on it. She worked determinedly, even though she felt off-colour for much of January and February. Prolific as she was, she did not consider herself a fast writer. The day she wrote 1200 words of her novel she considered noteworthy enough to record in her diary. By mid-February she had two-thirds down: 'Aren't I fruitful since I left Frank,' she wrote breezily to Bertrand Russell on the anniversary of her marriage to his brother.

The frigid conditions under which Elizabeth wrote much of *The Enchanted April* are a marked contrast to its balmy atmosphere of wisteria and sunshine. After the gothic blackness of *Vera*, the romantic and joyful novel that followed feels as if from a different pen. *Vera* and *The Enchanted April* are the two ends of the spectrum of Elizabeth's work.

The Enchanted April centres on four Englishwomen who rent a medieval castle in Italy for a month. Each is unhappy with their life: middle-class Mrs Arbuthnot and Mrs Wilkins with their marriages; the beautiful, single Lady Caroline Dexter with her lovers; the waspish, elderly widow Mrs Fisher with everything and everyone. Amid the bewitching Mediterranean beauty of San Salvatore—a fictionalised version of Portofino's Castello Brown—each rediscovers joy, love and generosity. While the book celebrates spring and regeneration, Elizabeth, at fifty-six, was in her autumn years when she penned it, closer in age to the sharp-tongued Mrs Fisher than to the three younger women.

As Elizabeth wrote her novel, her young lover in England bombarded her with letters, up to two a day. Frere had taken a position in London on the *Evening News* and was writing a column of literary criticism. He'd been invited to the South of France, where he would likely meet press baron Lord Northcliffe, his paper's proprietor. But Frere wondered whether he shouldn't abandon 'cheap' journalism and instead take a teaching job. He was keen for Elizabeth's career advice.

He narrated vignettes from his day. He had observed a 'super-Wemyss' on a train, bullying and manipulating his wife, taking the rack and coat hook for his belongings while commanding his wife keep her coat on in the hot carriage because there was no room to hang it.

His letters are those of an enthusiastic, excitable youth rather than the florid declarative letters Frank had penned her. Frere's youthful enthusiasm was nowhere more apparent than when he blithely related how an acquaintance, impressed by *Vera*, had inquired who had written it. Told it was by the author of *Elizabeth and Her German Garden*, the acquaintance responded: 'Oh, *that* book, my mother has it.' Elizabeth may have flinched at Frere's unwitting reminder, not only of how much time had passed since she began writing but of how many years separated her from her young lover.

Katherine's latest book arrived. Elizabeth eagerly read her copy of *The Garden Party and Other Stories*. Elizabeth was effusive in her praise to Katherine—there would be no repeat of the 'pretty little story' clanger. Elizabeth thought Katherine's 'The Life of Ma Parker' her finest and the most harrowing of the fifteen short stories. She was impressed too with 'The Daughters of the Late Colonel' (the colonel based on Ida Baker's father). '[I] felt so proud of you [. . .] I might be your mother in my pride,' Elizabeth wrote to Katherine. In Paris, Katherine was so overjoyed by Elizabeth's letter she 'kept taking peeps at it all day'. Elizabeth reiterated her maternal pride in her cousin to Frere. 'I'm beautifully proud of her—just as if I had hatched her!' Although Frere did not like Katherine, he acknowledged her talent.

In early March, Katherine's treatment was underway and she painted an alarming picture. After five doses of x-ray treatment she felt 'hotted up inside like a furnace and one's very bones seem to be melting.' After this, Katherine's letters made no mention of her health or the progress of her treatment, so Elizabeth begged her for news: 'Are you busy writing, or are you too much excited at the nearness of May? Perhaps you are plunged into despair.' Katherine continued to avoid the subject: 'it only wakens the Furies to speak of one's health before one is out of their reach.'

Elizabeth invited Katherine and John to stay with her at the chalet once the treatment was over. Elizabeth was soon imagining Katherine 'walking up the path to the chalet in August with a smiling husband carrying your fountain pen.' Katherine seemed much improved towards the end of her first course of treatment. Her cough had subsided and she'd gained weight. Katherine was in better health than she had been in more than two years.

John had recently met James Joyce in Paris, whose *Ulysses* had just been released. Elizabeth tried to read it but didn't get far. She wrote to John: 'nothing will induce me to read a thing—anything—even God's first novel, if it bores me. *Ulysses* made me feel as if I were shut up with a lunatic who was doing what the courts call "exposing himself". I got as far as the detailed account of the man's (morning?) visit to a lavatory and then boredom so profound fell upon me that I went to sleep.'

Elizabeth spent much of the spring with Frere in England. He showered her with carnations and lilies, and squired her to the theatre and opera. She was increasingly out in public with him. They played endless games of chess, and he was her match. The young man attended balls and dances—he was a nimble dancer—without her.

Elizabeth revisited places associated with her past, including East Lodge in Acton where she had lived as a girl. The grand lodge had been demolished, replaced by houses. She glimpsed the remains of the garden in which her father, a keen gardener, had happily pottered. It was full of weeds, rubbish and derelict motors.

She also revisited Goring-on-Thames and looked on Hazel Cottage, where Henning had courted her as a young woman. This time, it was Frere who came a-courting. For three idyllic days over Whitsuntide, he paddled her up and down the river, reading her Keats, and they drifted back by twilight and wandered through fields yellow with buttercups.

Elizabeth was not the only member of her family enjoying a romance with a lover of another generation. Her nineteen-year-old son H.B. in America was engaged to an older woman. Elizabeth was pleased he was engaged—she thought it might encourage him to work. But he was not yet old enough to marry without her consent, and she was not about to give that. About the age difference she was non-judgemental.

Elizabeth was eager to see Katherine and John when she arrived back at the chalet in June. They had returned to Switzerland and were staying at the Hotel d'Angleterre in Montana. Elizabeth was hoping they would soon come to stay at her chalet.

But from the hotel, Katherine wrote with distressing news: her health had declined. 'I suppose my enthusiasm was too much for the Furies [. . .] For they have turned about their chariots and are here in full force again [. . .] But here I am with dry pleurisy, coughing away.'

Katherine's exhausting trip from Paris would not have helped her condition. Unable to find railway porters at Gare de Lyon, she and John struggled with their luggage to board a crowded and filthy train. When they stepped out of Randogne station, a cold mountain downpour soaked them as they bumped their way in an open cart to their hotel. Katherine was feverish by the time she was shown into a cheerless single room—she and John had separate rooms—in the chilly, empty hotel.

Katherine had glimpsed the Chalet Soleil with its distinctive blue shutters as she made her way in the rain to the hotel. Elizabeth's little writing chalet looked so enchanting she thought it should have a star on the top. But that would be as close as Katherine would get. She would not come up in August: 'I am too much of a bother to have in a house, my dearest cousin [. . .] Fancy meeting me on the stairs, very short of puff, or seeing me always about. One can never get invalids out of one's eye.'

Katherine did not want sympathy. Her main concern was for her husband. 'He ought to divorce me, marry a really gay young healthy creature, have children and ask me to be Godmother. He needs a wife beyond everything. I shall never be a wife and I feel such a fraud when he still believes that one day I shall turn into one. Poor John! It's hellish to live with a femme malade.'

On a cold, grey afternoon, Elizabeth walked up to the hotel. Katherine was alone on a glass-enclosed veranda when she arrived. Katherine had put on weight and talked animatedly, but she coughed throughout. Elizabeth returned to the hotel a few days later with her house guest Marie Mallet. With her huge hat and lace veil caught with a diamond brooch and her gossip about her former mistress, Queen Victoria, Marie left an indelible impression on Katherine. But she suspected Elizabeth would quickly tire of the loquacious Marie. Katherine was right. Elizabeth soon found herself reading *The Times* through Marie's long-winded anecdotes, and was relieved when Marie's equally prolix sister-in-law also came to stay and they could be left to talk at each other.

Elizabeth continued to visit Katherine every few days. Finding her alone and pinched with cold in the gloomy hotel, Elizabeth begged her to come to the chalet. When John arrived, Elizabeth found him vague and awkward. She may have sensed the growing rift between the couple.

John appeared at the chalet a few days later with some news: Katherine planned to leave her hotel. She intended moving down to the Bellevue Hotel in the town of Sierre—the lower altitude being better for her heart. Ida Baker would care for Katherine at the Bellevue while John would remain at the Hotel d'Angleterre. Elizabeth and Katherine spent the morning of her departure talking at her hotel and rode together in Katherine's oxcart to the railway station. Elizabeth was sad to see Katherine go; she would miss her regular company. Elizabeth could walk to the nearby Hotel d'Angleterre but the Bellevue was a train ride away.

The silence at the Chalet Soleil was pronounced after the talkative Marie and her sister-in-law departed. John dropped by often and she welcomed his visits. 'John, who is my one comfort during this phase of *spiritual* loneliness,' she wrote in her journal.'

Elizabeth finished *The Enchanted April* in early July, but without the focus of a book, loneliness and depression overwhelmed her. She wrote a candid letter to Liebet, striking in its melancholy. Gone is her typical breezy, witty, acerbic tone. Even her handwriting, notable for the airy, abundant space between each line, is cramped and dense. In it, she acknowledged she had found no joy in marriage.

> What a pity I wasn't so lucky—it must be heavenly, that happy life with someone one can utterly trust. I'm completely alone here, & am ashamed to say I hate being alone. I thought I'd love it, & was strong enough & free enough of spirit to rejoice in it. To my disgust

> & disappointment I find I'm nothing of the kind [. . .] I find difficulty in growing up in lots of ways. You see, Lieb, nothing matters in the long run except love. There must be someone in the world who loves one *more* than anyone else, & the person who hasn't got that background is a forlorn thing. The love of children & sisters & things is very precious, but they love other people *more*, so it isn't the one warm comforting thing which alone makes one happy.

She began a couple of writing projects, but these went nowhere. And then she took off to Lake Geneva's shores, first to the majestic Palace Hotel at Caux near Montreux. But the hotel was deserted and she rattled around in it, eating alone as melancholy music echoed around the elegant but empty dining room. Then she went to Lausanne, a place of bittersweet memories.

A happy part of her childhood had been spent at Lausanne, with her mother and siblings—while her father sailed off to Australia. She found the old church she attended as a girl and hoped to see inside, but the door was closed. She recalled her mother there, looking pretty in a pale blue bonnet.

But Lausanne was where she had sent Felicitas to the school that later expelled her, which had triggered such a tragic train of events. Memories of her daughter flooded back as she sat alone over chocolate and sandwiches in a café where she had once shared food with Felicitas, she noted in her journal. The journal reference Elizabeth made to Felicitas is rare. She barely mentioned Felicitas after her death.

In contrast, Elizabeth frequently evoked memories of other family members long after they died. She would note in her diary the anniversaries of their births and deaths. Decades later, she would even note the anniversary of traumatic days, such as when Henning was arrested, or days she regretted, such as the day she married Frank.

But one looks in vain in Elizabeth's journals for any reflections on Felicitas. The anniversaries of the girl's birth and her untimely death pass without comment. In periods of distress, Elizabeth's diary often fell temporarily silent. As she wrote, towards the end of her life: 'Who wants to write, or think, of ancient griefs? Put them on one side; cover them up with silence.' Her silence on Felicitas lasted for the rest of Elizabeth's life.

Elizabeth could not dispel the cloud of depression that lingered throughout the summer, even as she corrected the proofs of her most upbeat book and her guests arrived. She often felt physically unwell too and her usual boundless energy and enthusiasm had flagged.

Although nights at the chalet were filled with music and dancing, Elizabeth frequently retired to bed early, leaving her guests to entertain themselves. Perhaps her mood infected Frere. Usually so agreeable and eager to please, he seemed nervy and petulant when he arrived for the summer. He occasionally read aloud to Elizabeth, but when they sat one hot afternoon on a grassy slope above the chalet she became irritated as he rattled on about the British character and revolutions.

Down at the Hotel Bellevue, Katherine's painter friend Dorothy Brett arrived. But her deafness—she carried an ear trumpet—made conversation difficult and exhausting for Katherine. It was like talking to someone for two hours on the telephone, Katherine told Elizabeth. Katherine had decided to return to London to see her doctor about her heart before pursuing further medical treatment with Dr Manoukhin in Paris. Katherine was short of money and Elizabeth loaned her £100. Katherine insisted she would pay it back from the earnings of her book, writing: 'You've lent that £100 to a fearfully desperate character.'

Katherine looked pitiful when Elizabeth visited in early August and they sat over afternoon tea in the hotel garden. Katherine must have known her recovery from tuberculosis was increasingly unlikely. Shortly before she departed the hotel, she drew up her Will. She gave John a free hand to do what he wanted with all her manuscripts, letters and papers. She left Elizabeth her copy of Shakespeare, full of her margin notes.

Elizabeth came to say goodbye. The cousins had lunch in the shade of an acacia tree in the Bellevue's garden before Katherine left for London in mid-August. Elizabeth would miss the cousin she had come to care for deeply. 'I hate to think you are nowhere within reach,' Elizabeth wrote to Katherine soon after her departure. 'There are so many moments I want to run and talk to you in, and such lots of things I want to tell you—but of course this is the selfishness of a pig.'

The arrival of Bertrand and Dora Russell at the chalet lifted Elizabeth's spirits. She always enjoyed Bertrand's conversation. She was amused to overhear him telling her guests how, as a seven-year-old, his brother Frank used to torture him because he was little and weak. But at times she became impatient even with her brother-in-law. As Bertrand and Dora 'hissed out annoying political theories' one night, Elizabeth pointedly fled to her piano. She tuned out when Dora spoke, but 'Bertie, that great brain, simply sits listening to her in rapture'. She felt more kind about them towards the end of their visit when she danced and sang with Dora.

As guests came and went throughout August, she was surprised when, alone in her room one afternoon, it dawned on her that not one of them had sought out her company. Many of her guests had already gone by the time of her birthday, her fifty-sixth, which she felt was the dreariest she'd experienced in a long time. She continued correcting proofs of *The Enchanted April* but was dissatisfied with the pallid, bloodless result: 'It's like a thin flute playing all by itself on an empty afternoon,' she wrote to Frere.

She learned that her dear friend Cobbie had died in London in early September. He was integral to the joyful spirit of summers past at the chalet. Reminders of him were everywhere around her—his chair, his red umbrella, and what she called Cobbie's path.

As summer neared its end, Elizabeth recalled how twenty-two years had passed since Henning had been arrested at Nassenheide. The day remained vivid in her mind; she even recalled the clothes she'd been wearing. As she thought of her late first husband, she was snapped back into the present by news of her second. Frank was writing his memoirs. Elizabeth figured he must be short of money.

When Frank's *My Life and Adventures* appeared in 1923, it contained a lengthy account of his many legal battles, his first divorce and his bigamy trial. It had sections on how 'my first wife did ensnare me', 'I fell in love with another', 'I was put in prison by my Fellows'. But nowhere in its more than three hundred pages is any mention of Elizabeth. She had been written out of his history. The book included photos of one of his white dogs, his cat, his yacht and his car and one captioned The Countess Russell. It was of his second—and by then divorced—wife Mollie.

Chapter 16

MORTAL LONGINGS

Elizabeth celebrated the publication of *The Enchanted April* over dinner with Frere at the end of October. It was as well she did so promptly. The first reviews of what is today considered her most loved and joyful book soon gave her little reason for cheer.

Rebecca West, who had admired *Vera*, was unimpressed. She considered the new novel a pastel-hued disaster, in which four grotesque females were transformed into 'dear little women' under the influence of almond blossom, she wrote in the *New Statesman*. *The Spectator* too was withering, arguing that the characters developed a condition of 'fatuous beatitude'.

In contrast, Edward Shanks in *The Queen*, who had found *The Caravaners* too savage and *Christopher and Columbus* too saccharine, thought *The Enchanted April* struck the right balance of sweetness and sharpness, as in a good cocktail. Elizabeth was delighted when *The Nation* admired her talent for gently puncturing pomposity and described the book as 'a gentle assertion of the claims of life against duty'. It was, after all, the creed by which she lived.

The Enchanted April would become her first book to be turned into a movie. Directed by Harry Beaumont—a prolific filmmaker who had worked with Joan Crawford and John Barrymore—it was released in 1935 by America's RKO Pictures. *The New York Times* considered it a gem and a howling comedy.

After she had read *Cosmic Anatomy* at her chalet, Katherine Mansfield became increasingly interested in a spiritual dimension to her illness. Since then, she had learned of a Caucasian mystic called George Ivanovich Gurdjieff, who emphasised expanding consciousness, self-transformation and developing balance. Today we might call him a new-age guru.

Gurdjieff was a charismatic figure with piercing eyes, a luxuriant moustache and a shaved head topped at times with a fez or astrakhan. He would eventually influence a range of arts figures including director Peter Brook, architect Frank Lloyd Wright and P.L. Travers, the Australian-born author of *Mary Poppins*. Gurdjieff had established his centre, the Institute for the Harmonious Development of Man, at Avon, just outside Fontainebleau, south of Paris. By autumn of 1922, Katherine had joined him there.

Elizabeth missed her candid conversations with her cousin: 'letters are such laced-in things—no comfortable overflowings and easy indiscretions,' Elizabeth wrote to Katherine. She received no reply. After a couple of months and with still no word, Elizabeth wrote again. 'Won't you send me one little line? I like to imagine that you are suddenly going to walk in, radiant and well, and that is what you've been saving up for and that is why you haven't written [. . .] I *miss* you so!'

As Elizabeth begged for news, Katherine in Avon was penning a long letter to Elizabeth and enclosed a cheque for the £100 her cousin had loaned her. Katherine apologised for not writing earlier, it was not for lack of love. Like Elizabeth, Katherine too had fallen into depression:

> A black fit came on me in Paris when I realised that X-ray treatment wasn't going to do any more than it had done beyond upsetting my heart still more that I gave up everything and decided to try a new life altogether. [. . .] When I came to London from Switzerland I did [. . .] go through what books and undergraduates call a spiritual crisis, I suppose. For the first time in my life, everything bored me. Everything and worse everybody seemed a compromise, and so flat, so dull, so mechanical.

She had 'burned what boats I had' and come to Avon, where she lived with about sixty others, mostly Russians. 'I cannot tell you what a joy it is to me to be in contact with living people who are strange and quick and not ashamed to be themselves.'

Katherine had not written a word since October and didn't intend to until the spring. 'I am tired of my little stories like birds bred in cages.' She thanked Elizabeth for *The Enchanted April*, for which she was full of praise. 'It is a delectable book; the only other person who could have written it is Mozart [. . .] How do you write like that? How? How?' Katherine signed off with a note of finality. 'Goodbye, my dearest Cousin. I shall never know anyone like you; I shall remember every little thing about you for ever.'

Katherine's poignant letter, penned on the final day of 1922, was the last she ever wrote. On the evening of 9 January, just after John arrived at Avon from England, Katherine climbed the stairs to her bedroom and began to cough. Blood gushed from her mouth. She was helped to the bedroom, where she died of a pulmonary haemorrhage. She was thirty-four.

John telegrammed Elizabeth with the news the next day. She wrote back to him in words that echoed those Katherine penned following the death of Elizabeth's brother. 'There *is* nothing to be said or done. But I feel inside like one huge ache of impotent sympathy and love.'

Elizabeth felt keenly the deaths of Katherine, Cobbie and Sydney. Yet the depression and loneliness she had felt for much of the past year began to lift. Her losses gave her a singular and lighthearted perspective on a Christian afterlife. 'All my friends are dying, so that the next world is becoming thickly packed with the best people, & from a great empty place of harps & unknown bearded people is changing in my mind to a very interesting & convivial sort of well-attended party.'

As she made light of mortality, she became enraptured by an opera entitled *The Immortal Hour*. The tale, based on Celtic legends, is a twist on the Orpheus and Eurydice myth. A beautiful fairy, Etain, is beguiled into leaving her Land of the Ever Young where she has a fairy lover. Soon she is wooed by a mortal king. But at a feast to celebrate their union, Etain's fairy lover appears. She recognises him as her true love and returns with him to the Land of the Ever Young.

The opera brought worldly mysticism and lush music to a country recovering from the misery of war. The opera was a huge success after its London opening in October 1922, with Gwen Ffrangcon-Davies as Etain. Rutland Boughton's now largely forgotten opera attracted a loyal following, with many patrons returning again and again.

Night after night Elizabeth took her seat in the auditorium of the ornate Regent Theatre, opposite St Pancras Station. Sometimes she went alone, sometimes with Frere, at other times with her friends including philosopher George Moore, and Thelma Cazalet, a feminist and later a Conservative politician. Each time, Elizabeth found it more enchanting than the last. When the opera's initial run ended in April, she had seen it about a dozen times. When it was revived later in the year, she returned again and again. Whether it was the Wagner-influenced music, the romantic tale of a woman recognising her soul mate, or the idea of returning to a land of eternal youth, Elizabeth was gripped by the opera.

She was also seized by a 'cannibal yearning' for her own flesh and blood. So great was her longing that, in summer, she set aside her aversion to Germany and decided to pay her daughter a surprise visit. She had not seen Trix for four years, since her third daughter had been newly married; now, Trix was the mother of a three-year-old daughter. Elizabeth had not yet met her granddaughter or Trix's husband.

Trix was out when Elizabeth arrived at her daughter's Bavarian home in the old part of Bamberg. Elizabeth waited in the drawing room, amid brocade curtains and silver knick-knacks. She thought the house, staffed with a cook and housemaid, looked comfortable.

Trix was astonished and delighted to discover her mother, who had arrived without warning. For the next two days they shared meals and walks through the old town's medieval streets full of timber-framed houses with steeply pitched roofs. If Elizabeth hoped to find herself reflected in her daughter, she was disappointed. Elizabeth found so little trace of herself 'she might just as easily not have had me for a mother at all'.

In Munich, former housekeeper Teppi was waiting as Elizabeth alighted from her carriage. They had not seen each other in nearly a decade—when Teppi left the chalet on the eve of the outbreak of war. Teppi's hair was grey, her face more fox-like than Elizabeth remembered, and she had gained weight, but her vitality was unchanged. She had prospered and was running an expensive finishing school for girls.

They had only one evening together and they made the most of it, talking and laughing until late. Much as she loved Teppi's company, Elizabeth's view of Germany was unchanged. She caught a train the next morning to Switzerland, happy to see the beastly country receding.

Wasps found their way through a hole in the floor of the little writing chalet. Elizabeth slew them with a prayer book she kept especially for the purpose. One of her guests proved an equally unwelcome, but more resistant, intruder. The talkative Marie Mallet took to barging in while Elizabeth was working.

Although Marie was a painter—one of her watercolours of Portofino appeared in the first edition of *The Enchanted April*—she had no understanding of a writer's need for solitude. Elizabeth exhorted her not to interrupt. When Elizabeth asked why Marie supposed she shut herself up there, her guest's response was: for a rest. Elizabeth was not resting, but working on a new novel. One that would draw on her affair with the younger Frere.

She worked even as her summer guests arrived, among them Maud Ritchie, Augustine Birrell, Liberal feminist Lady Nellie Sandhurst, Hugh Walpole, Irish diplomat Shane Leslie and John Middleton Murry. Elizabeth acquired a gramophone and asked Frere to bring with him some dance records such as the latest Roaring

Twenties jazz hit, 'Hot Lips'. Elizabeth was eager to be reunited with Frere—'Tuppence', as she had taken to calling him. As she waited for him, she sent him ardent letters—up to three a week.

Elizabeth was an indefatigable correspondent throughout her life. Sometimes she wrote up to thirty letters a day. She typically penned two-page letters, writing on both sides of the creamy paper. She frequently turned her notepaper sideways to write extra lines in the margins or upside down to squeeze additional thoughts across a corner. With few crossings out or amendments, and in a sloping cursive—more nimble than neat—the impression is of words tumbling from her fountain pen.

Her letters to Frere were full of longing, but it was expressed in a playfully idiosyncratic way. She addressed her most intimate feelings not to Frere directly but via an imaginary figure called Doris. Elizabeth's letters are full of entreaties to Doris, such as: 'Tell Doris I love her very much & she is hardly ever out of my thoughts' and 'what I want *really* want, & all I want is to be alone in this heavenly beauty with Doris'. Doris is part-messenger and part-Frere's alter ego. It may have been a mark of Elizabeth's unease about their romantic relationship that she did not address her more intimate yearnings directly.

The dynamic shifted repeatedly in their relationship: at times Elizabeth appeared maternal towards Frere—anxious about his health and his inclination to overwork—at other times he adopted a parental tone, advising Elizabeth to exercise and eat properly. From the diffident, under-confident young man who arrived at the chalet three years earlier, he had grown into an assured figure at ease in the literary circles into which Elizabeth had drawn him.

They were confidantes, who shared a love of literature and exchanged candid opinions on books and writers. She told him she found Rebecca West's *The Judge* 'quite strangely bad'; she thought

D.H. Lawrence was 'submerged in that ugly treacle of bad things & people'; her verdict on Henry James was: 'How *nearly* he was great.'

Their relationship brought joy to each of them. But Elizabeth knew they had no future together, and that eventually Frere would commit elsewhere. That much was implicit when she urged him, if he ever had children, to bring them up properly. She became more explicit over time: 'I really don't know what I'll do when she [Doris] marries, which of course she's sure to do. I must find her a nice husband who'll like me, so that I can still be friends.' As for Elizabeth, she had no desire to remarry. She valued the independence she had fought hard to achieve. She had 'outlived the alien authority of husbands'.

She found herself irritated by Frere's moods during his time at the chalet: 'He is always tiresome here sooner or later.' Nonetheless, the moment he departed, she missed him. Her reaction, while considerably less extreme, recalls her response to Frank's comings and goings.

As most of her summer guests departed, her former housekeeper arrived. Teppi read aloud stodgy German books to Elizabeth, which sent her to sleep. They conversed in German, but Elizabeth had forgotten much of the language in which she once was fluent. Elizabeth felt unwell one morning and, unable to work, she returned to bed. There she became absorbed in D.H. Lawrence's *Kangaroo*, his novel based on his journey to Australia the previous year. In it, he conjured the beauty of Sydney's harbour and terror of the immense landscape.

Elizabeth, who was always keenly attuned to landscape, may well have been intrigued by Lawrence's evocation of her birthplace. Certainly, she was impressed by his writing: 'He is on the way to greatness, unless he is tripped up by going mad.' If Lawrence's book made her curious about the land he described, she also knew that to reach it entailed a long sea journey. And she had no love of the sea.

The four-funnelled RMS *Arundel Castle* steamed out of Southampton on a bitter cold, late December afternoon. Elizabeth was heading for balmy Cape Town. Her doctor had ordered a rest cure of silence, solitude and no work. For much of the past two years, she had suffered bouts of unspecified ill-health. Her energy flagged, she frequently went early to bed or fell asleep during the day. Not that she had much faith in her new doctor. She missed her brother's advice. But the idea of doing nothing for a few weeks appealed to her.

She regretted her decision to embark on a sea voyage almost immediately. A gale blew up in the Bay of Biscay and she ached in her hard bed. She was soon convinced that a week in her New Forest cottage—which she had rented, with Ida Baker installed as housekeeper—would have been every bit as beneficial as a long, lonely, expensive journey by ship. 'Why did I ever come? Am an idiot, and one incapable of learning.' Christmas Day aboard was grey, rough and 'horrid'. She helped judge the fancy dress ball on New Year's Eve, then retired early to her tiny cabin, where she could hear the riotous party continuing until the early hours.

This was the longest sea voyage she had undertaken since as an infant she had sailed with her family from Australia. Unlike her father, she would never find joy on the ocean waves. She was relieved to reach dry land and the elegant Mount Nelson Hotel. When her ground-floor room was invaded by ants, she moved upstairs to a flower-filled room with a view of Table Mountain from one window and of the sea from another. 'It really is rather unfair the way one gets things, all the best things, in places like these merely by having a title,' she wrote to Frere. She enjoyed the benefits of being a countess.

She was feted with invitations to tea parties and high-society receptions. It was hardly the rest-cure prescribed and she was invariably exhausted by the end of each day. 'Dried up English people with colonial accents everywhere—all very cock-sure, because in their hearts they're *not* sure,' the colonial-born Elizabeth wrote to Liebet.

She was disoriented by the southern hemisphere flora, full of strange proteas and cacti. She'd trade them all for a pansy. She loathed Cape Town's raging winds, which blew for much of her three-week stay. The place was full of corrugated iron, baboons and elderly spinsters. She returned to England in mid-February after nearly two months away, unimpressed by her first adult encounter with colonial society, and resolved never again to undertake an ocean voyage. 'I'll never go away again unless I'm forced to by something terrific.'

The rooms were full of gracious ghosts. Elizabeth stood within the Château de Coppet above Lake Geneva. During her childhood, it had been the home of her Uncle Frederic Lassetter and his large family. Unlike her own family, they had nearly all returned to Australia. She was surprised by how clearly she remembered the rooms.

Another reason likely drew her to the once-familiar château in early June. Long before the Lassetters inhabited it, Château de Coppet had been a refuge during the Napoleonic era for two of Europe's most extraordinary women. Elizabeth had become increasingly fascinated by them. Outspoken writer Madame Germaine de Staël made her home there after Napoleon banished her from Paris and wanted her silenced. In response, she had turned the château into what the French writer Stendhal called the 'headquarters of European thought', as it attracted artists and intellectuals from across the continent.

Madame de Staël also gave refuge to Madame Juliette Récamier, who ran a leading Paris salon. Madame Récamier had also been exiled by Napoleon and the two women formed a deep friendship. As Elizabeth wandered the familiar rooms, Elizabeth thought of Madame Récamier's romantic connection with the von Arnim family. Considered one of Europe's greatest beauties, Madame Récamier had been courted, unsuccessfully, at the château by Henning's grandfather, Prince August of Prussia.

The castle had newly opened to visitors in 1924, and Elizabeth noticed how the rooms had been restored to reflect its two celebrated female occupants.

She was joined on her journey around Lake Geneva by Ida Baker, who accompanied her back to the chalet where they listened to the gramophone and talked late into the evening. From Ida, Elizabeth was delighted to learn that Katherine Mansfield had dedicated a book of poems to her cousin. The dedication read: 'Elizabeth of the German Garden, who loved certain of these poems and their author.' It was public affirmation that, despite the tetchiness that had at times blighted her relationship with Katherine, her cousin had cared deeply for her.

'Darling little house of happiness. May this summer be blessed,' Elizabeth wrote in her journal. She had high expectations for summer at the chalet. Two of her daughters were coming, Liebet from America and Trix from Germany. Elizabeth had unexpectedly sold the serial rights to her yet-to-be-completed novel, and the windfall meant she could pay for Liebet's trip.

Elizabeth was as excited as the new puppy she had acquired. She made her way early to Sierre to meet Liebet's train, waiting under the acacias in the Hotel Bellevue's garden, where she had once sat with

Katherine. She had not seen her daughter for seven years, not since her American escape from her disastrous marriage to Frank. They talked until the moon rose.

Trix arrived four days later. She and Liebet had not seen each other for more than a decade. Now both were married and young mothers. 'It was like a dream hearing those two children eagerly telling each other about their babies!'

The sisters played golf while Elizabeth worked on her novel, *Love*. The three women danced and listened to recordings of Italian soprano Amelita Galli-Curci, whose voice reminded Elizabeth of her mother's. They walked together with the puppy as it leapt after butterflies, and sang old German songs Elizabeth had taught them as children at Nassenheide. As Elizabeth's other summer guests began arriving, Liebet accompanied Trix to her home in Germany, returning in time for her mother's birthday.

The star of *The Immortal Hour,* Gwen Ffrangcon-Davies, was among Elizabeth's summer guests. At the time, Gwen—who was also an actress—was the toast of London. She had just been hailed for her performance in *Romeo and Juliet*, opposite a young, little-known John Gielgud. Gwen sang for Elizabeth and her guests at the chalet after dinner, and read aloud sonnets they had composed.

Elizabeth travelled to Paris with Liebet to farewell her daughter as she set out on her return journey to America. While there, Elizabeth went to nearby Avon, intending to visit Katherine's grave. But she was unable to find it. John had forgotten to pay for a permanent burial plot. She had been dug up and moved to the unmarked pauper's section. Not until 1929, after Katherine's father learned of what happened, was she reburied in a marked grave. Today she lies near Gurdjieff, with a headstone that refers to her not as a writer but simply as the wife of John Middleton Murry.

Elizabeth read works by John and Katherine in the wake of her Paris trip, and wrote candidly to Frere about both. She was not impressed with John's novel *The Voyage*. 'When one thinks of K.M. splashing out in a single sentence more than he continues to get across in a whole laboured book! I wonder why he persists.' But Katherine's newly published short story collection *Something Childish and Other Stories*, which John had edited, impressed her deeply. 'I believe if she had lived, she would have done great things.'

Chapter 17
A WORMY BUSINESS

'Should a Woman Marry a Man Much Younger than Herself? And if so—How Much Younger? The author of "Elizabeth and Her German Garden" and "The Enchanted April" answers both these perplexing questions in this, one of the finest of her novels.'

That was how the mass market *Good Housekeeping* magazine introduced its serialisation of Elizabeth's new novel, *Love*, in September 1924. Such was her popularity as a novelist that the magazine touted only one item on its cover: Elizabeth's new book. The serialisation ran for six months in America and the UK. Elizabeth was thrilled but under pressure. The serial began appearing even as she was still writing the book.

Elizabeth was about to place a sexually active older woman centrestage. This was a daring move, even given the shift since the war that had ushered in greater independence for women. Her novel, which drew on her affair with Frere, would also address ageing and the double standards by which women were—and are—judged.

Elizabeth was aware of how much literary tastes had changed since she began her writing career in the prim Victorian era. Just how much was brought home to her when she started reading a novel by Victorian-era author Anne Thackeray Ritchie while she completed writing *Love*. She found the Ritchie novel anaemic and its gentility hideous. 'From her writing one would suppose she had never in her life become aware that under one's clothes there was such a thing as a real naked body. And I can hear the genteel applause of all her friends, when her books came out—"Dear Anne—charming, charming." Christ, the gentility of the genteel Victorians,' Elizabeth—who rarely used profanities—wrote in her journal.

Love opens at a performance of *The Immortal Hour*, where a middle-aged woman and a young man are among the patrons drawn repeatedly to the opera. Seated near each other one night, they begin to talk. Catherine is forty-seven and a genteel widow who has never known passion. Christopher is twenty-five and has little experience of women. Christopher ardently pursues Catherine, and they marry. Marriage soon shifts the dynamic in their relationship. She becomes dependent and anxious while he wants a round of golf and male company.

Counterbalancing the central couple are Catherine's daughter Virginia and her husband Stephen, a clergyman thirty years her senior. Stephen is the embodiment of hypocrisy, as clergymen often are in Elizabeth's novels. But Elizabeth hints at something more unsettling in her description of Stephen and Virginia's courtship: '[Stephen] had his thoughtful eye on Virginia from the beginning. When he went there she was five and he was thirty-four [. . .] She wasn't nineteen when he married her. He loved her with the excessive love of a middle-aged man for a very young girl.'

While the age gap between Virginia and Stephen raises no eyebrows in the novel, the gap between Catherine and Christopher does. As the book unfolds, Catherine becomes obsessed by her age, her appearance and her flagging energy. Desperate to reverse the effects of time, Catherine embarks on a course of radical beauty treatments at the hands of an expensive quack. These involved x-rays.

Elizabeth may have had in mind Katherine Mansfield, who had undergone x-ray treatments in Paris. But it is also possible Elizabeth herself underwent a similar radical procedure as she contemplated the book. Her diary for early 1923 contains numerous appointments for x-rays. At the time, radium quackery was a lucrative trade, with the newly discovered element touted as a miracle cure for everything from fatigue to impotence. Cosmetics and other goods appeared that advertised radium as an ingredient—in face creams, toothpaste and even haemorrhoid ointment.

When the novel was published in the spring of 1925, she sent a copy to H.G. Wells. The acrimony she once felt towards him had long vanished when she wrote to ask him if he had received his copy. 'Did you get my Love? Indeed, you have it always, but I mean my book?' The warmth and wit of the woman Wells called 'Little e' had returned to their relationship.

The reviews were favourable. *The Times Literary Supplement* thought her subject 'so painful one shudders to think what a less sophisticated artist would have made of it'. *John O'London's* literary journal considered Elizabeth 'a pessimist by conviction who has cultivated the delightful gift of burying life's harder facts beneath a veil of fun and fancy'. Her ability to combine bitter with laughing matter gave the book its piquancy. *Love* was a story that 'few women would have the courage to write, and no man could have written'.

Elizabeth was walking back to the chalet on a grey late-winter afternoon when she slipped on ice. She fell backwards, hit her head and the sound was like the crack of a pistol. She feared she had fractured her skull and felt unwell for days afterwards. The fall and the danger of spending so much time alone at the chalet, especially in winter, may have contributed to her restlessness about where to live.

In England, she bought land in Virginia Water, Surrey, and began building a house she called White Gates. She rented an apartment on Venice's Grand Canal during the spring of 1925. Although she intended to work on a new book there, she fell into the temptations of gondolas, lagoons and the company of Frere, who joined her.

The ability to work that eluded her in Venice returned once she was back in her little writing chalet for summer and she was happy with her early progress on what became her *Introduction to Sally*. 'I am afraid I was pleased—afraid, because it is a bad sign and means the stuff is probably very bad and silly,' she wrote in her journal. But she recognised the work ahead. 'Such a mountain to climb up tiring step by tiring step.' She struggled increasingly with her novels, often tearing up ten pages for each one she kept.

She was also occupied with editing her old friend Cobbie's voluminous diary, all 800,000 words of it. Elizabeth persisted; she did not want to disappoint his widow Anne who had asked her to take on the task. Frere made only a brief appearance among the summer guests. He was about to go to America, where Elizabeth had arranged an introduction to her friend and publisher Frank Doubleday.

Elizabeth learned that Charlotte's son Guy, an army captain, had drowned while bathing near Beijing. She was desperately sad for her sister, who had now lost another son. Within a week of Guy's death, Charlotte's former husband George Waterlow shot himself in a Plymouth hotel. An inquest found he had taken his life while temporarily insane after learning of his son's death.

In autumn, Elizabeth went to visit Trix in Germany and together they revisited Nassenheide. But the iron gates to the property had been locked for so long that trees had grown through them. The driveway was thick with grass and shrubs. Elizabeth persuaded a reluctant housekeeper to let them peep inside the downstairs rooms. Henning's old library was being used to store wood and coal; the schoolroom was turned into a kitchen and the beautiful brickwork in the hall was covered in lino. The sight was far more dispiriting than when she had visited five years earlier. She vowed never to return. 'It is a wormy business digging up past and gone things.' Next day, Elizabeth's journey was as melancholy as the weather. In pouring rain, she and Trix drove to Criewen. After almost a decade, Elizabeth was at last able to visit the grave of her daughter Felicitas.

Elizabeth became embroiled in a trans-Atlantic literary stoush early in 1926. Her friend Poultney Bigelow had just published his memoir, *Seventy Summers*. In it, Bigelow described meeting H.G. Wells at Elizabeth's London flat. As they chatted over tea and admired Elizabeth's splendid view of the Thames, Bigelow claimed Wells boasted about the fabulous amounts of money showered on him by various publishers as they clamoured for his writing. And he described Wells as resembling a 'lucky stockbroker'.

Wells was furious. He hit back in the *Daily Express*, which ran his account of the meeting on its front page. Bigelow had not only sought an introduction to Wells, but at the tea party he had peppered the British author with vulgar questions about his income. Wells considered Bigelow's account malicious twaddle and Bigelow a bore. The escalating storm over a teacup was soon picked up across the Atlantic, including in *The New York Times* and *Time* magazine.

Bigelow took umbrage at Wells calling him a bore. 'How am I going to make a living as an after-dinner speaker if I am slandered by being called a bore?' he told *The New York Times*. The paper reported he planned to sue for $50,000 damages. But a few days later he backed down, claiming his threat had simply been a joke: 'I am a Quaker and Quakers do not bring suits.'

It was a clash of large, bruised egos that could have stepped from the pages of one of Elizabeth's novels. Amid the war of words, the publicity-averse Elizabeth took the surprising step of entering the fray.

She leapt to Bigelow's defence. She was sure Bigelow's comments were simply his way of expressing admiration. 'He gilds one with his own warm rays,' she wrote in a letter published in the *Daily Express* and *The New York Times*. Americans simply had a different way of expressing their admiration, she added. Anyway, she too had been stung by *Seventy Summers*. 'I was going, however, to suffer dumbly if I hadn't been encouraged by Mr Wells' example to do it out loud,' she wrote.

Bigelow had claimed in his book that whenever Elizabeth entered a drawing room, all conversation flagged unless she was in the mood for talking. 'Could anything be more damaging?' she asked. She continued:

> I have been into many rooms, and never has conversation flagged in them, except when the room was empty. What would Mr Wells have said if this had been written of him? On the other hand, I would very much like to be described as having the appearance

of a lucky stockbroker. To me the terrible adjective is usually applied of 'dainty'. As if I were a lace frill. Perhaps Mr Wells wouldn't mind being called dainty. I am ready to exchange.

Elizabeth gave the only substantial interview of her career a few months later to the popular American women's magazine *The Delineator*, which was about to serialise her new book *Introduction to Sally*. The article, by author and war correspondent Sir Philip Gibbs, promised to lift the veil on the mysterious Elizabeth. It did nothing of the sort. After describing her as dainty—the adjective she loathed—Gibbs may well have found getting information past wartime censors easier than extracting information from Elizabeth. She was not about to satisfy any public hunger for knowledge about her life. She stonewalled all questions.

'But *why* should they know? What is there to tell them anyhow? They can find me in all my books,' she said. Her marriages, her 'uneventful' years, her habits did not matter, she argued. And Gibbs colluded, writing: 'We made a little conspiracy over the teatable. We laughed at the thought that we would refuse, firmly but politely, to satisfy public curiosity about people like ourselves.' The article reveals little about Elizabeth's life not already known, in a piece long on flowery descriptions—'this dainty lady [. . .] like a miniature painted on ivory in the eighteenth century'—but short on insight.

Behind the scenes, Elizabeth had been at pains to ensure no information about herself reached the magazine. She was furious to learn that her daughter Evi had been contacted for the magazine article and had provided material. 'It is too impertinent of them, not having been able to get all they want out of me to try these back-door ways with my children. I hope you will always turn the deafest ears & a shut door to any newspaper person,' she wrote to Liebet. She hoped her daughter destroyed her letters. 'You do burn my letters, don't you. I'm terrified to say or write anything now for fear of those awful papers.' Liebet did not obey her mother's command. She preserved hundreds of Elizabeth's letters and our understanding of her today would be vastly different otherwise.

Elizabeth destroyed many of her love letters. Before she did, she copied out passages from them by hand, on nine closely written pages. Whether these were from Frank, Wells or another lover she did not say. She added a note: 'These are bits out of some love letters written to me once. The letters were burned. But it seems sad to save nothing. So these bits were extracted before the holocaust.'

Elizabeth wanted as little known about herself as possible. 'I have a most deeply rooted aversion from [sic] publicity,' she once wrote. Such was her loathing of the limelight that she had been a bestselling author for nearly three decades before *The Delineator*'s profile appeared.

She went to great lengths to conceal aspects of her life and career not just from the public, but from friends and family. She disavowed authorship of her books (even to her publisher in the case of *Christine*); she kept secret details of her life from her family—such as the birth of her son—and ordered her children not to share details of her life even with each other, including of her second marriage and its demise.

Silence was often her first response to traumatic events. Yet, paradoxically, Elizabeth treated her life as raw material for her semi-autobiographical writing, putting it into the most public of arenas as bestselling novels.

Beverley Nichols once observed:

> Very few people have ever managed to get behind the mask of anonymity, and they all come back with different stories of what they have seen [. . .] to the public she is only a pen, and not a person [. . .] they never think at all of Lady Russell, because they simply do not know she exists. They are caught up in the fascination of her work, they wonder for a moment what manner of man or woman produced it. And all they have to guide them is a blank title-page.

Elizabeth was also rarely photographed. In surviving family photographs, her face is nearly always in profile, in the shade or hidden by a large hat. On the rare occasions when her face is visible, she hardly ever meets the camera's gaze.

Long after her death, aspects of Elizabeth's life and even her appearance continued to confound. Her 1986 biography stated she was born in New Zealand and used for its cover a John Singer Sargent drawing of a wavy-haired aristocratic-looking woman that the book claimed was an image of Elizabeth. It was not. The drawing was of British art historian Clare Stuart Wortley, as its author Karen Usborne acknowledged to *The Times Literary Supplement*. The cover was replaced.

Elizabeth did not want herself exposed to the light. But what lay behind this aversion? Clues lie in an unpublished essay she penned about poets and poetry. It mounts a witty, spirited, even spiritual, argument in favour of authorial anonymity.

In it, she argues that great poets are godlike, and that 'the divine should be veiled in mystery'. That divine, mysterious power is destroyed by learning the details of a poet's life and all-too-human frailties. It is better not to know that Shelley had the voice of a peacock, that Milton was an impossible husband and a brutal father, or that Wordsworth's handshake was limp, she writes. 'Why should the saucepan in which our spiritual food was cooked be pushed upon our notice also.'

With their words, poets give the world their best. But the world, once invited behind the scenes, turns its gaze on their worst: 'How vital it is that their works should be separated from the blinding confusion of personal detail by a veil of thickest anonymity.'

Nothing should be known of poets except what they choose to tell us in their works, she argues in her essay, 'The Anonymous in Poetry'. She mistrusted biographers bent on feeding a public hungry for gossip. Nonetheless, throughout her life Elizabeth was an avid reader of biographies—not least of poets.

The undated essay was likely written when she was a young woman in Pomerania. Elizabeth would never have equated herself with a great poet—she was modest, even disparaging, about her talent. But the argument she mounted in her magazine interview—know me through my books—is the same she advanced in her essay. As the wife of a Prussian aristocrat, Elizabeth may have needed the cover of anonymity to publish. But long after that need disappeared, she held tenaciously to its protective shield.

'I shall be told I'm vulgar & indelicate. So I am, & thank God for it,' she wrote to Frere ahead of the release of *Introduction to Sally*. There was too much sex in her new book, her American agent had recently informed her, much to her amazement. 'It seems to me totally without any love making.'

Social class rather than sex is at the heart of the book. The eponymous heroine is a grocer's naïve daughter who is unaware of her magnetic beauty. A Cambridge student, infatuated with Sally, woos and weds her. But he soon realises they have little in common. Pygmalion-like, he attempts to 'improve' her—including the way she speaks—with the aid of his social-climbing mother. The book's tone is more lighthearted than its predecessor, *Love*.

The book was released in September 1926, in the wake of a nine-day general strike—then the largest industrial dispute in British history—when class division was in the spotlight. As Elizabeth predicted, 'vulgar' was the verdict of the *New Statesman*, while *The Spectator* considered it 'a little coarse'. *The Times Literary Supplement* acknowledged her gift for 'airily malicious portraiture' but feared she was becoming too kindly. But far worse, in Elizabeth's eyes, was the *Daily Express* review—which found the book boring. She felt dejected and feared for her sales. When she reached London in autumn, she visited her British publisher Sir Frederick Macmillan, to see about advertising the book better.

She particularly needed this book to sell. She wanted to help her daughter Evi, who was experiencing financial and marital troubles. Evi's husband Eustace, deep in debt, had abandoned her and their children. Elizabeth could support Evi as long as her books sold. But Elizabeth did not want Useless Eustace, as she called him, getting his hands on the money. She urged Evi to get divorced.

Elizabeth spent little time with Frere during the year and he had even been absent from the chalet's summer party. Although they wrote to each other regularly, there was less heat in their exchanges. As the year ended, Elizabeth decided to spend Christmas not with Frere or her family but among strangers.

She went as a paying guest to a private party at an Elizabethan mansion in Sussex. The mansion's proprietor had assured her that care was taken to ensure only the 'right people' attended their house parties. The snobby tone of the letter should have sounded alarm bells. Perhaps Elizabeth was hoping for material for a new book. But three days of festive cheer among strangers chirping 'cheerio' to each other proved too much. She cut her losses. 'Made up my mind flight was essential.'

Elizabeth fled to the South of France, where Charlotte had taken a cottage in Peyloubet, near Grasse. Elizabeth hoped for quiet, sunshine and time to work. She found sunshine, but quiet and work eluded her. Elizabeth's room in the cottage had no door, only a curtain, which made noise and draughts unavoidable. Charlotte's son Cecil, known as Puddle, joined them. Elizabeth and Puddle played chess together, but he was liable to become angry if he lost. He was otherwise given to long silences. Elizabeth found herself unusually irritated by Charlotte and starved of intelligent conversation.

The latter at least could be remedied. Beyond an olive grove near the cottage, Elizabeth could see a huge pink house under construction. H.G. Wells was building a new trophy home. She thought it worthy of Kublai Khan—although its name was Lou Pidou, not Xanadu. After a few frustrating days unable to work, she walked across to see Wells in his stately pleasure-dome and joked that she expected to see it filled with dulcimers and maidens.

On the latter, she was not disappointed. Elizabeth was captivated by a striking and slender young woman. Odette Keun was Wells' newest and most unusual lover. Odette was a Dutch author, adventurer and a one-time novitiate nun who was prone to jealousy and salty conversation. Odette had travelled among North African tribes in the Algerian desert, and through Russia and Georgia, where she had an affair with a Georgian prince. She had been arrested as a spy in Istanbul and met Wells after he favourably reviewed one of her books. Once again, Jane Wells was aware of her husband's affair with a woman twenty years his junior, and the two women exchanged letters and gifts.

Elizabeth was amused by their love nest and the engraving over the fireplace: 'Two Loves Built This House'. She was less impressed by Wells' new novel, *The World of William Clissold*, which he dedicated to Odette. 'Head of a genius, two enormous feet of clay,' was her verdict on the book to Frere.

Part of Elizabeth's purpose in spending the four months around the Riviera was to look for somewhere to live. Since her fall at the chalet, she had been considering a move to a warmer climate. The French Riviera in the 1920s and 1930s drew many artists, writers and socialites, among them F. Scott and Zelda Fitzgerald, D.H. and Frieda Lawrence, Aldous Huxley, Somerset Maugham, Pablo Picasso, and Coco Chanel. The elegant *Train Bleu* travelled from Calais (where it picked up British passengers from the ferry) via Paris to the Riviera, which was thus in easy reach for its well-heeled passengers.

Several of Elizabeth's friends lived near Charlotte's cottage, including Bridget Guinness, whose husband was part of the banking arm of the prominent Anglo-Irish Guinness family. Bridget was an artist and society hostess, and she and Elizabeth had become friends in London. In the South of France, Elizabeth and Bridget were frequently together, and shared the odd flutter at the casinos of Cannes. Bridget was the social glue in an aristocratic English crowd who'd settled into villas there or migrated to the Riviera each winter. These included the elderly Duke of Connaught, one of Queen Victoria's sons, who showed Elizabeth his Villa Bruyeres gardens.

Elizabeth had not yet decided to buy a house there by the time she left on the Blue Train in spring. But she had decided to give up her London flat. She visited Jane Wells, who spoke vehemently about the Italian fascist leader Benito Mussolini, then tightening his grip on power. It was their last conversation. Elizabeth was stunned to learn soon after that Jane had cancer. Elizabeth thought often of the many walks and conversations she and Jane had shared over the years, she wrote to Wells. Jane died in October.

Elizabeth arrived in Bayreuth with Trix for the summer Wagner festival. No music drew Elizabeth more consistently than his. She attended performances of his music throughout her life, and her responses were invariably passionate. Yet Wagner was not an unmitigated joy for Elizabeth. Her patience could run as thin with the composer as it could with her friends.

At times, Wagner's long-windedness and pomposity overshadowed for her the beauty of the music. When it did, she would threaten never to attend a production again. But, like her threats never to revisit Germany, she kept returning. Her reaction to *Parsifal*, the first opera she attended in Bayreuth, was typical. She enjoyed the first act, but as the hours passed her pleasure diminished. 'If Tolstoy had written operas he'd have written this one.'

The composer's son, Siegfried Wagner, was now artistic director of the festival. Elizabeth cared little for Siegfried Wagner's direction, but she was keen to hear the tenor Lauritz Melchior in the title role in *Siegfried*, the third part of Wagner's epic Ring cycle. She had met Melchior over the years through Hugh Walpole and was impressed with his performance. She joined the Wagner table for supper afterwards and a few days later went to visit Siegfried Wagner's English-born wife Winifred.

It was a dispiriting meeting. Elizabeth found the ugly mausoleum of a house little changed since Henning first took her there nearly forty years earlier. Elizabeth disliked Winifred, whom she found 'English by birth but nothing else'. Winifred would become a controversial figure when she took over the festival after her husband's death in 1930. A prominent supporter of Adolf Hitler, she shared his anti-Semitism—and provided the paper and typewriter on which he composed *Mein Kampf*.

One hot morning, Elizabeth drove to the late composer's villa, Wahnfried. Sitting on the balcony was Wagner's elderly widow, Cosima. But the figure Elizabeth glimpsed was a far cry from the once formidable woman before whom she had performed so long ago (and from the romantic figure Australian writer Henry Handel Richardson immortalised in her final novel *The Young Cosima*). Elizabeth observed: 'She held a black fan before her face but I saw her masses of white hair. The last of Cosima.'

Chapter 18

A VULGAR LITTLE MIND

Elizabeth lay in her hammock at the chalet in June 1927 reading Virginia Woolf's *To the Lighthouse*. She was enraptured. Elizabeth thought it better than anything Woolf had written. 'No one, I think, who wasn't acquainted with madness, could have written it. It says the things that are really unsayable, in the way poetry does.' How strident, vulgar and coarse her own writing felt in comparison.

As she questioned her abilities as a writer, another book seized her attention. Katherine Mansfield's journals, edited by her husband, had just been published. Elizabeth was shocked to see herself described there as possessing 'a vulgar little mind'. Katherine had penned the comment after one of Elizabeth's visits to her chalet in 1921.

Elizabeth, who had prided herself on her vulgarity as she penned *Introduction to Sally*, was appalled. 'If it is true, was I not born with it? Can I help it? I was very shy always with her, *afraid* of her while intensely admiring. Perhaps embarrassment made me say vulgar things. But I don't know—probably she is right. [. . .] One has so many sides, and it is possible K.M. drew out the vulgar one,' Elizabeth wrote in her journal.

Much as she loved her cousin, Elizabeth had never felt at ease in Katherine's company. Elizabeth wrote the next day to John saying she now realised that Katherine too felt their meetings were unsatisfactory. Elizabeth was constantly afraid of displeasing her cousin. So anxious was she in Katherine's presence that she felt all fingers and thumbs. 'I always came away feeling as if my skin were off, and miserable with the conviction I must have bored and repelled her. Yet I adored her.' Only when she wrote to Katherine could she feel at ease. 'If only I hadn't been so much *afraid* of Katherine! [. . .] I felt so gross when I was with her, such a great clumsy thing, as if my hands were full of chilblains.'

Elizabeth was more sanguine a week later when she wrote to Frere: 'I do know K.M. was fond of me, & no one knows better than myself how one splashes out things into one's diary which are just of the moment's mood, & with no relation to one's real feelings. Fortunately we don't all have J.M.M.'s [John Middleton Murry] to publish one's casual vapours.'

Elizabeth became increasingly ambivalent about John's decision to publish posthumously Katherine Mansfield's private musings, including her letters: 'It is somehow disgraceful that Middleton Murry should fatten on K.M.'s remains, for she would particularly have loathed them being published, but yet we are the gainers by it.' But perhaps John took the long view, looking past decency to the claims of posterity, she wrote to Liebet.

Frere remained Elizabeth's main literary confidante and he was among the summer guests at the chalet. Now in his mid-thirties, he was writing theatre reviews for London literary magazines and was poised to become a director of publishing house Heinemann.

He was integral to her life, but she feared she had become clingy. She could not live without him, even if he married, she wrote to him soon after he departed. She alluded all year in her letters to him to the possibility that he might marry, although nothing indicated there was a contender on the horizon. Nonetheless, she warned him repeatedly against embarking on the 'awful adventure' of marriage without being in love.

She shared with Frere her struggles to write. Some days she found this so difficult, 'black despair comes & perches like a crow on my heart, picking out the eyes of hope'. She struggled especially with endings. But she was never short of words. They tumbled from her pen: 'My way of working is to spill freely & then break my back spooning it all up again.'

She shared too her joys. She thanked God, who first put it in her head to write stories. 'Writing is the best fun in the world. One may & does curse & complain, but just the stringing of words together into artful necklaces is "so amusing". I'm glad God made me a scribbler instead of anything else. How I'd have hated it if I'd had a passion say for cooking.'

Adultery was the theme of the novel she worked on through the summer. Elizabeth knew the topic was risky. She had side-stepped the issue in her book *The Pastor's Wife*. Now she feared the subject might threaten a hoped-for lucrative American serialisation deal for her new book and the £6000 this would bring, she told Frere.

A gale blew as Elizabeth crossed to England in late October. She was filthy and exhausted by the time she reached her Surrey home, White

Gates. Frere arrived two days later—and plunged her life into despair. 'He told me things which were distressing to me, and the bottom was knocked out of life. No good pretending it isn't.'

He probably told her that he was involved with a young woman and considering marriage. Although Elizabeth and Frere continued to see each other, the stress was evident. Frere often arrived looking haggard, and Elizabeth was bewildered by his behaviour. Frere took months to tell her why.

As she made her way to London in April 1928, after again wintering in the South of France, Frere met her in Paris. There he broke the news. He had married the previous November. His wife was Jessica Rayne, the daughter of a London theatrical costumier and shoemaker. Jessica was thirty years younger than Elizabeth and a divorcee, a status that still carried considerable stigma.

Despite this, Elizabeth still wanted Frere in her life. As with Wells and Frank, she seemed unable to extricate herself. She and Frere attended *Götterdämmerung* together and he continued to visit her at White Gates. When he had his appendix removed, she visited him as he recovered at a nursing home, where on one awkward occasion she encountered Jessica. When Elizabeth returned to her chalet for summer, he accepted her invitation to recuperate there. She celebrated with Frere the release of her adultery book, *Expiation*, in early 1929.

In it, she had created her most unlikely heroine, Milly Bott. Middle-aged, middle-class, mild-mannered and 'cushiony', Milly hardly fits the scarlet woman stereotype. Milly's vengeful husband has died suddenly, and her secret, long-standing affair is revealed as the book opens. Much of what follows pokes fun at her horrified in-laws—pillars of suburban society—and their efforts to save Milly and themselves from public disgrace. Images of Milly as both a dove and serpent are threaded through the book. There is an echo of

Elizabeth's father's long-ago observation about his daughter's nature. The book's disapproving lawyer damns Milly as: 'A serpent masquerading as a dove.'

Forgiveness for Milly ultimately comes in the form of a sympathetic elderly mother-in-law, a figure previously pilloried almost as much as parsons in Elizabeth's fiction. Most striking is how Elizabeth deals with the liaison itself—an affair in which the heat of passion has long tempered into a companionable routine and has made an unhappy marriage bearable. The sudden ending of the affair—and Milly's attempt to hide her pain—is moving and prescient.

The controversial book was widely reviewed. The literary journal *John O'London's* recognised the author's courage. But its admiration was not for her willingness to tackle adultery. It was for creating a plump heroine.

Other reviews considered how the author's worldview had changed over three decades. J.B. Priestley in the *Evening News* thought the characters in her recent novels no longer believed in love. *Punch* argued that disillusion characterised her recent books, her cynicism a far cry from her 'pretty and intriguing' pre-war temper. The book was 'a one-sided quarrel with a world inadequately understood'.

The Yorkshire Post viewed her ripened vision vastly differently. The author had cast off her 'graceful garden attitude'; her observations had become sharper, their scope bigger. *Expiation* was the work of a woman with a mature philosophy and penetrative eye for comedy and the book had a 'harsh brilliance'.

Elizabeth was pleased to learn that Sydney Waterlow thought it her best book since *Vera*. Sydney had taken over from Elizabeth's father as the family critic whose opinion she most valued. Her fears that her book would not be serialised were unfounded. The American magazine *The Delineator* promoted her on its cover. Elizabeth was relieved by the critical and commercial response. She was satisfied that the appetite remained for her books. She knew literary tastes and styles had changed and some of her pre-war contemporaries were now considered 'old hat'.

Elizabeth had dreamed for years of seeing her three children in America. But work was always an obstacle. She had not seen Evi nor son H.B. in a decade, nor Liebet for five years. With *Expiation* released, she decided to cross the Atlantic aboard SS *Leviathan* in March. The ship was originally German, called *Vaterland* (Fatherland), but it had been seized during the war by America and renamed. Elizabeth would have appreciated the twist of fate that saw her sailing in the vessel to see her German-raised children in their new American home. But she was barely out of English waters before she fell ill and came to question the wisdom of embarking on a hastily arranged trip. She never conquered her loathing of ocean journeys.

Her doubts melted away when she saw Liebet waiting on the dock in New York. Liebet, her husband Corwin and their two daughters were living at Sunset Farm, in Hartford, Connecticut. She was reunited at the farm with H.B. and Evi. Elizabeth enjoyed spending time with her son, who was now married and had two daughters, but she found Evi unhelpful and ungracious. There was little affection in their parting.

Elizabeth remained closest to her daughter Liebet. Together they travelled to New York for several Wagner performances, including seeing Melchior in *Tristan und Isolde*. She wept as her Liebet saw her depart on the *Berengaria* after a two-week visit. Elizabeth stored the memories of their time together 'as a squirrel stores nuts & brings them out in bad days & gloats over them'.

The chalet's pleasures were many: long summer evenings on the terrace listening to the gramophone, lying in the bath with the window open beneath a yellow moon. Or winters curled up by the fire, as snow fell beyond. She had built it as a young widow determined to make her own way. Wells, Frank and Frere had all come courting in its honey-scented air. And left. Gone too was Katherine Mansfield, the cousin she had grown to love there. With the chalet, Elizabeth had balanced the conflicting strands of her nature: her need for solitude and society. She would fill the chalet with her guests, and then retreat down the path to her writing chalet and close the door.

None of that was conveyed in the advertisement Elizabeth prepared as she put the chalet up for sale in the autumn of 1929. It spoke of its four oak-panelled living rooms, sixteen bedrooms and such mod cons as central heating, telephone, electric lighting and ready access to a funicular railway.

With the sun about to set on the Chalet Soleil, Elizabeth wanted one last summer house party. She invited about a dozen guests, among them composer and suffragette Ethel Smyth, who was friends with Vernon Lee and Virginia Woolf. Ethel played and sang excerpts from her opera *The Wreckers*, which had debuted at Covent Garden some years earlier. The composer was taken with Elizabeth's intellectual curiosity: 'She continually makes me stretch my eyes and gives me the feeling of standing under a cool and gentle waterfall on an extremely hot day.' Elizabeth would later liken Ethel to a thunder-storm, and the pair would develop a turbulent friendship.

Elizabeth's enthusiasm for so many guests had run its course. Some days she felt like she was running a boarding house. As the guests departed, Trix and Teppi arrived to help her pack up the chalet. Elizabeth paused to read old diaries and letters and was swept back to Nassenheide days. 'How *happy* I've been! Inside so happy. All my unhappiness, of which I've had quite my share, came from *people*.' She re-read too some of Frere's letters. 'That has been a funny business! And a sweet one.'

She ordered a huge bonfire to be built in the garden. From her bedroom, Elizabeth watched as the flames leapt and engulfed so much of her past. She turned her back on the chalet and left for England. As the decade ended, she spent New Year's Eve alone at White Gates, buried in a book. It was Robert Graves's *Goodbye to All That*.

In the chaos of the last days of the chalet, Elizabeth lost a section of the new book she had been writing, *Father*. She feared it had been accidentally consigned to the flames as she cleared out her little writing chalet. She was relieved to find it again. But then she left the entire manuscript in a hotel room en route to England.

It was retrieved, but she was no sooner back at White Gates before she faced another difficulty with her draft. It had been rejected for serialisation in the *Ladies Home Journal*. It was a blow to her confidence and finances. She may have wondered if this book was cursed. She dusted off her disappointment and began rewriting it.

The book began, as many of hers did, with a heroine escaping male tyranny. Her heroines had run from war, domestic drudgery, motherhood, wrathful fathers, vengeful—or simply dull—husbands. They had escaped from palaces and parsonages and sought refuge in caravans, chalets, castles and California. This time her heroine, Jennifer, would seek to escape the iron rule of her widowed father.

Father may well have prompted memories of her relationship with her own father. For, as she toyed with the idea for the book, she reflected on Henry Beauchamp. 'My father was terror itself to me all my life, & yet I was very fond of him after I grew up, & much appreciated him, & felt he was right not to be able to endure me when I was small.' It is a surprising observation, given Henry's journals suggest he took great pride in his youngest daughter.

Elizabeth also reflected on the difference between how her parents had raised their children and the way she and Henning had. She wondered if she and Henning had been too zealous in their own children's upbringing, anxious to give them the best possible education. Elizabeth felt her parents rarely gave her a thought and left her to her own devices. She considered this a great blessing. 'With no book learning to hamper me, no spoon feeding by teachers, I spread such little wings as I had & flew off on my own.' In contrast, her sister Charlotte—who had become pregnant at thirteen—considered their parents' hands-off approach neglectful.

The book was not all Elizabeth penned over winter. She wrote a review of Virginia Woolf's *A Room of One's Own*. The review was so harsh, its tone so patronising and dismissive of women's creative aspirations that it raises questions about her purpose in penning it. Elizabeth's review appeared in the journal *The Graphic* under the pseudonym of Oliver Way. It was scathing of the premise of the seminal feminist essay—that in order to write, a woman needed £500 a year and a room of her own. Elizabeth disagreed. 'Rooms don't make writers. Streetsful of rooms of their own won't turn women into poets,' argued Elizabeth, the owner of a sixteen-bedroom chalet with a separate writing retreat.

Her review asserted that women should be content to give birth, especially to male geniuses: 'The only time Shakespeare was born he was a man.' Women were like taxis, she added, their role was to safely carry passengers. She dismissed as 'footstools of learning' Cambridge women's colleges (including Girton where Elizabeth sent two of her daughters to study) since they were not yet large or developed enough to be called 'seats'.

Was she serious? Or was this literary mischief on Elizabeth's part? Was she using the cover of a masculine pseudonym to skewer male entitlement and pomposity? For Oliver Way seems to damn himself with every line, in much the way the arrogant Prussian baron did with every utterance in *The Caravaners*.

It is a curious piece, not least because Elizabeth had long admired Woolf's writing, which she considered exquisite. And some months after her review appeared, she wrote to her daughter that since the release of *A Room of One's Own*, there had been no book worth getting excited about.

At White Gates, she developed a fractious friendship with Ethel Smyth, who lived close by at Hook Heath, Woking. Ethel's late friend, suffragette Emmeline Pankhurst, had famously been arrested at the cottage while recovering from a hunger strike in 1913. It was also where Pankhurst had learned to throw stones, before she aimed them at the windows of 10 Downing Street.

A missile of a different sort greeted Elizabeth as she arrived at Hook Heath in the spring of 1930. Ethel showed her a letter she had received from her friend Virginia Woolf. In it, Woolf described how she had observed hatred and scorn written all over Elizabeth's face when the two women had met. Ethel thought Elizabeth would be amused by the letter. She was 'amazed, horrified and shocked'.

Elizabeth was still reeling when she and Ethel went for a walk, during which the composer berated her for not being a 'real fierce feminist'. Nonetheless, Elizabeth stood by—albeit grumpily—the next day as Ethel conducted 'The March of Women', her anthem of the suffrage movement, while a statue of Pankhurst was unveiled near the Houses of Parliament.

Deeply wounded as Elizabeth was by Virginia Woolf's comment on her appearance, Woolf respected her as an author. Just a few months later, Woolf wrote to Ethel Smyth praising Elizabeth's novels, which made her shout with laughter. Woolf considered some of Elizabeth's writing as good as Dickens'.

The old pink house perched on a hillside inland from Cannes. Elizabeth had fallen in love with the home on land belonging to her friend Bridget Guinness, just above the medieval village of Mougins. Elizabeth bought the house and called it Mas des Roses. (Mas is a Catalan word used in Provence to describe a traditional farmhouse.)

Despite its charming name, there was not a rose to be seen. For much of 1930, it was a building site, and an expensive one. Elizabeth's architect had been overly optimistic in his estimates of costs and timing.

She arrived with high hopes in September. She had been assured the house was nearly ready for habitation. Instead, the property was full of workmen; the non-existent garden was full of stones, planks and bits of iron. But the long, narrow house had enough spare bedrooms—four at a pinch—for guests. There was also a study, drawing room and, in what would become the garden, a separate writing room, which she again referred to as her little chalet. On an outside wall, she had inscribed the same Greek motto that had long ago greeted her at Nassenheide and that she had reproduced at the chalet. Once again, she invoked the gods, graces and muses to reside within.

As work continued, she stayed with Bridget and Benjamin Guinness at their villa, Mas de Notre Dame de Vie. (Picasso later bought this villa and spent his final decade there.) She met writer Edith Wharton, who lived nearby, and visited Wells and his lover Odette Keun. Wells, Elizabeth observed, had grown enormously fat. 'One marvels how ever one could have ever . . . !'

Elizabeth was at White Gates over New Year when she learned Bridget Guinness had died in Cannes after an operation. Elizabeth was heartbroken. 'I loved her so very much, and was so happy to think I had gone to live near her [. . .] she was the best & truest of friends,' she wrote to Hugh Walpole. Elizabeth had lost not only a good friend but one of the inspirations for her move to the South of France.

Elizabeth acquired a puppy, Chunkie, taking to three the number of dogs she had at White Gates. She already had a large dog called Pincher, who had been given to her as a present a few years earlier. But Pincher had grown fat and indolent after she'd had him castrated in an effort to curb him chasing chickens. He had been replaced in her affections by Knobbie, a fox terrier acquired the previous year. Now she was smitten with little Chunkie.

She took Chunkie with her when she left behind England's wintry gloom and returned to the South of France in late January 1931. The dog was her companion on walks around Mougins. She visited

Bridget's tomb at Notre Dame de Vie. There she blessed the memory of her friend for leading her to so heavenly a place, where she was daily warmed by the sun and greeted by a bright blue sky.

Elizabeth was at home at Mas des Roses in early March when her friend Marie Mallet arrived with her husband. They greeted her with startling news. Frank Russell was dead. The 65-year-old, who'd had a weak heart, had been found dead in a Marseille hotel room four days earlier, on 3 March. He had been returning to London from the Riviera, where he had been recovering from influenza.

Britain's prime minister, Ramsay MacDonald, paid tribute to the man he had known since Frank was a boy. Frank, who was Parliamentary Under-Secretary of State for India when he died, was a valued colleague, a great intellect and 'one of the most charming men I have ever met'.

Elizabeth's reaction was rather different. For her, Frank's death was a 'blessed release from a wicked cruel man', she wrote in her diary. Elizabeth's friends were unsure what note to strike in response. They knew that Frank's death would cause her little sorrow. Although some sent condolences, others, including Frere, sent congratulations. Her sister Charlotte shared Elizabeth's relief: 'I've always feared he might do you some deadly harm.'

Santayana later sent Elizabeth a copy of a letter Frank had written to him weeks before his death. Penned on Valentine's Day, Frank claimed Elizabeth had never realised how much he worshipped and loved her. He blamed her for his suffering, poor health and loss of the will to live. Frank ascribed his bad heart to the anguish he suffered and described her betrayal as a Judas kiss.

Elizabeth wrote immediately to Bertrand Russell. When he went through Frank's belongings, would he please return her letters? But Frank had left all his papers, as well as his estate valued at £10,000, not to Bertrand but to an old friend, Amy Elizabeth Otter. 'How characteristic of Frank,' Elizabeth wrote to Bertrand. 'I shall make no effort to get my letters back. May Miss Otter read them to her heart's content. They are the record of a great love and a great betrayal.'

Chapter 19

DOG DAYS

Elizabeth was now the Dowager Countess Russell. At least that is how she was titled in a rare photograph in *The Illustrated London News*. In it, the camera-wary Elizabeth looks, for once, straight down the lens. Her steely eyes command attention in an otherwise restrained image. She is slim—leaner than as a younger woman—with her hair sleeked across her forehead and tightly coiled around her face. Her only jewellery is a single string of opera-length pearls.

The photograph appeared in the paper's Fiction of the Month column and coincided with the release of Elizabeth's novel *Father*. The paper noted Elizabeth's trademark malicious humour: 'She is violently prejudiced, and she rejoices in prejudice. She creates certain characters simply in order to get her knife into them and turn it round and round in the wound.'

Elizabeth did not rejoice in the book itself, which she regarded as her worst. 'Read it, and dislike it—as I have always done.' Rebecca West too was unimpressed. She thought Elizabeth had written the book with 'half her mind'. Elizabeth was surprised most reviewers thought otherwise, including prominent critic Cecil Roberts who described Elizabeth 'the finest literary miniature artist of our day'.

The book appeared a few weeks after Frank's death, after which Elizabeth further expunged him from her life, burning most of his letters. She kept a few reminders, including letters from his lawyers over *Vera*, which she hoped would one day amuse Frere—she had appointed him her executor—when he went through her papers.

She was mindful of what she left to the future and in whose hands material was entrusted. She had seen what had happened to her cousin. Elizabeth already had reservations about John Middleton Murry's role in posthumously publishing Katherine Mansfield's journals. Elizabeth was furious when John's biography of Katherine appeared a couple of years later. 'Gracious heavens how angry K.M. would be!'

Now, as she read John's book *Son of Woman*, about his friend D.H. Lawrence, she was appalled. In it, John argued that Lawrence's fierce love devoured him and turned to hate. Elizabeth thought his book unctuous and wicked. 'MM [Middleton Murry] is Lawrence's Judas, betraying him with an oily kiss,' she wrote in her journal.

Lawrence had died a year earlier in Vence, about thirty kilometres from Elizabeth's Riviera home. After she'd finished John's book, she decided to visit Lawrence's German-born widow Frieda, who was still living at Vence. Frieda showed Elizabeth her late husband's paintings.

Lawrence had become an enthusiastic—if not particularly skilled—painter of erotic and exuberant nudes late in life. His paintings had been exhibited in London two years earlier. Condemned in the press as disgusting and obscene, the crowds flocked and the police swooped. They seized the paintings, which were later returned to him on condition they were never again exhibited in Britain. Elizabeth returned from her visit with a copy of Lawrence's controversial *Lady Chatterley's Lover*, then only available in France and Italy.

As she spent more of her time at Mas des Roses, Elizabeth decided to sell her Surrey home, White Gates. She no longer needed a house in England. Its upkeep, as well as the chalet's—which had still not sold—was more than she needed.

Her energy and health had flagged for much of the year and she skipped meals. A few years earlier, she weighed more than fifty kilograms. By May, her weight had dropped to just thirty-nine kilograms. Even for her tiny frame, she was significantly underweight.

Little wonder her American granddaughters struck her as enormous when they arrived for summer with Liebet. They had clearly been eating the 'Food of the Gods', she quipped in a letter to Wells, invoking the title of one of his books. The two girls were left with a governess while Elizabeth and Liebet travelled to Germany to see Teppi, at her school in Bavaria, and Trix. As ever when she visited Germany, she was relieved to return home afterwards.

Other guests arrived for the summer, including Charlotte's pretty twenty-year-old granddaughter Janet, Elizabeth's great-niece, as well as Frere, whose marriage was in trouble.

Elizabeth invited Frere for Christmas, her first at Mas des Roses. They drove to Vence to visit D.H. Lawrence's grave on Christmas Day. But Frere's mood deteriorated and he became increasingly cantankerous as the days passed. Elizabeth was relieved when he left on New Year's Day, 1932.

Afternoon tea at H.G. Wells' Lou Pidou the next day quickly took her mind off Frere. Wells greeted Elizabeth as she drove up in her new Hillman. Inside a smoke-filled room was one of the era's richest men, the third Aga Khan. Karachi-born, Eton-educated, the Aga Khan was an influential figure among the subcontinent's Muslims, as leader of the moderate Isma'ili sect. He was also a race-horse enthusiast and thoroughbred breeder. Elizabeth thought him an 'all conquering oriental male' as he sat with his attractive but silent wife: 'His Begum sabelled and jewelled, pretty and more or less speechless.'

Also present was Anthony West, Wells' then-teenage son with Rebecca West. Anthony later recalled that Elizabeth and the Aga Khan had been present at Lou Pidou—possibly at this gathering—when the mercurial, salty-tongued Odette turned the conversation in a sexually explicit direction. She expanded on the part incest played in horse-breeding.

Elizabeth thought of Frank—as she often did—on their wedding anniversary. 'Lord, what a fool I was! And how I paid for my folly! But my wretchedness during my time with him is the dark shadow that makes my present happiness all the more radiant.' She was content with the company of her dogs, Knobbie and Chunkie—Pincher had been put down—her maturing garden and books.

But as she curled up one evening with Beverley Nichols's new novel *Evensong*, she was furious. The book was about an ageing, ruthless prima donna, her artistic powers waning, and was based on Australian soprano Dame Nellie Melba, who had died less than a year earlier. Nichols, who had been Melba's private secretary, had previously ghostwritten her autobiography. He was privy to much information about her.

Elizabeth was not the only one angered by his novel. It prompted an outcry in Melba's native Australia, where Nichols was condemned by *The Sydney Morning Herald* as irresponsible and indiscreet. Even artist Norman Lindsay weighed in, slamming the book as celebrity gossip.

Elizabeth considered the book base and ungrateful. Melba had been kind to Nichols: 'Moral is never be kind and generous to a young man. They invariably sooner or later bite the hand that fed them.' She read the book at a time when she wondered if her own career was waning, and as Frere's behaviour continued to distress her.

Frere was by her side at *Parsifal*, the *Messiah* and the *St Matthew Passion* when she returned to England in spring and put White Gates up for auction. Frere's moods left her sleepless and unwell. When they returned to her home one night after the theatre, a furious row ensued. 'We sat in the hall till after midnight smashing up everything.'

Elizabeth already suspected he was romantically involved elsewhere; but then she had a conversation with her niece, Margery, who asked if Frere was a 'safe' friend for her daughter Janet. The pair had been corresponding and seeing each other a great deal in London, Margery told her. The betrayal—with her young grand-niece—cut to the quick. Elizabeth left for the Riviera the next day and promptly changed her will. She revoked his appointment as her literary executor. 'This is my final cutting off from him, and high time too. I have been a fool, and an exploited one.' After more than a decade she drew a line under her relationship with Frere.

Elizabeth sat playing chess at Mas des Roses with her son in the warm July air. He had arrived earlier that day from America. Elizabeth had paid his fare over, so eager was she to see him after their happy reunion a few years earlier. H.B. left behind his wife, daughters and chicken farm in Buffalo, upstate New York, to join his mother.

H.B. had acquired an American accent, which Elizabeth struggled to understand. She was sorry he had lost his well-modulated English accent, so expensively polished at Eton. Elizabeth was struck by her son's resemblance to Henning. She thought him the image of her late husband.

The resemblance was not only physical. He had no sooner arrived than financial problems back in Buffalo threw him into a panic—he thought he might have to return immediately—and turned his holiday plans with Elizabeth into chaos. H.B.'s money woes reminded her of Henning's. 'I might be back in Nassenheide, in the middle of imminent financial crashes,' Elizabeth wrote to Liebet. Elizabeth was keen for H.B. to meet Trix, the sister he barely knew. She knew the chance might not come again. Elizabeth had grave fears about events unfolding in Germany. 'I believe Germany, as always, is the danger, & should never be surprised if she set us on fire again.'

Elizabeth and H.B. drove to Germany to visit Trix and Teppi and attend a Wagner music festival in Munich. Elizabeth spent a sleepless first night in Germany worrying about the political situation. Her visit coincided with elections that saw the Nazis become the largest parliamentary party. The atmosphere was tense. She feared revolution was afoot and they might have to flee.

The festival continued to attract foreign music lovers and Elizabeth ran into several acquaintances, including Somerset Maugham, Thomas Beecham and his lover Maud Cunard. Elizabeth loved seeing H.B. so absorbed in the sweeping music that he appeared in a dream after the concerts. He seemed hungry for intelligent conversation, which Elizabeth suspected he lacked at home.

'H.B. & I are as happy as happy, for though outside he is like Papa, inside he is *so* like me!'

Elizabeth had hoped she could encourage H.B. to move his family from America to France and take up farming near her—she even showed him a house she had picked out for him near her own. But before he sailed home, she had abandoned that plan. Instead, she wrote to Frank Doubleday and his son, Nelson, who was then president of their publishing company, to see if they could find an opening for her son. She arranged to send H.B. to Nelson as he passed through New York on his return. She had, after all, smoothed a path for Frere, who was hired on her recommendation.

No matter that H.B. was a chicken farmer without publishing experience. She wanted to liberate him from what she considered his slave-like existence. Despite the apparent financial chaos on his farm, Elizabeth was convinced H.B. was good at managing people. She drove him to Cannes to see him off after his five-week visit. She'd adored having him and wondered if they would ever see each other again. She had no wish to sail to America again. She was furious when she learned Nelson had turned her son down for a job.

At H.B.'s departure, her dogs and garden were her greatest joys. Knobbie and Chunkie mated and the result was a litter that Knobbie delivered on Elizabeth's bedroom sofa. She kept two of the puppies, Winkie and Woozie. They went in the car, on walks, on visits to friends. Elizabeth, who had objected to Frank sleeping with seven dogs on his bed, now slept surrounded by four.

Mas des Roses at last lived up to its name. She oversaw the creation of an extensive garden. As well as roses, she had planted orange, olive, almond and mimosa trees, and flowering bulbs and plants, including irises and stocks. 'I feel that this house is the little crown of my career, & the final result of all my toilings at writing books.'

She had begun another book, *The Jasmine Farm*, but lamented her slow progress. She lived like a 'cloistered slug, bursting out in the afternoon into teaparties, & relapsing thankfully into sluggishness afterwards.'

She was shaken out of sluggishness when she received a letter from Odette Keun. Distressed and frustrated with her lover, Odette was considering leaving Wells. Odette insisted their relationship was intolerable and blamed Wells. She wanted to speak with Elizabeth alone. Unwilling to be caught in the crossfire of a curdled liaison, Elizabeth replied with caution. Soon, Wells called on Elizabeth and poured out his woes, insisting he was poised to leave Odette. Elizabeth was not convinced.

She heard the news about another of her former lovers. Frere was planning to remarry as soon as his divorce was through. 'How happy I am now that I have finally cleared so-called loves out of my life!' she wrote in her journal. She ran into Frere a few months later in Cannes, where he introduced her to his fiancée, writer and theatre critic Patricia Wallace. She was the daughter of British writer and *King Kong* creator Edgar Wallace. They planned to marry the following week. 'I'm so glad it is she and not I,' Elizabeth wrote in her journal.

Without the anxiety of a romantic relationship, Elizabeth seemed content; she put on weight and her health improved. It was the 'first whole year since I was sixteen without a lover of some sort in it. Great peace and freedom,' she noted as the year ended.

She bumped into her Sydney cousin Arthur Lassetter in Monte Carlo. He had left his Woollahra villa, St Brigid's, and moved to the Riviera after the closure of Lassetter's store in 1926. Her cousin had grown fat and old, she noted in her journal: 'Thank God for Pa's blood, mitigating the Lassetter stuff.'

Unlike her father, Elizabeth did not retain any particular affection for Australia and likely retained few, if any, memories of it. She saw herself as British, as she made clear after an inquiry from an Australian academic in the mid-1930s. 'Alas, I cannot claim to be an Australian. I was born in Australia because my mother happened to be there at the time, & was brought home to England, I understand, when a few months old,' she wrote to the Vice-Chancellor of the University of Tasmania, Professor E. Morris Miller. At the time Morris Miller was preparing a bibliographic survey of Australian literature. Elizabeth's reply suggests she knew little of her Australian roots, unaware even that she had left as a three-year-old.

Elizabeth mixed with the Riviera's artists and aristocrats. She lunched at Somerset Maugham's villa at Cap Ferrat together with a corpulent J.B. Priestley. She went swimming—her new enthusiasm—with E.H. Shepard, the illustrator of *Wind in the Willows* and *Winnie the Pooh*; she joined essayist Michael Arlen for meals and invited friends to stay. One woman invited herself. Molly Mount Temple was an English society hostess who lived in grand and eccentric style. Molly presided over dinners where flowers were designed to complement the colour of her gown and where she kept a gavel to bang on the table when her guests got too noisy. Elizabeth was furious to discover that at Mas des Roses, Molly had taken her baths entirely in milk.

Despite Elizabeth's leisured life 'embedded in jasmine' on the Riviera, events in Germany increasingly alarmed her. Hitler had been appointed Chancellor in January 1933 and began transforming

Germany into a Nazi dictatorship. Anti-Semitism was spreading: by April, Jews were forbidden from holding official positions and attacked with impunity. Attacks on Albert Einstein—whose writings were being cast into the flames in mass book burnings—particularly horrified Elizabeth. So too did her daughter's refusal to grasp what was unfolding. 'Trix writes that she can't understand why the foreign papers tell such tales about Jews being beaten, & that there's not a word of truth in it,' Elizabeth wrote to Liebet. 'The fact is the German press is completely muzzled, & she hears nothing of these things [. . .] What will she do if they begin to inquire into her ancestry, & find Marie Arndt?'

Marie Arndt was a reference to her children's great-grandmother, Henning's grandmother. She was the long-time mistress of Prince August of Prussia, with whom she had several children, including Henning's father. She was a commoner of Jewish background who had been given the title Baroness von Prillwitz. Elizabeth feared that the baroness's Jewish background posed dangers for Trix and her family.

She found it difficult to write to Trix 'while people are being whipped to death in her fatherland. I know she can't help it, but I so hate cruelty, & am so full of dread of what that lot is going to bring of horror on the world that it is almost impossible to write to her of dicky-birds & roses. Yet if I say a word of criticism it might land her in a concentration camp.' Elizabeth needed to be cautious about what she wrote; she knew letters between her and Trix were opened by German authorities.

The more she observed of human cruelty, the more Elizabeth preferred the company of animals. She became involved in animal welfare and was increasingly preoccupied with her dogs. Towards the end of the year, one of her dogs caused concern. Woozie had become aggressive, and started attacking her other dogs, and developed severe eczema. She decided to have him put down. She took him to the vet, who promised a peaceful, painless demise.

But the procedure was botched. Elizabeth watched in horror as the trembling, terrified dog struggled to the end. The image haunted her.

> I ought to have snatched him up and brought him home. But I didn't know. I thought he would drop off to sleep in a minute. I hadn't an idea that brute [the vet] was going to dash at him with ether and hold it over his poor little sore nose [. . .] the very things I most loathe and shrink from I allowed to be done to my helpless little Woozie.

She felt sick and wretched long after she buried the little dog, wrapped in linen, in her garden and begged his forgiveness.

Elizabeth read widely about the political situation, including Hitler's *Mein Kampf*. She was horrified at his savagery. She read a collection of essays edited by Leonard Woolf entitled *The Intelligent Man's Way to Prevent War*, but concluded 'alas, the unintelligent men are too many and too mad'. As a counterbalance, she devoured books about Dorothy and William Wordsworth and her friend Orlo Williams's book on essayist Charles Lamb, which she thought a fine work.

Her own work struggled along. She dubbed *The Jasmine Farm* her 'gooseberry' book, in part because of its opening scene involving a sour, indigestible fruit tart, which sets the flavour of the book. The book centres on the aristocratic Lady Midhurst and her errant daughter Terry and interweaves themes of class conflict, infidelity, ageing and heartache. Yet amid the comedy of manners, there is a darker thread in the form of an amorous German count whose pedigree provides 'an ancestry completely Jewless', as well as references to concentration camps and Germany's 'great new Leader'.

After three years working on *The Jasmine Farm*, she was at last 'curling its whiskers and sticking flowers behind its ears' by late spring, 1934. She received a £1500 advance and handed the manuscript to her new British publisher Heinemann, where Frere was managing editor.

She had parted from her long-time English publisher Macmillan, believing the company had lost interest in her. She later claimed to be surprised to learn of 'dear old Freddy' Macmillan's dismay at her departure. 'If I had known he would mind & that the firm was quite fond of me really, I'd have stayed with them until my last syllable. One likes, you know, *signs* of affection. Strength & silence aren't enough for the hungry female heart.'

With the book off her hands, she went to England to see her sister. Charlotte was worried about her youngest son Puddle (Cecil), then in his mid-forties. The man whose silences and tempers Elizabeth had witnessed a few years earlier had become manic depressive. Elizabeth took Charlotte away for a few days to the Lake District, where Elizabeth was keen to embark on a Wordsworth pilgrimage. But Charlotte, fearful for Puddle in her absence, cut her trip short and returned home.

Elizabeth soon had fears for a child of her own. She arranged to meet Trix on the German border in October. There, the young woman painted a terrifying picture of her daily life under the Nazi regime. 'She sees the husbands of her friends suddenly disappearing, & the wives without an idea why, or where, & they never come back. They're all in the power of any servant or person owing them a grudge, for all such persons need do is denounce them, & off they go to heaven knows where,' Elizabeth wrote to Liebet. Trix and her husband held their tongues, even as their teenage daughter Sybilla, known as Billy, became enthusiastically pro-Nazi.

Against a backdrop in which racial 'purity' was emphasised and persecution of Jews was increasing, Trix was being forced by Nazi authorities to trace her ancestors back to 1750 in search of Jews. Elizabeth feared again the discovery of Trix's great grandmother, Marie Arndt, and what the consequences might be. Elizabeth believed war was inevitable. 'It's like a barrel of gunpowder, & the beastly Germans will apply the match [. . .] I feel this will be the last Christmas in a world as we know it.'

Elizabeth went to Italy over Christmas, where she visited old friends Max Beerbohm and the ailing, but still witty and caustic Vernon Lee. There she also attracted a new admirer. Charles Strong was a philosopher and psychologist who had married one of J.D. Rockefeller's daughters. He was a friend of Santayana's and had moved near to Florence after his wife's death. And there he entertained Elizabeth for several days.

He soon paid Elizabeth a return visit. But the 72-year-old had more in mind than a polite social call. At Mas des Roses Elizabeth was stunned when he told her he had fallen in love with her long ago when he first read her books and had fallen all over again now that he had met her. He wanted to marry her.

She was initially amused that at sixty-eight she had received a marriage proposal. But her amusement faded when he would not take no for an answer. He made several more insistent visits to Elizabeth, courting with a 'terrifying energy'. Even two years later, he was still insisting to Santayana that their two hearts beat as one. 'It is distressing to hurt him, but I'll get involved in no more men.' She planned to live and die a widow.

As she repelled a new admirer, she encountered an old one. At lunch at Somerset Maugham's villa, among the guests was H.G. Wells. He had parted from Odette, left Lou Pidou and had returned to live in England. Elizabeth invited him to join her for a few days with her other house guests. It had been more than twenty years since Wells last stayed under her roof. The heat of their relationship had long tempered into friendship, but it retained its playfulness. That was evident—together with some frank criticism—in a letter he sent soon afterwards about *The Jasmine Farm*, which had recently been released.

'Dearest little e,' he began, using his pet name for her. At the top of the page was a childlike sketch of her surrounded by her three dogs. Wells thought *The Jasmine Farm* was twenty times better than her previous book *Father*, for which he had not cared. The new book was fun with subtle characterisations and strong storytelling. The ever-flirtatious Wells wasn't sure if this was her best book, but he would like to 'roll again in the wild thyme' of her earlier works. 'I could spank you (very lovingly & wanting to kiss the place afterward) for some of your involved sentences & the careless way you made some of it up as you went along. But it's all part of you.' He signed himself 'Geak'—her nickname for him.

Elizabeth, in turn, had reservations about Wells' writing. He had recently published his two-volume *Experiment in Autobiography*. But she shared her opinion not with Wells, but with her journal: 'His gift is being funny and finding the happy word or phrase. I don't believe he's anything like as clever as he thinks he is [. . .] But it is full of brilliant brief descriptions, and also full of very foolish judgments on people. This is the autobiography of a small clever man!' she wrote.

After an evening spent reading Wells' first volume she dipped into another autobiography, by writer John Cowper Powys, about whom she noted spikily: 'How these men love to talk about themselves!' As she penned this comment, she had made a stammering start on her own memoir. She called it her 'dog book'. What would become *All the Dogs of My Life* would tell her story via the canines she had owned. Elizabeth was not the first writer to use dogs to illustrate a literary life. Virginia Woolf had recently published *Flush*, which Elizabeth had read, about Elizabeth Barrett Browning's cocker spaniel.

She set her memoir aside as the weather warmed to make her first, and only, trip to Greece. She wanted to visit her favourite nephew, the newly knighted Sir Sydney Waterlow. He was Britain's ambassador, and living amid much splendour and ceremony in Athens like an 'uncrowned king of Greece'. He had certainly earned his nickname, Monarch.

She found him erudite and indiscreet—an unusual mix for a diplomat. He had 'a most delightful mind. A most peculiar heart.' She revelled in the splendour of a national day ceremony, sat at night observing the lights on the Parthenon and drove with Sydney into the hills outside Athens where they ate suckling pig in an inn before an open fire and drank wine that smelt of turpentine, presumably retsina.

As Elizabeth settled down to work on her memoir over summer, her youngest dog Winkie became listless. Initially, she put his languor down to the August heat. Despite repeated visits from the vet, Winkie was getting worse. He had a tick. By the time this was discovered Winkie could take only liquid from a teaspoon and it was too late to save him. She called the vet to put him down rather than see the dog suffer further. It had been two years since little Woozie was destroyed, fighting until his last breath as the procedure was botched. She wanted no repeat of that.

She sat on the grass with Winkie in a chaise longue holding his paw until the vet arrived. She was distraught for weeks afterwards. Her only consolation was that Winkie died peacefully and quickly. 'He had eyes and heart only for me.' He was buried among the irises, beside Woozie.

Chapter 20

HELL IS LOOSE

The police phoned at lunchtime. Elizabeth's troubled nephew Puddle had been arrested in Avignon after travelling without a ticket or money. He would be jailed as a vagabond if he wasn't removed, she was informed. Elizabeth knew Puddle had recently been in Monte Carlo and was gambling heavily. He had visited her for lunch at Mas des Roses a week earlier, in late October, where his odd appearance and erratic behaviour alarmed her.

Elizabeth set off for Avignon. Charlotte was contacted in England and she despatched a male relative and doctor. By the time they all reached Avignon, Puddle had been released and had fled to Marseille, where they found him at the home of the British consul. Assuming the men had the situation in hand, Elizabeth took herself for lunch before heading to the train station. As she caught a taxi to the station she saw Puddle, a rose in his coat and a cigarette in his mouth, smiling as he crossed the street in front of her. He had absconded again. He was escorted back to England and placed in a mental asylum.

Elizabeth went back and forth to England over the following months, in part to spend time with Charlotte, who was in anguish over her son. Puddle was in and out of the asylum. Each time he was released, his erratic behaviour deteriorated. He spent wildly, including on expensive cars. Elizabeth took Charlotte to Oxford for a few days over Christmas where, as they wandered the colleges and attended services, she hoped her sister had a 'little breathing space from torment, bless her darling little brave heart'. Charlotte worried what Puddle would do next.

The death of King George V on 20 January was a sad and ominous beginning to 1936. It was the end of the twenty-five-year reign of the well-loved monarch. The heir to the throne, his unmarried playboy son Edward, Prince of Wales, was a vastly different character.

Unlike his father, who had abandoned the Saxe-Coburg name, Edward was proud of the family's German origins. He was sympathetic towards Hitler and Nazi Germany and had quipped that 'dictators are very popular these days and we might want one in England before long'. He had argued that Britain had no business interfering in Germany's internal affairs, including over its treatment of Jews. By the time Edward's accession was proclaimed, this treatment included banning marriages between Jews and Aryan Germans.

Elizabeth received a letter in late January from a Berlin publisher who wanted to secure the rights to Elizabeth's novel *Expiation*. Before he could take this further he needed two assurances, the publisher explained. He needed a certified declaration that Elizabeth was of pure Aryan race and she needed to provide her sworn assurance that she would never make unflattering comments about the German government. She wrote back briefly: the rights were not for sale.

Elizabeth listened to Hitler's 'ravings' on her recently acquired radio. As a German speaker, she understood every word. The grotesque absurdities of his claims did not make them any less terrifying. She switched back to the calm, smooth tones of the BBC, which struck her as the voice of order, decency and civilisation. 'I don't see how we are going to dodge a marvellous final bust-up in which everyone, including the dictators, will go equally to hell [. . .] We live in a world choked by lies,' she wrote to Liebet.

Elizabeth tuned in to Nazi propaganda minister Joseph Goebbels' speech on the eve of Hitler's birthday in April. Goebbels painted the Führer as godlike, a builder of miracles who had taken on his nation's burdens and earned the love and blind allegiance of his people. Elizabeth was sickened at what she heard. Not all in her Riviera social circle shared her views. Elizabeth was shocked at the bloodthirstiness of one society hostess who sided with dictators.

She had sent off her dog book to her publisher and she toyed with a new novel. But she found herself devoid of energy and ideas. She wondered if her writing days were done. 'Have I finished forever?' She distracted herself amid the Riviera social scene, but even this gave her little pleasure at times. 'Why should I have to go and try to animate exhausted house-parties? The whole burden of talk was on me. Got home tired, depressed, and bored myself.' She had made little progress on her new novel, which she tentatively called *The Birthday Party*, when she left for England in mid-year and visited her sister Charlotte.

Puddle, who had been released again from the asylum, drove Elizabeth to the railway station after a few days with her sister. Charlotte was now in her late seventies and frail, but attempting to care for her mentally ill son at her home. As Elizabeth and Puddle stood on the platform on a damp June morning, she pressed a sixpence coin into her nephew's hand for good luck and boarded the train.

Elizabeth had been back at Mas des Roses just a few days when she learned the news. Puddle was dead. He had thrown himself under a train near his mother's home. Charlotte had now lost three of her four sons: Jack, killed in the Battle of Jutland; Guy, drowned in China; and now Puddle. Only Charlotte's diplomat son Sydney Waterlow remained.

Elizabeth returned to England. She knew the toll that caring for Puddle had taken on her elderly sister. Even as she comforted Charlotte, she confided to her diary her unflinching response: 'Poor little Tit so shaken and all of a tremble [. . .] Yet it is a solution to her terrible troubles and perplexities over poor Pud.' Elizabeth laid roses on Puddle's grave. An inquest found that Puddle—like his father George Waterlow—had killed himself while of unsound mind.

Amid her sorrow for her sister and anxiety over Germany, Elizabeth turned seventy. On her birthday, she wrote, tongue-in-cheek: 'Am now definitely an old woman, and I must bear it in mind. One is so much used to being young that one goes on taking it for granted. I must remember. And my looking glass helps.' Elizabeth retained her lifelong ability to appreciate her blessings. 'I count over my past and present happinesses as if they were jewels on a thread of gold.'

She was overjoyed by the arrival on her birthday of Frere and his wife, Pat. Elizabeth's pain over Frere had mellowed into affection for him and Pat. Frere, with whom she was working on her dog book—had recently given her yet another dog, a dachshund puppy named Vickie.

For her birthday, Frere arrived bearing flowers. He was sun-tanned and still good-looking. Elizabeth thought him, 'A pleasing contrast to the underdone old men who abound here'. Trix joined Elizabeth a couple of days after her birthday. They swam together; they went on picnics and drives, sometimes with the Freres, and walks with the dogs. Yet another dog was added to Elizabeth's menagerie, a Scottie named Emily—a gift from Trix and her husband Tony. Liebet, Corwin and their daughter Ann arrived from America in late October. They planned to spend a year in Europe, including in Germany, aware that the political storm clouds on the horizon might soon make this impossible.

'I wish I could write a truthful autobiography,' Elizabeth wrote as she awaited the release of her memoir. 'But hardly anyone can do that.' She was apprehensive about the release of the book, which she considered trivial and foolish.

Despite its title, *All the Dogs of My Life* is no more about dogs than her first book was about gardens. But nor is it autobiography. Her dog book is a strange crossbreed, a witty, lighthearted tale that conceals as much as it reveals about Elizabeth. In it, her career as a writer barely gets a mention and the many dramatic and painful episodes of her life are skipped over. She deflects throughout with such lines as, 'this isn't autobiography, so I needn't enlarge' and, 'If I weren't writing about dogs, I might say a few words about widows'. And yet she does say a great deal about widows. She gives pithy pencil sketches of her childhood, parents, husbands and suitors in a book that begins by stating that 'though parents, husbands, children, lovers and friends are all very well, they are not dogs'.

Even as an account of the lives of her dogs, events are embroidered and fabricated. Neither Coco nor Woozie, for example, died as she writes in her memoir. Coco did not immediately die on her return to the chalet after her five-year absence. He kept her company there for three more years. And Woozie did not die after being hit by a car. Woozie had become so aggressive, Elizabeth had him put down. Literal truth strains at the leash.

The reviews were overwhelmingly positive, including Gladys B. Stern in *The Sunday Times*. 'The style is that of a clear, small voice delivering sentiments always well-mannered and formal as a Court Minuet, and sometimes deadly as a phial of poison,' Stern wrote. *The New York Times* considered it a light and lively account of 'not all the days of her life, but enough to make agreeable reading'.

But H.G. Wells was quick to take her to task: 'Dearest but very inaccurate little e,' he wrote. 'The Dogs live again and it is as good a dog show as heart could desire [. . .] Some of your dates seem wrong to me.' Yet dates are largely absent from the book. So Wells' ire may have been aroused by another aspect of the book—such as his thinly disguised portrayal as an ardent but unwelcome suitor madly pursuing her around her chalet. Certainly, his later version of their vigorous affair—replete with broken beds and secret sliding doors—presented a vastly different account.

England was agog. The new king, Edward VIII, wanted to marry his American lover, Mrs Wallis Simpson. Elizabeth too was gripped by the unfolding drama when she reached London in December. Mrs Simpson was a twice-divorced American socialite who had become Edward's mistress while he was Prince of Wales. Opposition to their marriage was widespread, including from the Church of England. Edward was the nominal head of the Church of England, which did not allow divorcees to remarry while their spouses were still alive. Not since Henry VIII wanted to marry Anne Boleyn had the Crown faced such a crisis.

News of the controversial royal romance had only just broken in the British papers (although it was not news to readers of the international papers) in which Mrs Simpson was seen as a gold-digger and unsuitable as a royal consort. In the high society circles in which Elizabeth moved, the affair had been an open secret. Elizabeth may also have heard titbits from her nephew, Monarch, in Greece where Edward and Mrs Simpson had made a secret summer cruise a few months before news of their affair became public.

Little more than six months after his coronation, Edward planned to relinquish the throne. Elizabeth was dismayed, portraying it as a betrayal: 'King chucked us for Mrs Simp. Am completely ashamed of him.' Elizabeth's fury increased when, on a winter drive through Devon, she joined guests in her hotel drawing room to gather around the radio to listen to the King's abdication speech. In her journal that night she wrote: 'To those who know what Mrs Simp. is like one can feel nothing but shame and regret.'

Elizabeth was in a mood as bleak as the weather when she walked to Gordon Square in December and looked at the house she once shared with Frank, the house where 'he tortured me'.

Elizabeth had not seen Bertrand for some time. She decided to hear him speak at the Fabian Society, where, to her dismay, he did not recognise her at first. 'I've grown so old—it's dreadful.' She later visited him at Telegraph House, where he had set up a progressive school called Beacon Hill. His marriage to Dora was over and he had taken up with his children's governess, Patricia Spence, whom he had since married.

Bertrand had been editing for publication his parents' papers, known as the *Amberley Papers*. If only she had read them before she married Frank, 'for then I wouldn't', she wrote to Bertrand. 'I wonder what that gentle, civilised father & that highly intelligent mother would have done about Frank if they had lived to see what he was like later.' Bertrand replied with his verdict on his late brother. 'Frank as a boy seems just like what he was later; one gets an impression that it was nature, not bad education.'

Elizabeth was unrelenting in her hatred of Frank. She often remembered bitterly the anniversary of their wedding—she hated Fridays for that reason, she once quipped. She attempted to visit the Russell family's ancestral tomb in Buckinghamshire. She found it locked, surrounded by prohibition notices and barbed wire. 'Imagine having barbed wire in one's blood.'

Her attitude to Frank was in contrast to the genuine affection she felt for Wells and Frere. She rejoiced that she and Wells had enjoyed themselves in that 'lovely, spacious past before 1914'. She was glad they had become friends so long ago 'for there is still a pleasant backwash, like a warm, cosy, Gulf Stream,' she wrote to him.

She invariably found Wells fun, even if she did not always appreciate his lunch companions. She found the influential press baron Lord Beaverbrook boorish. She was increasingly irritated by older men, particularly those who talked over her. 'Most old men are bores.' She enjoyed the company of Frere and his wife, Pat, who stayed with her in summer. And she became godmother to their daughter, whom they named Elizabeth after her.

Where once she surrounded herself with people, she now surrounded herself with dogs. She had five, having added a cocker spaniel puppy to her unruly pack. Billy was an impulse buy while walking through Harrods just before Christmas. She transported him to the Riviera at great expense and organisation. The details of her garden that had filled her journal since she moved to the Riviera were replaced by the minutiae of canine walks, fights and mishaps. She wrote less about what plant was in flower and more about which bitch was on heat.

Dogs, family visits and travels took up most of the year, during which she did little work on her book. She was particularly taken with a young family member who visited her in summer: Trix's seventeen-year-old Billy. Elizabeth was enchanted with the slim teenager who had a mane of red-gold hair. 'Of course if she had two more legs and a golden tail, she would be even more perfect,' she wrote to Trix.

A mid-year trip to the Salzburg Music Festival with Trix and Liebet, who was soon to return to America after her year in Europe, was a chance to see the brilliant and avowedly anti-Nazi maestro Arturo Toscanini conducting. Elizabeth sat as if in heaven through his concerts and legendary performances of *Die Meistersinger von Nürnberg* and *Fidelio*. Both were performed as acts of defiance in a politically charged atmosphere.

Wagner had become something of a house composer for Nazism. Hitler was by then a regular guest at Bayreuth, while Wagner's music was the backing track to the Nuremberg Rallies. More than any other Wagner opera, *Die Meistersinger von Nürnberg*—with its expression of German cultural supremacy—had been hijacked by Hitler. Its performance at Salzburg was a way to reclaim the opera for humanity. Beethoven's *Fidelio* is about a political prisoner who triumphs over tyranny. The resonance with events in Germany could hardly be missed. It would be the last time Toscanini would ever conduct at Salzburg, for Nazi Germany soon took control of Austria.

Throughout her life, Elizabeth loved the grandeur of church architecture and the beauty of the music and the services. But she was also content to sit in silent meditation. The denomination was not important, she attended Catholic and Protestant.

Only the austerity of Calvinist churches, with buildings bare of beauty, left her cold. In London, St Paul's was often her first port of call whenever she arrived from the Continent. Sometimes, she would spend entire days there in contemplation. Amid the music and services under Christopher Wren's magnificent dome, she 'smoothed out'. With Charlotte, she toured English cathedrals in autumn, including in Liverpool, York, Lincoln and Durham.

Elizabeth had a deeply spiritual side, but her expression of this appears more pantheistic than conventionally Christian. She did not doubt the existence of God, although she occasionally thought he had much to answer for. She saw the divine in the beauty of a flower, a lake, a pearlescent sky. She was drawn to the poets who celebrated nature, among them Thoreau, Wordsworth, Keats. She often peppered her journals with a line from *Psalm 23*: 'Surely goodness and mercy shall follow me all the days of my life.' It reflected more her determined optimism than piety.

Elizabeth's optimism and her faith in the future were tested as she sat in the House of Lords shortly after the Armistice Day anniversary to hear a debate on events unfolding in Europe. Where once she had enjoyed listening to the eloquent Frank debate here, this time she was filled with dismay. The various lords insisted that Hitler not only wanted friendship with England but that he would never break any treaty he made. 'All the old dodderers seemed inadequate as dealers with the fierce swift Nazis,' she wrote in her journal.

Despite her anxieties about Germany, she accepted daughter Trix's invitation to join her family in Murnau, Bavaria, for Christmas.

The chance to celebrate Christmas in Germany—for the first time since having it at Nassenheide in 1909—overcame Elizabeth's reservations. Trix was waiting when she alighted from her train. Elizabeth greeted with great enthusiasm a man standing with Trix. She assumed he was Trix's husband, Tony. The man was a taxi driver.

She incorporated the incident in a short story she quickly drafted, *Christmas in a Bavarian Village*. The story initially captivates with its images of glittering snow and candlelit Christmas trees, as a foreign visitor arrives after nearly thirty years to spend Christmas with her relatives. The story has a sting as it is revealed that the family members are gripped by political fears that they are too frightened to express.

Elizabeth sent the story to *The Times*, hoping it might be suited to a pre-Christmas issue. But it reached England too late for publication. Had it arrived in time, the paper would have published it, wrote *Times* journalist and author Peter Fleming (and brother of James Bond's creator) who reluctantly returned the story.

Elizabeth left Germany via Munich, where she went to see a notorious exhibition, the anti-Semitic *The Eternal Jew*. It presented Jews as engaged in a conspiracy against Germany, bent on global domination, and displayed images of 'typical' Jewish features, using Leon Trotsky and Charlie Chaplin as examples. The exhibition was among several Nazi-sponsored so-called degenerate art exhibitions, including the infamous *Entartete Kunst*, which had closed in Munich a few weeks before Elizabeth arrived. That exhibition presented works confiscated from art museums that 'insulted' German feelings—including by Otto Dix, Kurt Schwitters, Paul Klee, Pablo Picasso, Piet Mondrian and Marc Chagall.

She bought a catalogue of *The Eternal Jew* exhibition and a copy of the anti-Semitic newspaper *Der Stürmer*, whose Nazi editor, along with Goebbels, had opened the show. She planned to send the material to Bertrand Russell. She perhaps hoped to change Bertrand's pacifist mind on appeasement.

'What I really am by nature is an Escapist, which is only another word for a monk or hermit,' Elizabeth wrote to Liebet. At the start of 1938, Elizabeth chose to live her monk-like existence first on the shores of Italy's Lake Garda and then at a hotel near a monastery above Menton in France. She wanted to write, read and turn her back on the gathering political storm clouds. 'Of what is going on in the world I say nothing here, for it makes me too sick,' she wrote in her diary.

She re-read Jane Austen's *Pride and Prejudice*. The more she revisited the book—she had read it many times over the years—the more she discovered in it. 'That small, sly Jane, scribbling away about entirely ordinary people, and behold immortality!' She chronicled the local dogs she encountered on her daily walks, and fed them with sugar and croissants.

But it was impossible to ignore events unfolding. At Lake Garda, Teppi arrived from Germany with disturbing news; her brother had been sent to a concentration camp. Soon Hitler had annexed Austria in an effort to unite German-speaking nations. 'I expect you are horrified by the news of Hitler's goings-on,' she wrote to Liebet. 'I rub my eyes in amazement that there should exist politicians who still think they can come to an understanding with him.'

Elizabeth told her daughter of her deadly plan. 'Directly the first bombs start I shall put myself to sleep. The *only* thing that worries me is my dogs, & whether there'll be time to put *them* to sleep before *I* go.' She attempted to soften the impact of her letter the next day.

While not pulling back from her plan, she explained to her daughter that 'it would be absurd to take trouble to hide or get away or things like that at my age, & I shall stay quiet in my garden till the last possible minute, & then with immense dignity settle down to sleep.' It was a follow-up hardly likely to placate its worried recipient.

Meanwhile, in America, her son H.B. had just produced the first boy in the family, her only male grandchild. Far from being overjoyed at the news, Elizabeth was dismayed at what she considered her son's financial fecklessness and for having more children than he could adequately support. H.B. was constantly crying poor and regarded her as a soft touch. She was convinced that the financial drama that nearly upended their travel plans when he visited her at Mas des Roses had been a trick to extract more money from her. She feared her son had inherited Henning's lack of financial scruples rather than her father Henry's honourableness.

Other male relatives also caused her concern. In England, her elderly brother Ralph needed money to help to pay for his medical care after a fall. She was more willing to help her ailing elderly brother than her able-bodied son. Elizabeth's nephew Monarch—Puddle's only surviving brother—arrived to stay in May and promptly slipped and injured his ribs. Frustrated at having to care for a less than ideal patient, she was amazed at 'the incapacity of men to bear *anything*'.

All year, as tensions in Europe increased, she struggled with her book. What she initially called *The Birthday Party*—about a rich and once-beautiful woman poised to turn fifty—she now called *Fanny*. It would eventually become *Mr Skeffington* and crown her career. 'I can't help being distracted by the threats of war. Yet I try to go on at *Fanny*, if only as a gesture of defiance.'

She listened to Hitler's radio broadcast from the Nuremberg

rallies in mid-September. Having annexed Austria, he had turned his attention on Czechoslovakia, threatening war if the 'oppression' of Germans living in its northern part, Sudetenland, did not end.

In mid-September, British Prime Minister Neville Chamberlain flew to meet Hitler to seek a solution. Elizabeth applauded Chamberlain's move—anything was better than war. But she suspected that was what Hitler was gambling on. The talks broke down and Chamberlain left without a guarantee that Germany would not take military action against Czechoslovakia.

Elizabeth listened to Hitler's chilling ultimatum broadcast in late September. He would fight Czechoslovakia if it did not give up Sudetenland by 1 October. She felt her death warrant, and that of her dogs, had been signed. With her dogs dozing trustfully around her she lay in bed unable to sleep, thinking about how best to kill them. As she contemplated this dramatic step, she received a desperate plea from Trix in Germany. Trix wanted to obtain narcotics to kill herself and her family. She begged Elizabeth's help to acquire them. Such was Elizabeth's despair, that she did as Trix asked.

Amid Elizabeth's desperation, there was a glimmer of hope. With the signing of the Munich Agreement on 30 September 1938, Germany, Britain, France and Italy agreed that the Reich would take control of Sudetenland, but make no further territorial claims. With Hitler appeased, Chamberlain flew home, fatefully declaring 'peace for our time'.

Along with much of Europe, Elizabeth was relieved that bloodshed had been averted, for now. 'Profoundly distrusting Hitler and his crowd of gangsters, I don't believe in more than a respite [. . .] Monstrous that one man should be able to keep us all dangling over a pit of fear.' Such were her fears for Trix—whose letters continued to alarm her—that when she talked about her daughter with friends at a lunch a week later, Elizabeth broke down. Her tears were greeted by an unsympathetic silence.

Elizabeth was desperate to see Trix in person so her daughter could unburden her heart of all she could not put in writing. And she wanted to put to her daughter an escape plan. Elizabeth wanted Trix and her family to emigrate with her to Canada. She arranged to meet Trix at the end of October at Romanshorn on the Swiss–German border. Trix had asked Elizabeth to bring her a lipstick. After so many troubling letters from Trix, Elizabeth viewed the request as a sign of hope: 'no one wants a lipstick whose outlook is completely black.'

But when they met, Trix was too terrified to speak openly, even in her hotel room. Trix was convinced a man typing in the next room was recording what they said. She would speak only in the middle of a field. Trix told Elizabeth how a woman had stood at her gate, loudly denouncing her and shouting that she should be put in a concentration camp. Trix clearly had enemies. 'She got a real scare & is going to be very careful in the future and shout *Heil Hitler* wherever she goes.' Elizabeth no longer complained about Trix's politics—indeed Trix and husband Tony regarded the Nazis as loathsome.

Fearful as Trix was, she rejected Elizabeth's Canada plan. Trix returned to Germany from where she wrote loud praises of her country, knowing her mail would be opened, but also knowing Elizabeth would read the opposite into them. In Germany, Trix was under pressure to produce baptismal certificates of her parents and grandparents. But Elizabeth knew little of her family background, as she wrote to Liebet. 'I, who was born in Australia, may for all I know have been baptised in the drawing room, as was frequent in those days. As for my parents, I only know granny [Louey Beauchamp] was born in Tasmania, Deepa [Henry Beauchamp] in or near London, but more than that is a blank.'

'Hell is loose,' Elizabeth wrote just after Kristallnacht, the pogrom that spread across Germany, as Jewish businesses, buildings and synagogues were destroyed. Nazi spies were everywhere, she was convinced. Even within the walls of the elegant Riviera villas of her well-connected circle.

Elizabeth's great fear was that Trix would be sent to a concentration camp. Elizabeth worried that something she might do or say might filter back to Germany with terrible consequences for her daughter. Even as she tried, without success, to take in a Jewish refugee from Germany as a cook she worried what would happen to Trix if this became known.

Elizabeth was accustomed to speaking candidly among her friends. But at a Riviera party, she spoke critically of Germany to a fellow guest, an Italian aristocrat. She was filled with anxiety afterwards when she remembered the woman had German ancestry and adored the country. Her fears for Trix were well-founded, although Elizabeth did not live to see them realised. Trix spent six months in a concentration camp towards the end of the war.

As the atmosphere of suspicion spread, Elizabeth worried her actions might have consequences closer to home. She had invited Teppi to visit Mas des Roses but then wondered about the wisdom of doing so, particularly if war suddenly erupted. 'The French would hurl themselves upon her—& upon me too for having her.' She adored Teppi, her oldest friend, and desperately wanted to see her. Elizabeth steeled her resolve.

Elizabeth's Riviera circle embraced Teppi and hung on her tales of Germany. For light relief, Elizabeth took Teppi to see a new film, *Snow White and the Seven Dwarfs*. Their escape from reality was short-lived. As Teppi readied to return to Germany, Hitler invaded Czechoslovakia. The Munich Agreement was in tatters.

Chapter 21

LIFE BENEATH THE SMILES

Elizabeth arrived at Menton on a cool spring morning in March 1939 to attend a memorial for her cousin Katherine Mansfield. A plaque was to be unveiled at Villa Isola Bella, where Katherine had lived nearly twenty years earlier. The little villa was part of a large property overlooking the sea and was owned by Elizabeth's wealthy cousin Connie Beauchamp. Katherine had come to Menton at Connie's behest.

Like Elizabeth and Katherine, Melbourne-born Connie had inherited the independent and unorthodox spirit that ran through the Beauchamp women. Connie had sailed from Australia to Europe as a teenager, chaperoned by Elizabeth's father, who was then on his second around-the-world jaunt. Connie's parents wanted her to complete her education in Europe. The rebellious Connie never returned to Australia.

Connie had a long-time companion, Jinnie Fullerton, who dressed as a man in pin-striped suits, and together they ran a nursing home in England and spent their winters at Menton. Villa Isola Bella was dilapidated when Katherine had moved in, but it was the first home she ever loved. Within its shabby walls she wrote some of the stories that Elizabeth most admired, including 'The Daughters of the Late Colonel' and 'The Life of Ma Parker'.

Elizabeth too was charmed by the little villa, less than two hours' journey from her home. She joined the guests, most of them French, who gathered in the garden for speeches underneath what was once Katherine's bedroom window. As Elizabeth watched the plaque being unveiled and joined in on a celebration lunch, she wondered what Katherine would have thought of it.

Elizabeth was walking near her home the next day when she came across a stray dog. Little more than a puppy, the scrawny creature began to follow her. There was no one around she could ask about him. She put him in her car, took him home and added another dog to her pack. She called the starving mutt Tuppence—the name she had once called Frere. Acquiring another canine seems a perplexing act at a time when she was convinced war was imminent. Even in Mougins, the streets were full of French soldiers.

H.G. Wells sent Elizabeth a copy of his latest novel. *The Holy Terror* was about a dictator bent on world domination. 'Have you sent a copy to Hitler?' she asked, when she wrote to thank him. Wells had not long returned from Elizabeth's birthplace. While in Australia, Wells had become the centre of controversy after he called Hitler a 'certified lunatic'. This aroused the ire of Prime Minister Joe Lyons. 'I would prefer that Mr Wells should exercise his undoubted gifts for the promotion of international understanding rather than international misunderstanding,' he said. Wells' views were not those of the Australian government, the prime minister added. Lyons' response brought cheers from Nazi Germany.

Elizabeth treasured her quiet evenings reading in her sitting room, the Orange Room, as she called it. 'Usual peaceful evening. How many more of such evenings shall I have?' The spring flowers, her visits to friends and their gardens, all took on a poignancy as if she was seeing them for the last time. Some of her friends were leaving. But she was determined to stay put. 'The plight of refugees is not for me. Besides really, what does it matter if one dies a few years sooner?'

Two French officers arrived at her door in mid-April. They wanted to quarter soldiers at Mas des Roses. Within hours, she had thirty soldiers bunking in her garage, plus officers in her spare bedrooms and reception rooms. Her dogs were excited by the arrivals. But the men barely made a sound and remained quieter than the frogs croaking in the garden.

Subdued and respectful as they were, the soldiers' presence could hardly be ignored. Soon there was a truck full of ammunition in the garden, an anti-aircraft gun in the rosemary bushes and a sentinel with a bayonet at the entrance to Mas des Roses, day and night. This was part of a secret mobilisation underway as isolated farms and houses filled with soldiers.

Elizabeth tried to carry on as normal. She had tea under the medlar tree, the dogs ran around on the grass, friends came to visit. She took herself off to her workhouse—as she dubbed her writing outhouse. Difficult as it was to concentrate, she was determined to finish *Fanny*. 'Hitler shan't come between me & it.' With officers taking over even her living rooms, she was confined to her bedroom in the evenings, where she tried to read on a sofa that was too short even for her. She missed her Orange Room. Her peaceful evenings had been replaced by 'usual imprisoned evening'. The walls were closing in.

Elizabeth had been working on her book when a letter arrived in late April. It was from Berlin, where her granddaughter Billy was studying acting. But Billy was not writing about her theatrical successes. Billy's letter was a desperate plea:

> I can't go on living in Germany. I hate it, oh I hate it, everything, the people, the government. It is impossible to live here. And darling little Granny, I don't know how I dare asking [sic] you, but could you adopt me, or do you know anybody who would adopt me, and give me an English name? [...] You can't think how awful they all are, those Nazis [...] marching on in their Prussian way over culture and civilization [...] what shall I do here in a war among those awful patriots in a country I hate?

The girl had come to detest the regime she had once admired. Billy's letter galvanised Elizabeth into action. Her plan to stay put and even take her own life was abandoned. She went immediately to Nice to consult an English lawyer to see if she could adopt Billy. When she learned that was not possible, she quickly developed another plan. She resolved to go to America and take Billy with her. She contacted Trix for permission and went to Cannes and booked their passages.

When she got no response from Trix she wrote to Teppi. It was worded in a way so as not to arouse the attention of German authorities. Elizabeth told her that because of 'poor Aunt Kitty'—her code for Hitler—she was leaving for America. 'You should see my garden now. It is not only full of roses but full of things hidden in the bushes—all getting ready to welcome Aunt Kitty if she should give us the honour of coming to see us.'

Elizabeth asked Teppi to phone Trix and beg her to let Billy come with her. Time was pressing. In the end, Trix would not agree to Billy leaving for America. Elizabeth would have to flee alone. Well, not quite alone. She planned to take a different Billy with her—her little Harrods cocker spaniel. She would rather die than go without him.

She could not take the rest of her pack. She found homes for the two foxies, Chunkie and Knobbie, and for Vickie, the dachshund. But she could not find anyone willing to take Tuppence, the scrawny stray, or Emily, the Scottie. She reluctantly called the vet. 'Would that he could put me [down] too,' she wrote in her journal. 'I can hardly bear it. I feel sick.' Tuppence and Emily were buried in the garden. She packed her bags, lay bunches of sweet william where the dogs lay and departed Mas des Roses.

Flowers and telegrams filled Elizabeth's cabin aboard RMS *Queen Mary*. The sight cheered her, even if the prospect of an ocean voyage did not. She intended her American odyssey to be an interlude until the gathering storm clouds of war dispersed. Just as she had sailed out through Sydney Heads as an infant with a father promising just a year's interlude abroad, Elizabeth planned to return. So when she sailed out of Cherbourg on 17 May 1938, she bid Europe *au revoir* not *adieu*.

The ship's manifest recorded her age as sixty-six—six years had somehow been lopped off. Elizabeth was in frisky spirits the first night when she dined with an elderly American widow. The woman told her she'd had two husbands. 'Which did you like best?' Elizabeth asked. 'Oh, the last one,' the woman replied. Elizabeth told her she too had had two husbands. 'Which did you like best?' asked the woman. Elizabeth replied: 'Neither.'

Elizabeth knew that taking her dog Billy with her would cause problems. These began immediately. She kept him in her cabin, where her shipboard neighbours complained about his barking. Either Billy must go to the onboard kennel or Elizabeth must upgrade to First Class. She upgraded. After that, she rarely ventured out of her cabin, taking all her meals with Billy.

Liebet met Elizabeth in New York after the six-day crossing and Elizabeth moved into a little house next to her daughter's in Hartford. She wrote to Bertrand Russell, who was in America, telling him she planned to stay in the country for about a year. She wanted to lecture on English literature at a university in some sunny part, such as California or the Carolinas. She asked him for advice on who to approach.

She bought a Chevrolet and passed her American driving test. The examiner waved aside the need to observe her behind the wheel and asked her to inspect his begonias instead. To keep her anxieties at bay, she filled her journal with the minutiae of tea parties and walks with Billy. 'These entries are very like Louis XVI's while [. . .] the most frightful things were preparing and happening.' The soon-to-be guillotined French king famously wrote the word 'Nothing' in his diary as the Bastille was stormed.

She saw her old friend Poultney Bigelow. But his political views alarmed her. The man she had once defended in print had become stridently anti-Semitic. She wrote to him bluntly: 'Your views on Jews shock me.'

She was disoriented by America—the cars were too big, the conversation too shallow—and soon felt an exile. But she did not want to live too close to her daughter's family, where friction arose between Elizabeth and her son-in-law, Corwin. After a month as neighbours, she decided to put distance between them and spent the summer several hours north at a hotel in Dublin, New Hampshire. Liebet came with her two daughters and H.B.'s daughter Caro to visit.

Elizabeth was in contact with her daughter Evi in California, but made no plans to visit. She made arrangements to see her son H.B.

in Buffalo, but put these on hold when she realised it entailed driving more than six hundred kilometres. Through summer she worked on her book and reworked the ending. The news from Europe—as Germany was poised to invade Poland—distressed her. But she had two pieces of good news from Europe.

She finally had a potential buyer for her chalet in Switzerland. The money offered was a fraction of what it had cost her to build; but, after a decade of expensive upkeep, she accepted. The chalet was finally off her hands. And she was overjoyed to learn that her granddaughter Billy—who had sparked her flight to America—was engaged to an Englishman. William Ritchie, twenty five, was a nephew of Elizabeth's old friend Maud Ritchie and worked in France for Barclay's Bank. 'I'm so happy for little Billy, whose problems would all be solved by this.' Elizabeth sent £100 for a wedding gift and urged haste. Billy married in London days before the war began.

Elizabeth was once again on the fault line of history as Britain entered the war against Germany. She was torn between her political allegiance to England and her love for Trix and her family in Germany. Her concise response encapsulates her conflict: 'England in the war. My poor little ones in Murnau!'

Elizabeth sent off what would eventually be titled *Mr Skeffington* to Nelson Doubleday and took a road trip through Vermont. So began a period of shifting from hotel to hotel, living like a well-heeled gypsy. She wrote a prescient, if self-pitying, letter to Liebet about her shiftless life motoring from place to place with her dog. 'It's so odd how what I write in my stories so often comes true. All unconscious of my doom, I wrote in my new novel of the end of my hero & heroine:

"The final summing up of their spectacular lives: One dog." Little did I dream this was going to be the final summing up of mine—my Billy—but it begins to look like it.'

Elizabeth wanted to winter somewhere warm, and Liebet joined her for a month for an autumn journey south through Virginia to South Carolina, scouting out somewhere to stay. She settled into the rambling waterfront Gold Eagle Tavern at Beaufort, part of the Sea Islands and midway between Charleston and Savannah. The choice of the tavern was partly determined by the owner's willingness to accept Billy, after Elizabeth had been asked to leave another Beaufort lodging because of the dog.

She settled into a ramshackle room with five windows and a four-poster bed so high she climbed into it using steps. The hotel's food was too heavy and greasy for her taste. It left her longing for a boiled potato. She survived on boiled eggs and milk. But she adored the pale serenity of Beaufort's light and sky, the water, vast marshes and golden reeds. She walked daily through woods and farmland and took to feeding a stray dog who appeared when she whistled. But Billy was her constant companion. He was not a placid dog, and was prone to chase chickens, rabbits, cats and pigs. Elizabeth was more inclined to dote on than discipline the dog, and was reluctant even to put him on a lead.

Her publisher Nelson Doubleday, who had a plantation called Bonny Hall nearby, may have regretted his offer to mind Billy while Elizabeth spent a couple of days in Savannah. The dog, so rarely apart from his mistress, howled for five hours. Elizabeth became a frequent guest at elegant Bonny Hall and on one occasion was charmed by Ted Roosevelt, son of the late president Theodore Roosevelt. On another, Elizabeth asked Nelson why he did not hire her son H.B. a few years earlier. Because he was dull, Nelson replied. She tried to persuade him otherwise, but in her heart she suspected Nelson was right.

Nelson had good news at a dinner in late November. Her forthcoming book, which she still called *Fanny*, had been picked by America's Book of the Month Club. The club sent its members a cut-price, hardback copy of a newly released book through the mail at a time when many, especially rural, Americans lacked easy access to bookstores. The club's membership and influence had soared to more than 350,000 members in the years since her book *Father* had been selected.

That meant a huge boost to sales, comparable today to being included in Oprah's Book Club. Elizabeth was overjoyed, not least because her money in Europe had been frozen. She spent Christmas at the Doubledays and was buoyed as the year—and decade—ended: 'In spite of the war horrors and the evil the Nazis have let loose on the world, as far as just my tiny life goes I can still say Thank You. In my immense upheaval from my roots, I have had every sort of blessing and luck. My Liebet. Kind Americans. Lovely places to stay in. Had *Fanny* [Mr Skeffington] chosen as the American book of the month.'

The book opens as the once-beautiful Lady Fanny Skeffington is suddenly haunted in her London home by the wealthy Jewish businessman she divorced more than twenty years earlier. Fanny had taken Job Skeffington's religion when they married and a large share of his money when they parted. She had barely given a thought to him since. Instead, she has frittered away her life, traded on her looks and been flattered by a string of admirers. On the cusp of fifty, her beauty and beaux have fled and she is told bluntly that her 'love-days' are over.

The book begins as a comedy of manners as the vain Fanny goes in search of her old flames and attempts to rekindle the embers.

Each former lover disappoints, and much of the book's humour is focused on this. But the novel veers sharply from comedy when Job Skeffington—no longer an apparition—re-enters her life. Fanny learns that Job had been living in Vienna when the Nazis arrived, and this has had shocking consequences. Fanny, until then devoid of compassion and political awareness, comes to a startling realisation: 'This, then, was life, beneath the smiles. While she, in the sun of its surface, was wasting months in shamefully selfish, childish misery over the loss of her beauty, Job was being broken up into a sort of frightened animal.'

Elizabeth had seen the act of writing her book as defying Hitler. But so too was the tale itself. In *Mr Skeffington* she had put two Jewish figures, Fanny and Job, centrestage. What had been conceived three years earlier on cheerful lines, possibly as a tale of an ageing beauty considering the consolations of her later years, had taken a different direction. As she worked on it, and especially as she reworked the ending, Elizabeth could not—would not—turn away from the horrors unfolding in Europe.

She waited anxiously for the book to appear, first in Britain in January and the US in April. She feared not just the critical reception, but what impact the book, especially the last part, might have on Trix in Germany. Elizabeth was relieved when *The Times Literary Supplement* considered it 'Elizabeth at her best'. But the book's startling ending divided critics. It left *The Spectator*'s Kate O'Brien feeling queasy. 'I do not think it is good manners in light comedy to make your heroine's curtains out of someone else's off-stage and too convenient tragedy.' Across the Atlantic, Charles Poore in *The New York Times* disagreed. *Mr Skeffington* 'begins as a cream puff and ends as a bomb'.

Time magazine noted the author's longevity, finding in *Mr Skeffington* the same 'diverting, lightly troubling, perfectly delicate and occasionally outrageous wit' that had distinguished her since her first book, and which had prompted British critic Alice Meynell to describe her as one of the three finest living wits.

The review added some biographical details, including that her record in not having been interviewed until 1926 was admired by connoisseurs. But the inclusion of her age infuriated Elizabeth. She cursed *Time* for stating she was seventy-four rather than sixty-six: 'seven years—no eight—stuck on to my 66 age by them, blast their eyes.' (She was in fact then seventy-three.)

Elizabeth was always meticulous in noting birthdays and anniversaries, not least her own. She would hardly have got her age wrong. More likely, Elizabeth was winding back the clock. She may have already begun to do so on the *Queen Mary*'s manifest, when her age was noted as sixty-six. *Mr Skeffington* was in part about a woman ceding the vanity of her earlier years, but its author retained her dissembling ways.

A few weeks later, the media-shy Elizabeth was photographed at the Gold Eagle Tavern for *Life* magazine. In one image, she sits facing a mirror, tending her once luscious, now thinning hair. Photographs of dogs surround the mirror, and her four-poster bed is glimpsed in the background. With her face reflected and refracted, it is an apposite image for a woman who eschewed the direct public gaze.

With the popularity of her new novel, Elizabeth was 'having some amusing experiences of what being loved by Americans is like', she wrote to her friend Maud Ritchie. She was becoming a celebrity. She was photographed for US *Vogue* magazine, with Billy perched beside her. Celebrity gossip about her began circulating, with the *San Francisco Examiner* claiming she was living in Hollywood. She wasn't, of course. But Hollywood had come calling, wanting to make a movie of *Mr Skeffington* and offering a $50,000 deal. The movie was eventually released in 1944; directed by Vincent Sherman, it took many liberties with the book, introducing new characters and plotlines, and transplanting the story to New York. It starred Bette Davis, then one of Hollywood's most bankable stars, and Claude Rains, both of whom received Oscar nominations for their roles.

The news from Europe was bleak in the first half of 1940, as Germany invaded Denmark, Norway, Holland and then Hitler's troops rolled into Paris. Amid it all, only the replacement of Neville Chamberlain as prime minister by Winston Churchill gave Elizabeth some hope. She felt guilty she was so far from friends and family in Europe. She wished she was back there rather than sheltering beneath the Gold Eagle's shabby wings, chatting with what she considered complacent Americans.

As the reality of returning to Europe receded, she kept despair at bay by tending to a series of stray dogs and trying to find homes for them. In her darker moods A.E. Housman's words echoed in her head: 'I, a stranger, and afraid / In a world I never made.'

But then she would double down. No devil—least of all Hitler—would break her. She would not surrender to despair. Several visits from Liebet also lifted her spirits. At times, she felt unwell and her energy flagged. She wrote a codicil to her will leaving her American money to Liebet. Her English will left her money in England, Switzerland and France to be divided equally between her children.

As the weather warmed, she travelled north, through the Smoky Mountains, and based herself at Charlottesville in Virginia. Her months there were enlivened by her acquaintance with the unorthodox American writer Amélie Rives, who lived nearby at her plantation

Castle Hill. In her earlier years, Amélie had had a pet wolf called Fang and a morphine addiction; after she was photographed voluptuously naked on a divan, she had given copies of this to her friends. Her steamy first novel, *The Quick or the Dead?*—about a widow's erotic desire for her late husband's cousin—was a bestseller. It was among several of Amélie's books Elizabeth read around this time.

Elizabeth visited Castle Hill plantation, where she invariably found the bewitching Amélie lying in bed and looking as delicate as the roses surrounding her. Elizabeth found her exquisite, intelligent company.

Liebet joined Elizabeth in Charlottesville and they drove north to Woodstock, in upstate New York. Liebet was considering buying a house there with a summer cottage for Elizabeth next door. Elizabeth loved it. She was in a buoyant mood when they reached Liebet's Sunset Farm on the eve of Elizabeth's seventy-fourth birthday. There Elizabeth played Wagner's 'Liebestod' on the piano and Liebet sang.

Elizabeth returned to Charlottesville dreaming of her Woodstock cottage. She envisioned arriving there next summer as the lilacs bloomed and staying until the blackberries fruited. She offered to pay for the purchase. But the sale did not go ahead, for which she blamed opposition from her son-in-law.

As winter approached, Elizabeth migrated to Summerville, South Carolina, about a thirty-minute drive from Charleston. She stayed at the gracious Halcyon Inn and settled with Billy into a pale pink cottage, a converted stable set amid pine woods. She wrote to H.G. Wells, who had just arrived in America, to let him know her whereabouts. Wells had become an unlikely celebrity after his novel *War of the Worlds*—about a Martian invasion—had been adapted for radio by Orson Welles. The broadcast had set off widespread panic two years earlier, when some listeners mistakenly took for real its fake news bulletin format. Elizabeth's note to Wells was brief but poignant.

'Here, in the pinewoods of the deep south, I keep the flag flying & defy Hitler by insisting on being happy. But I would be happier still if I were really happy.'

Much as she had treasured solitude throughout her life, now she found herself lonely and far from home. As December began, she confided to her journal how she 'Meditated on the growing silence and solitude that surrounds the end of one's life [. . .] I greatly long for my real flesh and blood'. She missed her extended family in England and Trix in Germany. 'I ache to be with those who laugh. Well, well. Such are the reflections that flow in on one on a dark, silent, dripping Sunday, alone in pine woods.'

She also reflected on her life as a writer. She drafted an introduction for a combined edition of three of her novels, *Vera*, *The Caravaners* and *The Enchanted April*. In it, she acknowledged how she had drawn on aspects of herself for her characters. 'Those who would beget anything must turn their attention to their own insides,' she wrote. Within one's self dwelled rascals, angels, and in-betweens. 'It is out of these odds and ends of my personality, out of these torn off bits, sometimes bleeding, of my very secret self, that the characters in my stories are made.'

Even the overbearing baron in *The Caravaners* was her in one of her more regrettable aspects, she wrote. The only character not based on a part of herself was *Vera*'s monstrous, abusive Wemyss. After she created Wemyss, she wrote, she vowed never again to go outside of herself for a character.

Driving rain prevented Elizabeth from joining the Doubledays for their Christmas Day celebrations. They would have had much to celebrate. *Time* magazine had just named *Mr Skeffington* as one of its books of the year. Its list also included Hemingway's *For Whom the Bell Tolls* and Thomas Mann's *Lotte in Weimar*.

Elizabeth spent Christmas Day alone. She felt desolate and cried tears she thought had long dried up. When a lizard crawled across her carpet, she sat down next to it for company. In the evening, her telephone rang. It was her daughter Evi phoning from California. Elizabeth was overjoyed to hear her voice and those of Evi's children.

A New York friend Beatrice Chanler arrived for New Year. Beatrice was an actress, sculptor and author, who had married into the Astor family. Elizabeth found her a comfort after sleepy southerners. The two women welcomed in the New Year with eggnog and listening to the radio; Elizabeth prayed for 'God's blessing on all I love in this next terrible but going to be glorious year. Amen 1940'.

Elizabeth listened to Wagner's *Götterdämmerung* (*Twilight of the Gods*) on the radio early in the new year, read Goethe and wondered how the Germans, who produced such greatness, could have produced Hitler, Goering, Goebbels and Ribbentrop.

In mid-January she felt unwell; she feared she had flu and called the doctor. She had a high temperature and he ordered her to bed. She defied the doctor but did cancel a couple of social engagements. She played down her illness in her journal: 'Not very bad—really hardly at all.' Nonetheless, when she telephoned Liebet, her daughter was sufficiently concerned to arrive the next day.

With her daughter's companionship, Elizabeth appeared to pick up after a few days. She played chess with Liebet, read and listened to music, including a shrieking *Madama Butterfly* on the radio. Elizabeth was not impressed. 'No wonder he wouldn't marry her.' Elizabeth's spiky wit remained intact. On 29 January, she wrote just one line in her diary: 'Lovely day, but raw—anyhow raw early. Don't feel well.' They were her last written words.

Liebet called a doctor, who advised transferring Elizabeth to hospital. Knowing Elizabeth's aversion to medical institutions, Liebet would not agree. Elizabeth fell into a coma and was taken by ambulance to Riverside Infirmary in Charleston on 2 February. She did not regain consciousness. With Liebet at her side, Elizabeth died just before dawn on 9 February 1941. Streptococcal septicaemia and influenza were recorded as the causes of death.

Her death certificate was littered with errors. Elizabeth would no doubt have been pleased to find her age recorded as seventy not seventy-four. Her birthday was given as 25 August 1870, rather than 31 August 1866. Her birthplace was recorded not as Australia but as New Zealand. The woman who had defied and dissembled throughout her life, who shunned fame and prying eyes, remained elusive to the end.

Elizabeth's death left obituarists scratching their heads as to what name to use. Newspaper tributes variously referred to her as Lady Russell; Mary, Countess Russell; 'Elizabeth' and Elizabeth, Countess Russell.

The New York Times acknowledged her brilliance, sparkling wit and storytelling skill that had sparked many imitators. She retained a 'passion for secrecy and anonymity, which never left her'. The *New York Herald Tribune* summarised her literary output: 'her early books were marked by charm and the author's love of nature, but showed the beginnings of her brilliant and often merciless character sketches. Her later works showed the same originality of outlook, but were marked by a growing cynicism.'

In England, *The Times* noted Elizabeth's vitality and an innate kindliness shot with irony. 'Everything that "Elizabeth" wrote was interpenetrated by her unusually vivid and loveable nature and her pervasive sense of fun.' She had 'a frank, gentle expression indicative of the peaceful beauty of her temperament'.

Elizabeth's friends painted a more complex picture. She was neither gentle nor peaceful, argued Hugh Walpole for the *Daily Sketch*. She was 'amused, cynical, ironic, loving, gay, ferocious, cold, ardent—but *never* gentle'. She was a whirlwind. She created around her the atmosphere of a Court at which her friends were either in disgrace or favour, a butt or a blessing. Walpole recalled his miserable months as a young tutor at Nassenheide, being teased and tormented by Elizabeth: 'When she was cruel she was very cruel [. . .] I doubt whether any experience in all my life did me more good, but, dear me, I *did* suffer!' Walpole began by hating her but grew to love her. 'English literature is not so crammed with wits that it can spare Elizabeth [. . .] She leaves, undoubtedly, some of the wittiest novels in the English language.'

Frank Swinnerton, in *The Observer*, considered Elizabeth kind but her 'judgments of men and women, being unsentimental, were often destructive'. What she seemed to be in her novels, she was in reality. 'The lucid ridicule of dullness and brutality that quickens nearly all her books was what produced for every hearer an awful delight in her more intimate conversation. I do not mean that she was spiteful. On the contrary, she was enchanting company. I have never known any other woman with the same comic detachment of mind.' Novelist Gladys B. Stern's assessment was succinct: 'What a devil she was, but *what* good company!'

Liebet travelled from America to England with her mother's ashes two years after the war ended. Elizabeth now lies with her brother Sydney in St Margaret's Church, Tylers Green in Buckinghamshire. On a stone tablet is inscribed 'Mary Annette Countess Russell "Elizabeth"'. Below is a Latin motto: *Parva sed Apta*. It translates as 'Small but Apt'. Absent from the memorial stone is the name by which she is known today: Elizabeth von Arnim. That name is a recent invention, created long after her memorial stone was carved.

Elizabeth's books fell out of favour and out of print after her death. In a world recovering from the second world war, it was a time of Angry Young Men. The name 'Elizabeth' came to conjure an image of Britain's monarch, rather than a once bestselling novelist.

But in the mid-1980s, change arrived when feminist publishing house Virago, founded by Australian Carmen Callil, republished some of Elizabeth's novels. They reappeared after writer Dora Russell, formerly married to Bertrand Russell, drew Callil's attention to *Vera*'s roots in Elizabeth's marriage to Frank Russell. And so, four decades after her death, the author 'Elizabeth von Arnim' was born.

While Elizabeth's gothic *Vera* is seen by many critics as her masterwork, *The Enchanted April*, with its atmosphere of wisteria and sunshine, remains her best-known and loved. It has certainly proved her most adaptable. Twice turned into a movie, most recently in Mike Newell's Oscar-nominated 1991 version with Miranda Richardson and Joan Plowright, *The Enchanted April* has also been a stage play and an opera. Elizabeth's novel has even been credited with putting on the tourist map the pretty Italian fishing village of Portofino. With its reassuring optimism, the book gained renewed appeal during the 2020 pandemic. Its sales increased dramatically in the UK, according to *The Guardian*, and by the end of that year *The Washington Post* commended the novel to lift holiday spirits.

Elizabeth's old Pomeranian schloss, Nassenheide, no longer stands. Allied bombers destroyed her German home towards the end of World War II. Near where it once stood, which is today in Poland, a couple of bronze statues of Elizabeth are reminders of where she first drew her literary inspiration.

No such reminders exist in her Australian birthplace, a country so fond of its monuments it has erected them to everything from explorer Matthew Flinders' cat to the musicians of the *Titanic*. Even Henry Beauchamp's fellow traveller, the opium-smoking scientist Nicholas Miklouho-Maclay, has a Sydney park named after him.

Elizabeth, one of the finest and wittiest writers of her generation, has vanished without a trace. Her early home, Beulah, and its gardens are covered in apartment blocks in the shadow of the Sydney Harbour Bridge.

On the Writers Walk that snakes around Circular Quay to the Sydney Opera House, metal plaques embedded in the footpath acknowledge Australian-born writers, and those who made fleeting visits to antipodean shores: the likes of Rudyard Kipling, Arthur Conan Doyle and D.H. Lawrence. But you look in vain for Elizabeth von Arnim's name along the walkway across from the Kirribilli Point foreshore of her childhood.

The colonial-born countess eschewed fame, and published her twenty-one books behind an authorial mask. Elizabeth lived her nomadic, free-spirited life on her own terms. But writers are best remembered not in metal statues and plaques but by their words—and many of Elizabeth's remain in print.

The witty, contradictory woman who wrote eloquently of nature, and satirically of people, had a rose named in her honour in Britain a few years ago. It has a magnificent apricot bloom. Beware the thorns.

Appendix

THE BEAUCHAMPS AND THE LASSETTERS: THEIR AUSTRALIAN BEGINNINGS

Reverend Matthew Lassetter was the first of Elizabeth von Arnim's forebears to set foot in Australia. At various times her grandfather was a baker, a farmer, an auctioneer, a teacher and a lay preacher. He was a master of reinvention who exuded a whiff of disgrace. It mingled with the odour of mock turtle soup, oyster patties, veal and ham in the small shop he opened in Sydney's King Street in early 1834.

Family lore says Matthew ambushed his wife—Elizabeth's grandmother—into marriage in Somerset, England. He took her to visit a church where a parson and witnesses were waiting. Elizabeth Bedford was a widow when she was frogmarched up the aisle. Matthew and Elizabeth soon sailed for Sydney with their infant son Frederic and arrived in 1832. They were accompanied by Elizabeth's teenage daughter from her first marriage, Georgina. Matthew emigrated at the urging of his wife's sister Kezia, who had sailed into Sydney years earlier on a boat laden with potatoes and married a former convict, Lancelot Iredale. He was a Durham blacksmith who had been transported for stealing iron bars. After receiving a conditional pardon, Lancelot set up an ironmongery and hardware business in George Street and began to prosper.

Matthew Lassetter did not fare well. Despite the encouragement of his wealthy brother-in-law, money was short and he was soon down on his luck. After his daughter, Annie Mary, was born, Matthew shut up his Sydney shop. He took his family south to the remote island of Van Diemen's Land, as Tasmania was then known. Van Diemen's Land was a hell hole, the harshest of Britain's penal colonies, to which seventy thousand souls were transported, many to be broken by floggings at Macquarie Harbour or solitary confinement at Port Arthur.

Transportation was at its height when Matthew arrived. He settled at Launceston, then a settlement of fewer than three thousand people. Miserable as life was for convicts, for a free man such as Matthew Lassetter, life in Van Diemen's Land seemed more secure for his growing family. Another daughter followed. Elizabeth Waite Lassetter—known as Louey—was born in Launceston in 1836. Louey would become Elizabeth von Arnim's mother. Matthew set up as a baker and became headmaster of an infants' school. The headmaster's position paid £100 a year, and came with a house as well as free coal and candles.

He soon made enemies as his dual role and income raised eyebrows. How could he give proper attention to the morals of the children under his care while running a bakery? An anonymous correspondent to the local paper demanded an answer. Matthew shot back. He arose around 4 a.m. to work in his bakery and could not be improving the morals of his little charges then since they were still 'slumbering on their pillows'.

But it wasn't long before Matthew was in strife again, accused of selling underweight loaves. Another anonymous newspaper correspondent—or perhaps the same one—claimed 'Reverend Mr Light-weight' had been seen pinching dough from his loaves after weighing them. Matthew strenuously rejected the claims.

He gave up his bakery and returned to farming at Longford, a hamlet outside Launceston. He was expelled for drunkenness from the Wesleyan Methodists in 1841. He eventually mended his ways and was readmitted to the Wesleyan fold.

The local Wesleyan Methodists were less forgiving of Matthew's stepdaughter. The devout Georgina was refused full membership because she had not 'manifested sorrow for being married to an unbeliever'. The unbeliever was an auctioneer named Joseph Bell. When Joseph became insolvent and moved with Georgina to Melbourne, Matthew reinvented himself once again and took over Joseph's auctioneering business. Calico, sailcloth, worsted stockings, pigs and cart horses all passed through Matthew's nimble hands.

Matthew's wife Elizabeth died suddenly in 1844, leaving him with three children. By now Frederic was fourteen years old; for a time he helped his father on the Longford farm, but he soon left for Melbourne and found work with an auctioneer. Matthew was ill-equipped to care for Annie Mary and Louey, who were left largely unsupervised to fend for themselves.

When news of this reached their older half-sister Georgina in Melbourne, she sailed to Tasmania and rescued them. It may have suited Matthew Lassetter to have his daughters off his hands. He soon left for California.

In Melbourne, young Frederic Lassetter had found working for an auctioneer named Mr Easy was anything but. Frederic toiled from 8 a.m. to 10 p.m. and had little more than a hard ship's biscuit to sustain him through. But his diligence impressed a Sydney businessman, George A. Lloyd, who offered him work as a clerk.

When Frederic's uncle, Lancelot Iredale, died in 1848, his widow, Aunt Kezia, asked her young nephew to join the family's Sydney hardware business. Frederic knew little about running a firm, but Lloyd encouraged his capable clerk to accept the offer: 'Go into that business, and you will run round your competitors like a cooper round a cask.'

Frederic became a partner in Iredale & Co in 1850. It was his big break—and his timing was perfect. The discovery of gold in New South Wales in 1851 meant demand boomed for spades, picks, revolvers and other tools would-be diggers needed. Gold fever spread as ragged bands of hopeful men headed to the diggings around Bathurst. So did the enterprising Frederic. With cartloads of goods, he bumped his way to the diggings at Turon.

The currency at the goldfields was gold dust, and Frederic's first payment was just over two ounces of it. He kept it for life. Frederic had the golden touch. A shortage of coin in the colony in the 1850s saw his company issue copper tokens. These were accepted as legal currency and known as Lassetter's Pennies.

Demand for his goods was strong, but obtaining stock was a battle. Shops with the best stock got the customers. Many goods had to be shipped from England. But merchants tightly controlled the shipping trade and onsold their goods by favour. Frederic developed an enterprising way of getting his hands on scarce merchandise and beating his rivals. He kept his pony saddled at his shop door. When a vessel came through Sydney Heads, he galloped down to Circular

Quay, where an oarsman rowed him out to the ship, often before it had dropped anchor. On board, he inspected the manifest to see what goods had been consigned to which merchant. He would then visit the merchant, tell him his goods were arriving and make the first offer on the consignment. His competitors were aghast at such unorthodox, ungentlemanly ways. But it helped make his fortune.

Frederic began courting his first cousin Charlotte, Kezia Iredale's daughter, and married the sixteen-year-old in 1852. He continued to prosper and was so successful that by the early 1860s he had taken over Iredale & Co. He renamed it F. Lassetter & Co., converted it to retail and built huge new premises that eventually covered three city blocks between George and Kent Streets. At the time of Elizabeth's birth, her Uncle Frederic's store, known simply as Lassetters, was the biggest in Sydney.

As Frederic was counting his Lassetter Pennies, a young Englishman sailed into Circular Quay. The captain of the ship that brought Henry Herron Beauchamp—Elizabeth's father—to Australia in 1850 doubted his 25-year-old passenger would amount to much in Sydney, but he wished him well.

Despite the captain's misgivings, Henry quickly set up as a Sydney shipping merchant trading in everything from flour and sugar to imported claret, English cheese and opium as well as kangaroo skins from Van Diemen's Land. Business was brisk in the colony, where goods were scarce.

Henry was a more astute businessman than his father John Beauchamp, a London silversmith said to have invented a way to make imitation silver. But John never managed to turn his plated silver into financial gold. John was dubbed the Poet of Hornsey Lane, fond of reciting verse and mixing with poets and painters.

Apprenticed at thirteen to a London firm of merchants and shippers, Henry was in his early twenties when the company sent him to Mauritius. There he went into business by himself, before deciding to seek his fortune and a better climate in Australia. Three of his brothers also left London for the antipodes: Horatio Beauchamp settled in Melbourne, while Arthur and Craddock Beauchamp went to New Zealand.

Energetic and enterprising, Henry had good prospects by the time he caught the eye of the vivacious Louey Lassetter, then in her late teens. No longer a dirty and near-destitute Tasmanian farm girl, Louey was living with her wealthy Aunt Kezia Iredale at Auburn Cottage—a mansion, despite its quaint name—in Sydney's Surry Hills. He courted her on the veranda, took her on outings around Sydney and soon proposed. Henry and Louey married at Frederic's Surry Hills home in January 1855. Henry was the second Beauchamp to marry a Lassetter lass. His brother Horatio had married Louey's older sister Annie Mary in Melbourne two years earlier.

Henry and Louey Beauchamp made their home along the Cooks River at St Peters. The now inner-city Sydney suburb was then semi-rural, and Louey gave birth to their first child in November. Their joy was short-lived. The boy survived just two days. Another son, Ralph, arrived two years later, followed by a daughter, Charlotte.

Henry prospered and by 1861, the family shifted across the harbour to Kirribilli Point. They moved into Woodlands, the first of three villas they occupied on the Point, where sons Sydney and Walter were born before the Beauchamps moved up the hill to Clifton, where a fourth son, Henry (known as Harry), was born.

Louey's wealthy brother Frederic probably encouraged the move to Kirribilli Point. The Lassetters had moved there a few years earlier. So too had Frederic's mentor, George Lloyd, whom Henry Beauchamp did business with. Family and business were intertwined.

The Lassetters occupied Beulah, while George Lloyd occupied the most prestigious house on the point, Wotonga. It had a view not surpassed in the colony, according to *The Sydney Morning Herald*. Frederic coveted the vista, not just for its beauty but for the opportunity it provided to keep his eye out for the arrival of ships. So when George Lloyd left Wotonga in 1865, his departure set off a series of house-swaps. Frederic Lassetter moved into Wotonga, while Henry and Louey Beauchamp prepared to shift into Beulah.

Frederic Lassetter made many trips to Europe, but Sydney remained his home. After his retail empire was taken over by two of his sons after his death, it closed in 1926 when its stock was bought by rival Anthony Hordern.

ACKNOWLEDGEMENTS

The grevillea caught my eye. Such a familiar sight in Australia, the shrub seemed so out of place on the edge of Los Angeles. But its lemon flowers nodded in the warm spring air when I arrived at the Huntington Library, which holds Elizabeth von Arnim's papers, diaries, letters and even photographs of her much-loved dogs.

Elizabeth was surrounded by mystery throughout her life, much of it of her own creation. Other myths have arisen since her death. I wanted to know what this intensely private person had written about herself. I had many questions. How had this woman who wrote the sunny, optimistic *Enchanted April* also penned the dark, troubling masterpiece *Vera*? Who was she?

Elizabeth's cursive handwriting felt hard to decipher initially. But in time, the sight of the black ink that flowed from her fountain pen became as familiar as the sound of a friend's voice. What didn't change was the feeling of intimacy as I held in my hand the pages on which Elizabeth's once rested. With hand-written letters virtually extinct today, I wondered what will replace that tactile immediacy for biographers delving into lives lived in the age of typed emails and text messages?

ACKNOWLEDGEMENTS

My gratitude in telling Elizabeth von Arnim's extraordinary story spans the globe. Her descendants on several continents have shared their knowledge and family photographs with me. Ann Hardham, Elizabeth's literary executor and great grand-daughter, allowed me to quote from the author's letters, journals and books, the biography by Leslie de Charms (Elizabeth's daughter Leibet) as well as from the papers of Henry Beauchamp (Elizabeth's father). Ann kindly answered my many questions and provided photographs.

Jamie Ritchie opened his family photo album to me and Caroline Gathorne-Hardy vividly evoked family memories. David Norton provided photographs and material on Elizabeth's Australian connections. Christopher Naylor shared background on the Beauchamps and his late mother's family history research.

I was assisted by the Huntington Library's Alan Jutzi Fellowship which allowed me to spend two months immersed in Elizabeth's archive. The library's staff were untiringly helpful. Archivist Gayle Richardson initiated me into the collection and was enthusiastic in her support and in sharing her detailed knowledge of Elizabeth's life and work. Gayle also read an early draft of this manuscript and made helpful suggestions. Others, too, kindly read early sections. Thank you, Gerri Kimber and Ken Blackwell. That said, any errors are my own.

Many others made time to talk, responded to my emails and generously provided background. I am indebted to Jennifer Walker, Isobel Maddison, Juliane Römhild, Ruth Derham, Dennis Sears, Carmen Callil, Elizabeth Frere Jones, Ian Hoskins,

Anne Bailey, Frank Murray and John Murray.

The Stella Prize and Springfield Farm assisted with a writer's residency in the New South Wales Southern Highlands, where Kinchem Hedegus and Peter Barge were my thoughtful hosts.

Elfriede Ihsen kindly translated German letters for me and Anne Boura Noordeloos translated French. Former colleagues and friends assisted in myriad ways. Thank you, Jenna Price, Peter Fray, Anne Coombs, Susan Varga, the late Peter Cochrane and Camilla Gill.

For copyright material, I gratefully acknowledge the Bertrand Russell Archives at McMaster University Library and the Bertrand Russell Peace Foundation Ltd for permission to quote from Bertrand Russell's letters and published works; the Society of Authors (UK) as the literary representative of the estates of Katherine Mansfield and of Gladys B. Stern; the Provost and Scholars of King's College, Cambridge, and the Society of Authors for permission to quote from E.M. Forster's diaries, letters and writings; and Eric Glass Ltd on behalf of the estate of Beverley Nichols. I thank Duff Hart-Davis for permission to quote from Rupert Hart-Davis' biography of Hugh Walpole.

My book would not have seen daylight without the encouragement, prodding, wit and insight of my publisher Richard Walsh at Allen & Unwin. Editorial director Rebecca Kaiser kept me on track and promised the book would look beautiful, and it does. Angela Meyer's careful editing saved me from myself.

Conrad Walters' faith in me is adamantine. He assisted with research, solved tech glitches, made astute comments on early drafts and celebrated each milestone with a confetti trail of party poppers.

BIBLIOGRAPHY

Elizabeth von Arnim's books

Elizabeth and Her German Garden, Macmillan & Co., London, 1898.
The Solitary Summer, Macmillan & Co., London, 1899.
The April Baby's Book of Tunes, Macmillan & Co., London, 1900.
The Benefactress, Macmillan & Co., London, 1901.
The Adventures of Elizabeth in Rügen, Macmillan & Co., London, 1904.
The Princess Priscilla's Fortnight, Smith, Elder & Co., London, 1905.
Fräulein Schmidt and Mr Anstruther, Smith, Elder & Co., London, 1907.
The Caravaners, Smith, Elder & Co., London, 1909.
The Pastor's Wife, Smith, Elder & Co., London 1914.
(Cholmondeley, Alice), *Christine*, Macmillan & Co., London, 1917.
Christopher and Columbus, Macmillan & Co., London, 1919.
(Anonymous), *In the Mountains*, Macmillan & Co., London, 1920.
Vera, Macmillan & Co., London, 1921.
The Enchanted April, Macmillan & Co., London, 1922.
Love, Macmillan & Co., London, 1925.
Introduction to Sally, Macmillan & Co., London, 1926.
Expiation, Macmillan & Co., London, 1929.
Father, Macmillan & Co., London 1931.
The Jasmine Farm, Heinemann, London, 1934.
All the Dogs of My Life, Heinemann, London, 1936.
Mr Skeffington, Heinemann, London, 1940.

Select Bibliography

Alpers, Antony, *The Life of Katherine Mansfield*, Penguin, Middlesex, 1982.

Baker, Ida, *Katherine Mansfield: The Memories of L.M.*, Michael Joseph, London, 1971.

Bartrip, Peter, 'A Talent to Alienate: The 2nd Earl (Frank) Russell', *The Journal of Bertrand Russell Studies*, McMaster University, vol. 32, issue 2, 2012. https://doi.org/10.15173/russell.v32i2.2229

Bell, Georgina, unpublished diary. Georgina Bell, Family Papers, MS Box 1874/5, held by State Library of Victoria.

Brown, Erica, *Comedy and the Feminine Middlebrow Novel: Elizabeth von Arnim and Elizabeth Taylor*, Pickering & Chatto, London, 2013.

Carey, Gabrielle, *Only Happiness Here: In Search of Elizabeth von Arnim*, UQP, Queensland, 2020.

De Charms, Leslie, *Elizabeth of the German Garden*, Heinemann, London, 1958.

Derham, Ruth, *Bertrand's Brother: The Marriages, Morals and Misdemeanours of Frank, 2nd Earl Russell*, Amberley Publishing, Stroud, UK, 2021.

Doubleday, F.N., *The Memoirs of a Publisher*, Doubleday & Co., New York, 1972.

Furbank, P.N., *E.M. Forster: A Life*, Harcourt Brace Jovanovich, New York, 1978.

Gathorne-Hardy, Robert (ed.), *Ottoline at Garsington: Memoirs of Lady Ottoline Morrell 1915–1918*, Faber & Faber, London, 1974.

Griffin, Nicholas (ed.), *The Selected Letters of Bertrand Russell: The Public Years 1914–1970*, Routledge, London, 2001.

Hart-Davis, Rupert, *Hugh Walpole: A Biography*, Macmillan & Co., London, 1952.

Holzberger, W.G. (ed.), *The Letters of George Santayana*, vols 1–7, MIT Press, Massachusetts, 2001–2006.

Jones, Kathleen, *Katherine Mansfield: The Story-Teller*, Edinburgh University Press, Edinburgh, 2010.

Lago, Mary & Furbank, P.N. (eds), *Selected Letters of E.M. Forster*, vol. 1, Collins, London, 1983.

Lago, M., Hughes, L. K., Walls, E.M., (eds), *The BBC Talks of E.M. Forster 1929–1960*, University of Missouri Press, Columbia, 2008.

Lowndes, Belloc, *The Merry Wives of Westminster*, Macmillan & Co., London, 1946.

McKenzie, Joan, *Silverleaf: The Story of a Pioneer Jessie Lloyd of Terembone, North Western NSW*, J.M. McKenzie, Coonamble, NSW, 1986.

Maddison, Isobel, *Elizabeth von Arnim: Beyond the German Garden*, Ashgate, Surrey, 2016.

Maddison, Isobel, 'The Curious Case of *Christine*: Elizabeth von Arnim's Wartime Text', *First World War Studies*, vol. 3, issue 3 2012, 183–200, DOI: 10.1080/19475020.2012.728740

Meyers, Jeffrey, *Katherine Mansfield: A Biography*, New Directions, New York, 1980.

Middleton Murry, John (ed.), *Journal of Katherine Mansfield*, Constable & Co., London, 1954.

Nichols, Beverley, *Being a Young Man's Candid Recollections of his Elders and Betters*, George H. Doran Company, New York, 1926.

Nicolson, Nigel (ed.), *A Reflection of the Other Person: The Letters of Virginia Woolf, Volume 4, 1929–1931*, Hogarth Press, London, 1978.

North, Marianne, *Recollections of a Happy Life*, Macmillan & Co., London, 1892.

O'Sullivan, Vincent & Scott, Margaret (eds), *The Collected Letters of Katherine Mansfield*, Oxford University Press, Oxford, vols 1–5, 1984–2008.

Pless, Daisy, Princess of, *From My Private Diary*, John Murray, London, 1931.

Potter, Jane, *Boys in Khaki, Girls in Print: Women's Literary Responses to the Great War 1914–18*, Oxford University Press, Oxford, 2005.

Roiphe, Katie, *Uncommon Arrangements: Seven Marriages in Literary London 1910–1939*, Virago, London, 2008.

Römhild, Juliane, *Femininity and Authorship in the Novels of Elizabeth von Arnim*, Roman & Littlefield, Maryland, 2014.

Russell, Bertrand, *The Autobiography of Bertrand Russell*, vols 1–2, 1872–1944, Little, Brown & Co., Boston, 1967.

Russell, Earl, *My Life and Adventures*, Cassell and Company, London, 1923.

Santayana, George, *Persons and Places: Fragments of Autobiography*, Holzberger, W.G. & Saatkamp, Jr, H.J., (eds), MIT Press, Massachusetts, 1986.

Scott, Margaret (ed.), *The Katherine Mansfield Notebooks*, University of Minnesota Press, Minneapolis, 2002.

Stead, C.K., *The Letters and Journals of Katherine Mansfield: A Selection*, Allen Lane, London, 1977.

Swinnerton, Frank, *An Autobiography*, Hutchison & Co, London, 1937.

Swinnerton, Frank, *Figures in the Foreground: Literary Reminiscences, 1917–40*, Hutchinson, London, 1963.

Tomalin, Claire, *Katherine Mansfield: A Secret Life*, Alfred A. Knopf, New York, 1988.

Usborne, Karen, '*Elizabeth*', *The Author of Elizabeth and her German Garden*, Bodley Head, London, 1986.

Walker, Jennifer, *Elizabeth of the German Garden: A Literary Journey*, The Book Guild, Sussex, 2013.

Wells, H.G., *H.G. Wells in Love: Postscript to an Experiment in Autobiography*, G.P. Wells (ed.), Faber & Faber, London, 1984.

NOTES

Abbreviations

EvA Elizabeth von Arnim
BRA Bertrand Russell Archives, McMaster University Library, Ontario, Canada.
CRP Elizabeth Mary Russell, Countess Russell Papers, the Huntington Library, San Marino, California, USA.
HHB Henry Herron Beauchamp
JMM John Middleton Murry
KM Katherine Mansfield
LB Liebet Butterworth
NYT The New York Times
TLS The Times Literary Supplement

Elizabeth von Arnim's journals and correspondence are held by the Huntington Library, except where marked. Henry Herron Beauchamp's letters and journals are held by the Huntington Library.

Chapter 1 Setting sail

p.3 Not until 1910: *The Sydney Morning Herald*, 6 Aug 1910. **p.5** 'quiet and good Milch Cow': *The Sydney Morning Herald*, 31 Dec 1869. **p.6** 'Made money, lost a great deal': HHB journal, Jan 1870. **p.7** 'Beauchamp waggishness': EvA to Bertrand Russell, 1919. BRA. **p.7** 'sweet, twining ways': *All the Dogs of My Life*, 13. **p.7** 'frisky little widow': HHB journal, 21 Jan 1870. **p.7** 'an hour on the sunny side of George Street': HHB journal, 3 Feb 1870. **p.7** 'Pa, are him bellied?': HHB journal, 3 Feb 1870. **p.8** 'All my nightmares': EvA to LB, 8 April

1930. **p.8** 'chatted and did a little scandal': HHB journal, 3 Feb 1870. **p.8** 'a decided outbreak of lovemaking': HHB journal, 24 Feb 1870. **p.8** 'Poor old captain': HHB journal, 19 March 1870. **p.8** 'Well, certainly Mrs Beauchamp': HHB journal, 20 March 1870. **p.9** 'or be playful': HHB journal, 20 March 1870. **p.9** 'began to wish for a new slander': HHB journal, 18 March 1870. **p.9** 'Our children's faith': HHB journal, 27 March 1870. **p.9** 'intoxicating several ladies': HHB journal, 6 April 1870. **p.9** 'Lovely placid day': HHB journal, 22 April 1870.

Chapter 2 A pert, unlovable child

p.11 'Feel ourselves like cuckoos': HHB journal, 7 May 1870. **p.12** 'First, giving you Scarlet fever': HHB journal, 11 May 1870. **p.12** 'Our coming home is a fine thing': HHB journal, 7 June 1870. **p.12** 'Wished them all to Jericho': HHB journal, 10 June 1870. **p.12** 'He wasn't a man': *All the Dogs of My Life*, 16. **p.13** 'Him's a rum one, Pa': HHB journal, 12 June 1870. **p.13** 'thought of the lovely month of September': HHB journal, 18 Sept 1870. **p.13** 'our Australians made their debut': HHB journal, 24 Dec 1870. **p.14** 'an Australian air and climate': HHB journal, 22 May & 26 May 1871. **p.15** 'Queer how sprightly life became': *All the Dogs of My Life*, 8. **p.15** 'I can be happy in Belsize Park': HHB to Louey Beauchamp, 3 March 1873. **p.16** '[Maclay] does not at all wonder': HHB journal, circa 12 April 1873. **p.17** 'Darling little May!': HHB to Louey Beauchamp, 22 March 1873. **p.17** 'After sowing my wild oats': HHB to Louey Beauchamp, 9 May 1873. **p.17** 'happy intelligence of dear Shad's return': HHB to Louey Beauchamp, 11 June 1873. **p.20** 'Sunday in Sydney is terribly quiet': HHB to Louey Beauchamp, 1 Aug – 1 Oct 1875. **p.20** 'I do not at all like the idea': HHB to Louey Beauchamp, 16 Oct 1875. **p.20** 'If you would but love me': HHB to Louey Beauchamp, 19 Dec 1875. **p.20** 'She has plenty of ability': HHB to Louey Beauchamp, 19 Dec 1875. **p.22** 'A pert, unlovable child': *All the Dogs of My Life*, 10. **p.23** 'All feeling acutely our loss': HHB journal, 18 Jan 1883. **p.24** 'very different from that of her birth': HHB journal, 31 Aug 1887. **p.24** 'bright, industrious, good': ibid.

Chapter 3 Smothered in babies

p.27 'All girls like love': *All the Dogs of My Life*, 20. **p.27** 'What a rich woman I shall be': Louey Beauchamp to Jessie, 22 June 1889, in Leslie de Charms, *Elizabeth of the German Garden*, 30. Jessie's surname is unknown. **p.27** 'I never was in such a lovely house': Louey Beauchamp to Jessie, 24 July 1889, ibid, 31. **p.28** 'They say the way to Madam Wagner's heart': Louey Beauchamp to Jessie, 24 July 1889, ibid, 32. **p.28** 'there's not a tree anywhere': EvA to Hugh Walpole, circa Aug 1924. **p.28** 'The more I see of him': Louey Beauchamp to Jessie, 24 July 1889, in de Charms, op. cit., 32. **p.28** 'There are times when she does not feel quite sure of herself': ibid. **p.29** '[I] shall stay with them': HHB to Jessie, 5 Oct 1889. **p.29** Years later, Henning attempted: *NYT*, 3 Jan 1894.

p.31 'a promising artist gone!': George Grove to Edith Oldham, 3 March 1889. In Giles William Edward Brightwell, '"One equal music": The royal college of music, its inception and the legacy of Sir George Grove 1883–1895', PhD thesis, Durham University, 2007, http://etheses.dur.ac.uk/2611/, p. 204, accessed 12 July 2019. **p.32** 'Do not kiss the dog': *All the Dogs of My Life*, 23. **p.33** 'casts herself on her poor mother': Henning von Arnim to HHB, 11 Dec 1891. **p.34** 'Poor little May smothered in babies': HHB journal, 3 May 1894. **p.34** 'Haven't a notion who he is': EvA journal, 30 Jan 1896. **p.34** 'Wrote F.W. am': EvA journal, 1 Jan 1896.

Chapter 4 A Pomeranian countess

p.37 'we were like Adam & Eve': EvA journal, 31 May 1896. **p.38** 'I can't express the love': EvA journal, 31 May 1896. **p.38** 'disgraceful scenes': EvA journal, 18 June 1896. **p.39** A dramatic, if fanciful, account: see Karen Usborne, *Elizabeth*, 61–2. **p.39** 'as usual': EvA journal, 23 July 1896. **p.39** 'H. very nasty': EvA journal, 26 July 1896. **p.39** 'Praise-worthy attempt to celebrate': HHB journal, 31 Aug 1896. **p.40** 'Came home & being too playful': EvA journal, 28 Mar 1897. **p.40** 'Began to write "In a German Garden"': EvA journal, 7 May 1897. **p.40** 'The garden is the place': *Elizabeth and Her German Garden*, Macmillan & Co., London, 1898, 28. **p.41** 'every flower and weed is a friend': ibid. **p.41** 'I never could see that delicacy of constitution': ibid, 59. **p.41** 'We know when spring is coming': ibid, 47. **p.41** 'What a comfort it is': ibid, 80–1. **p.41** 'Far from innocuous': Frank Swinnerton, *The Observer*, 16 Feb 1941. **p.41** 'wondering at the vast': *Elizabeth and Her German Garden*, op. cit., 40. **p.42** 'H & I quarrelled': EvA journal, 31 July 1897. **p.43** 'greatly upset and couldn't sleep': EvA journal, 11 Feb 1898. **p.43** 'It is the first thing I have done': EvA to Macmillan, 3 Mar 1898, Macmillan Archive, British Library, in Isobel Maddison, *Elizabeth von Arnim: Beyond the German Garden*, 53. **p.43** 'Got answer re G.G. accepting it': EvA journal, 30 March 1898. **p.43** 'I note I make no comment on this': EvA added this comment to her 1898 journal in 1937. **p.44** 'Great jubilation': EvA journal, 1 Oct 1898. **p.44** 'managed with the skill of a woman': *The Scotsman*, 26 Sept 1898. **p.44** 'A whimsical personality betrays itself': *The Manchester Guardian*, 5 Oct 1898. **p.44** 'English people will enjoy the sly quips': *The Sydney Morning Herald*, 12 Nov 1898. **p.44** Mary refused to have the book translated: See Maddison, op. cit., 59. **p.45** 'She sedulously cultivates': *Punch*, 8 Feb 1899. **p.45** 'The anonymous author': *The Derby Mercury*, 18 Oct 1898. **p.45** 'May chirrupy on favourable criticisms': HHB journal, 9 Oct 1898. **p.45** 'Chief thing that happened': EvA journal, 31 Dec 1898. **p.46** 'What you say & think of *Elizabeth*': EvA to HHB, 6 Jan 1899. **p.46** 'I want to be alone for a whole summer': *The Solitary Summer*, Macmillan & Co., London, 1899, 3. **p.47** 'like a cold in the head': ibid, 94–5. **p.47** 'Mixed feelings—chiefly disgust': EvA journal, 12 Jan 1899. **p.47** 'The author of *Elizabeth and Her German Garden*': *The Athenaeum*, 1 April 1899. **p.47** 'disgusted with me for being disgusted': EvA journal, 8 April 1899. **p.48** 'literary event': *Daily Mail*, 23 May 1899. **p.48** 'Our author has a knack': *The Sydney Morning Herald*, 8 July 1899. **p.48** 'a little too thin': *The Times*, 14 July 1899. **p.48** 'I hear the anonymous writer': *The Book Lover, A Literary Review*, Melbourne, Nov 1899. **p.48** 'Got a letter from Pa': EvA journal, 20 May 1899. **p.49** 'should help to open the eyes': HHB journal, 21 May 1899. **p.49** 'Ingraban's death had shocked me': *All the Dogs of My Life*, 44. **p.49** 'weighed in balance': HHB journal, 13 Aug 1899. **p.49** 'Wept much without any apparent reason': EvA journal, 31 Aug 1899.

Chapter 5 Dove and serpent

p.51 'each page containing at least one big crime': Henning von Arnim to HHB, 29 July 1900. **p.52** 'unguarded moment by her husband': *NYT*, 28 July 1900. **p.53** 'owing to the author's persistent modesty': *NYT*, 4 Aug 1900. **p.53** 'It would be superfluous to say': *The Critic*, Aug 1900, vol. 37, no. 2. **p.54** 'they merely prove': *The Academy*, 18 Aug 1900, no. 1476. **p.54** 'In your own ear, Mr Editor': *NYT*, 18 Aug 1900. **p.54** 'Just as they would neither confirm': ibid. **p.55** 'even though she still persists': ibid. **p.55** 'I care little whether': *The Critic*, Sept 1900, vol. 37, no. 3. **p.55** As argument continued: see *The Academy*, 1 Sept 1900, no. 1478. **p.55** 'I think with these relatives': *NYT*, 8 Sept 1900. **p.55** 'The fact that I published my misinformation': *The Critic*, Oct 1900, vol. 37, no. 4. **p.56** 'She has not had a train': *San Francisco Examiner*, 7 Oct 1900. **p.56** 'This may be a diplomatic denial': *Daily Mail*, 20 Oct 1900. **p.57** 'the supposed author': *Elizabeth and Her German Garden*, Laird & Lee, Chicago, 1900. **p.57** 'this charming book': Daisy Princess of Pless, *From My Private Diary*, 229. **p.57** 'whatever the temptation': *Punch*, 7 Aug 1901. **p.58** 'rare and fascinating combination': HHB to Henning von Arnim, 18 March 1901. **p.58** 'Oh so happy to get back again!': EvA journal, 8 April 1901. **p.59** 'flag of independent womanhood': *The Benefactress*, ch. 31. **p.59** 'saw its weaknesses depressingly clearly': EvA journal, 4 Oct 1901. **p.59** 'will fall very flat because it is bad': EvA journal, 11 Oct 1901. **p.60** 'agreeably malicious': *The Spectator*, 12 Oct 1901. **p.60** 'And however one may protest': EvA journal, 20 Oct 1901. **p.60** 'more than support her previous reputation': HHB journal, 20 Oct 1901. **p.60** 'I keep getting reviews': EvA to HHB, 23 Oct 1901. **p.61** 'there is nothing so absolutely bracing': *The Adventures of Elizabeth in Rügen*, Macmillan's Colonial Library, Macmillan & Co., London, 1904, 6. **p.62** 'her troubles going with her': HHB journal, 4 Dec 1901. **p.62** 'Can't get on with my Rügen book': EvA journal, 23 Oct 1901. **p.62** 'What a lovely world': EvA journal, 17 Dec 1901. **p.62** 'Took hot footbath but resultless': EvA journal, 4 March 1902.

Chapter 6 Tormenting the tutors

p.63 'The author of *Elizabeth and Her German Garden* and *A Solitary Summer*': *The Pall Mall Magazine*, Sept 1902, vol. 38, no. 113. **p.64** 'This is mysterious author': *Chicago Tribune*, 23 Sept 1902. **p.65** 'Great joy but May': HHB journal, 11 Dec 1902. **p.65** 'I am very glad': Henning von Arnim to HHB, 16 Dec 1902. **p.65** 'the gifted Kathleen': HHB journal, 25 Dec 1904. **p.66** 'Above them all I heard': KM to Edith Bendall, undated, in Vincent O'Sullivan & Margaret Scott (eds), *The Collected Letters of Katherine Mansfield: Volume 1: 1903–1917*, 22–3. **p.66** 'the blessed German baby': KM to Sylvia Payne, 26 Dec 1904. ibid, 15. **p.66** 'sketches so original, delicate': *The Spectator*, 12 March 1904. **p.66** 'A star danced when she was born': *TLS*, 19 Feb 1904. **p.66** 'I simply hate him': EvA to HHB, 9 Nov 1904. **p.67** 'Henning from Dolly': The copy is held by the Huntington Library. **p.68** 'or something of that sort': E.M. Forster to Alice Clara Forster, 4 April 1905, in Mary Lago & P.N. Furbank (eds), *Selected Letters of E.M. Forster, Vol. 1: 1879–1920*, 65. **p.69** 'How d'ye do Mr Forster': Mary Lago, Linda K. Hughes and Elizabeth MacLeod Walls (eds), *The BBC Talks of E.M. Forster, 1929–1960*, 457. **p.69** 'They don't like me': ibid, 458. **p.69** 'quartette of menials': E.M. Forster to Alice Clara Forster, 21 April 1905, in Lago & Furbank, op. cit., 72. **p.69** 'dumb devotion bound her': *The BBC Talks of E.M. Forster, 1929–1960*, op. cit., 460. **p.70** 'if she is meditating': E.M. Forster to Alice Clara Forster, 9 April 1905, Lago & Furbank, op. cit., 67. **p.71** 'The Man of Wrath listens': EM Forster to Alice Clara Forster, 2 July 1905, ibid, 76. **p.71** 'a little unwilling to be mixed: E.M. Forster to Alice Clara Forster, early June 1905, ibid, 73. **p.72** 'I hope that I shall never again': E.M. Forster's diary, 25 July 1905. In *E.M. Forster: A Life*, by P.N. Furbank, 131. **p.72** 'their feeble attempts at naughtiness were crushed': E.M. Forster, Nassenheide notes, circa 1960. CRP. **p.73** 'ragged plot and occasional heaviness': *The Academy*, 5 Nov 1905. **p.74** 'whistle a Bach fugue': *TLS*, 10 May 1907. **p.75** 'Keep bubbling': HHB to EvA, 28 May 1907 **p.75** 'I am—alas!—crawling': HHB to Emma Maunsell, 19 April 1907. **p.75** 'Dear Youth': EvA to Hugh Walpole, 7 Feb 1902 **p.76** 'what makes you think': ibid. **p.76** 'Oh, Mr Walpole': Rupert Hart-Davis, *Hugh Walpole: A Biography*, 49. **p.76** 'Charming, like her books': ibid, 50. **p.77** 'There in it are all his criticisms': EvA to Evi von Arnim, 5 July 1907. **p.77** 'I was so miserable, so homesick': Hugh Walpole, *Daily Sketch*, 24 Feb 1941. **p.77** 'He grows weirder visibly': EvA to Evi von Arnim, 5 June 1907. **p.77** 'I can't tell you how truly beautiful': EvA to E.M. Forster, 5 May 1907, Furbank, op. cit., 131. **p.78** 'I do not know why people': EvA to E.M. Forster, 18 Dec 1907, ibid, 151–152. **p.78** 'It does seem odd that one should be so anxious to please such a person': ibid, 131–132. **p.78** 'No; I don't like her': Virginia Woolf to Ethel Smyth, 21 Sept 1930. Nigel Nicolson (ed.), *A Reflection of the Other Person: The Letters of Virginia Woolf 1929–1931*, Hogarth Press, London, 1978, 218. **p.78** 'almost never': E.M. Forster to LB, 9 Dec 1951. CRP.

Chapter 7 The Gypsy queen

p.81 'I should very *much* like that,': EvA to H.G. Wells, 8 July 1907. H.G. Wells papers, Rare Book and Manuscript Library, University of Illinois. **p.83** 'never to live in a house': HHB journal, 31 Aug 1907. **p.83** 'to seek my fortune': HHB journal, 17 Sept 1907. **p.84** 'after much buffeting': *All the Dogs of My Life*, 16–17. **p.85** 'He hated lies and everything': EvA to Evi von Arnim, 11 Oct 1907, de Charms, op. cit., 125. **p.85** 'Nothing wakes her': EvA to Evi von Arnim, 6 Nov 1907, ibid, 126. **p.85** Mary wrote in great distress: EvA to Evi von Arnim, 13 Nov 1907. **p.87** 'entangled in tea-parties': *All the Dogs of My Life*, 57. **p.87** 'The brooding heaviness': *All the Dogs of My Life*, 75. **p.88** 'Write if you can': Henning von Arnim to EvA, 14 Oct 1908. **p.89** 'The water into which I'd get': EvA to H.G. Wells, undated circa 1908. H.G. Wells papers. **p.89** 'Not since Mr Bernard Shaw': *The Daily News*, 2 Dec 1909. **p.89** 'an achievement to make an arch bore': *The World*, 30 Nov 1909. **p.89** 'Intensely malicious, I now see': EvA journal, 15 Feb 1937. **p.90** He thought *The Caravaners*: David Marr, *Patrick White: A Life*, Random House Australia, Sydney, 1991, 145. **p.91** 'cleaning up my soul': EvA to LB, 27 Jan 1910. **p.91** 'the glow worms dance': EvA to LB, 26 May 1910. **p.92** 'To go to the theatre': *Daily Mail*, 24 June 1910. **p.93** 'You're not to shout author!': EvA to LB, 29 June 1910. **p.93** 'pleasantly ordinary': *The Manchester Guardian*, 29 June 1910.

Chapter 8 Emotions after breakfast

p.95 'It is very dreadful to see somebody die': EvA to Louey Beauchamp, 20 Aug 1910. **p.95** 'I know poor H couldn't ever get well': EvA to Louey Beauchamp, 21 Aug 1910. **p.96** 'Whenever I have had to do with death': EvA to Richard Curle, 7 Aug 1924, in J.H. Stape and O. Knowles (eds), *A Portrait in Letters: Correspondence to and about Conrad*, Rodopi, Atlanta, 1996, 248. **p.96** 'it is so good to be here': EvA to Beatrix von Arnim, 29 Oct 1910, de Charms, op. cit., 142. **p.97** 'What happened to them': EvA to H.G. Wells, 5 Nov 1910. H.G. Wells papers. **p.98** 'to me a baby has always been': EvA to LB, undated circa July 1911. **p.98** 'Christmas will see us all re-united': EvA to LB, undated circa Sept 1911. **p.99** 'it will give me great pleasure': EvA to H.G. Wells, undated circa 1910–11. H.G. Wells papers. **p.99** 'She talks very well': H.G. Wells to Jane Wells, in Jennifer Walker, *Elizabeth of the German Garden: A Literary Journey*, 126. **p.100** 'Never had she conversed with anyone': de Charms, op. cit., 143. **p.101** 'bright and original little lady indeed': G.P. Wells (ed.), *H.G. Wells in Love: Postscript to an Experiment in Autobiography*, 87. **p.101** 'We went for walks over the heathery hillside': ibid, 88. **p.101** 'It was a cheerful thing': ibid, 89. **p.101** 'I attracted her': ibid, 87. **p.101** 'made love all over Mrs Humphrey Ward': ibid, 89. **p.101** 'I cannot imagine a relationship': ibid, 88. **p.102** 'Our little house hanging': *All the Dogs of My Life*, 87. **p.103** 'He didn't want to enough': EvA journal, 8 Nov 1912. **p.103** 'bowing myself out': EvA journal, 17 Nov 1912. **p.103** 'A devil in G. of cruelty': EvA journal, 2 Dec 1912. **p.104** 'emotions after breakfast': EvA journal, 3 May 1913. **p.105** 'things all honey again': EvA journal, 16 May 1913. **p.105** 'more or less sick of me!': EvA journal, 5 Sept 1913. **p.105** 'Great catastrophes etc': EvA journal, 25 Sept 1913. **p.105** 'out of my life': EvA journal, 5 Nov 1913. **p.106** 'It was your fault': Wells, op. cit., 90.

Chapter 9 The wicked earl

p.107 'If he stayed': *All the Dogs of My Life*, 127. **p.108** 'an unwashed, ill-bred, impertinent little child': Earl Russell, *My Life and Adventures*, 22. **p.108** 'after I had been with him some time': Bertrand Russell, *The Autobiography of Bertrand Russell: 1872–1914*, 24. **p.108** 'a limb of Satan': ibid, 24. **p.108** One account says they met: See Usborne, 47–8. This appears to be based on Frank Russell's reference in his memoir to falling in love with an unnamed 'lady of artistic tastes' with whom he shared an admiration for Sarah Bernhardt. Frank Russell's biographer, Ruth Derham, has identified this woman as American poet Agnes Tobin. **p.110** 'Oedipus when he married Jocasta': *The Manchester Guardian*, 19 July 1901. **p.111** 'fat, florid, coarse Irishwoman': George Santayana, *Persons and Places: Fragments of Autobiography*, 476–81. **p.111** 'from her most devoted admirer': Elizabeth later added an inscription of her own. Beneath the author's name, 'Countess Russell', Elizabeth wrote: 'Not to be confounded with "Elizabeth".' Copy held by the Huntington Library. **p.112** 'I am volcanic inside': Frank Russell to EvA, 4 Jan 1914. CRP. **p.112** 'wondered if it wouldn't shine through': EvA journal, 7 Jan 1914. **p.112** 'Elizabeth will be alone': *The Journals of Thomas James Cobden-Sanderson*, journal entry 14 Jan 1914, Doves Press, London, 1926. **p.112** 'I lay in bed panting': Frank Russell to EvA, 11 Jan 1914. CRP. **p.112** 'F. & happiness instead': EvA journal, 16 Jan 1914. **p.112** 'Perfect sunshine': EvA journal, 6 Feb 1914. **p.112** 'Gradually it became my chief concern': *All the Dogs of My Life*, 128–9. **p.114** 'so extremely & delightfully': EvA to Liebet, 3 April 1914. **p.114** 'rude & horrid to Teppi': EvA journal, 14 April 1914. **p.114** 'surprising nuisance': EvA journal, 15 April 1914. **p.114** 'homosexuelle liebe': EvA journal, 16 May 1914. **p.116** 'horrid & degrading evening': EvA journal, 19 June 1914. **p.119** 'So am free': EvA journal, 24 Sept 1914. **p.120** 'readmitted to that blessed British fold': EvA to Walpole, 16 Nov 1914. **p.120** 'tiresome & cross': EvA journal, 30 Sept 1914. **p.120** 'hopelessness of marriage': EvA journal, 3 Oct 1914. **p.120** 'heavenly evening of happiness': EvA journal, 7 Oct 1914. **p.121** 'very extreme & unfair about F': EvA journal, 9 Oct 1914. **p.121** 'Watched for him all morning': EvA journal, 17 Dec 1914.

Chapter 10 A family fractured

p.122 He considered it: George Moore to EvA, 10 Dec 1929. CRP. **p.123** 'hitting below the gaiters': *Punch*, 18 Oct 1914. **p.124** 'furious ravings': EvA to LB, 19 Oct 1914. **p.125** 'I wish I were a man': EvA to Walpole, 16 Nov 1914. **p.126** 'what happiness I've had': EvA journal, 28 Dec 1914. **p.126** 'Now let's see what this one's got': EvA journal, 1 Jan 1915. **p.126** 'F & I very happy': EvA journal, 20 Jan

1915. **p.127** 'quaint memories': EvA journal, 5 May 1915. **p.128** 'horrid consequences': EvA journal, 27 April 1915. **p.129** 'So have the disgusting ways': EvA journal, 24 April 1915. **p.130** 'Found it such rot I left': EvA journal, 14 May 1915. **p.130** 'I greatly disappointed': EvA journal, 5 June 1915. **p.131** 'Gott strafe chemistry': EvA journal, 8 June 1915. **p.131** 'much motheaten & run to seed': EvA journal, 10 June 1915. **p.132** 'I fear if the French get back into Lilley': EvA to LB, 15 June 1915. **p.132** 'the snapdragons didn't care': EvA journal, 19 Aug 1915. **p.133** 'It took her breath away': Bertrand Russell to Ottoline Morrell, circa early Sept 1915, *The Autobiography of Bertrand Russell: Volume 2 1914–1944*, 62. **p.133** 'She drifted, said nothing definite': ibid. **p.133** 'She is a flatterer': ibid. **p.134** 'She loves to be loved': Cobden-Sanderson, op. cit., journal entry 12 Sept 1915. **p.134** 'Great & infinite bliss': EvA journal, 17 Sept 1915. **p.134** 'I never speak except': EvA journal, 8 Oct 1915. **p.134** 'Enjoyed being idle': EvA journal, 9 Oct 1915. **p.135** 'difficulty remembering that I have a separate spirit': EvA journal, 15 Nov 1915. **p.135** 'A cheerful jolly girl': EvA to LB, circa Dec 1915. **p.135** 'I full of doubts about the future': EvA journal, 28 Dec 1915. **p.135** '1915 was not nearly so happy': EvA journal, 31 Dec 1915. **p.136** 'render thanks for my great happiness': EvA journal, 23 Jan 1916. **p.136** 'quaking at the possibilities before us': EvA journal, 24 Jan 1916.

Chapter 11 The dregs of misery

p.137 'spoils me so completely': EvA to LB, 17 Feb 1916. **p.140** 'remarkable secret marriage': *The Washington Post*, 6 April 1916. **p.141** 'on which subject he may be considered': *The Age*, Melbourne, 28 March 1916. **p.141** 'Have made up my mind': EvA journal, 15 April 1916. **p.143** 'tasting the depth of desolation': EvA journal, 4 June 1916. **p.143** 'My little Martin!': EvA journal, 6 June 1916. **p.143** 'I can't bear it': EvA to LB, 7 June 1916. **p.143** 'Martin's death is just as directly': EvA to LB, 7 June 1916. **p.144** 'Did she say something about her mother': EvA to Teppi Backe, 22 June 1916. **p.144** '[I] feel she *must* go to Papa': EvA to LB, 16 June 1916. **p.145** 'I can't look at her little face': EvA to LB, 6 July 1916. **p.145** 'I got down to the very dregs': EvA journal, 8 June 1916. **p.145** 'I'm so eager to be happy': EvA journal, 15 July 1916. **p.146** 'The marvel was that so many women': Santayana, *Persons and Places*, op. cit., 483. **p.147** 'Love-making for him': ibid, 484. **p.147** 'His wives and his cats': ibid. **p.147** 'I'm practically in prison': EvA to LB, 6 Aug 1916. **p.147** 'In order to get him': EvA journal, 26 Aug 1916. **p.147** 'kicked to death by life': EvA journal, 22 Sept 1916. **p.148** 'Don't ever be surprised if you see': EvA to LB, 27 May 1916. **p.149** 'Suddenly the door opened and in came summer': *Christopher and Columbus*, Macmillan & Co., London, 1919, 234–5. **p.150** 'This year (1916) was the most wretched': EvA journal, Dec 1916. **p.151** 'now strictly ordered by a heavy hand': de Charms, op. cit., 190–1. **p.151** 'Life is getting very much whittled': EvA to LB, 21 April 1917. **p.152** 'All other happinesses are as pale': EvA to LB, 21 April 1917.

Chapter 12 'Alice' in propaganda-land

p.153 'A New Novel by a New Author': *NYT*, 29 July 1917. **p.153** 'true in essentials though it wears': *NYT Review of Books*, 5 Aug 1917. **p.154** 'the wretched taste of an author': *The Nation*, 23 Aug 1917. **p.154** Macmillan claimed not to know: *NYT Review of Books*, 16 Sept 1917. **p.154** The newspaper soon raised a quizzical eyebrow: *NYT*, 23 Sept 1917. **p.154** A correspondent to the paper: *NYT*, 30 Sept 1917. **p.154** Macmillan rejected arguments: *NYT*, 7 Oct 1917. **p.154** 'obvious fake, and ingenious': *NYT*, 14 Oct 1917. **p.155** 'Having no positive proof in their hands': *NYT*, 28 Oct 1917. **p.155** 'But nobody believed her': F.N. Doubleday, *The Memoirs of a Publisher*, 202. **p.156** 'I have indignantly repudiated such a charge': EvA to LB, 1 Nov 1917. **p.157** 'it is hard to believe it was written': *TLS*, 20 Sept 1917. **p.157** 'As propaganda for the outside world': *The Daily Telegraph*, 26 Sept 1917. **p.157** 'Elizabeth's contribution to the war effort': de Charms, op. cit., 188. **p.158** More than twenty publishers: For list of publishers, see Schedule of Wellington House Literature, in Jane Potter, *Boys in Khaki, Girls in Print*, 227. **p.158** Curiously, shortly after the war ended': See *NYT*, 18 March 1919. **p.159** 'bath of love': EvA to LB, 15 Aug 1917. **p.159** 'envelops me to the exclusion': ibid. **p.159** 'I like being with male creatures': EvA to LB, 23 Aug 1917. **p.159** 'a Christ & a devil': EvA to LB, 1 Nov 1917. **p.159** 'volcanic interest': EvA to LB, 3 Sept 1917. **p.160** 'arch, acid, charming self-portraits': Frank Swinnerton, *Figures in the Foreground: Literary Reminiscences, 1917–40*, 52. **p.160** 'Then one observed that the child': ibid, 53. **p.160** 'It is exactly like what happened to me': EvA to LB, 10 April 1918. **p.160** 'You have a proper decent husband': ibid. **p.161** 'Dad's very loving & overwhelming': EvA to LB, 25 Feb 1918. **p.162** 'One doesn't have a relation in prison': EvA to Bertrand Russell, 20 May 1918. BRA. **p.162** 'especially after that portion of you': EvA to Bertrand Russell, 6 June 1918. BRA. **p.162** 'I am very fond of her': Bertrand Russell to Ottoline Morrell, 1 Aug 1918. BRA. **p.163** 'London was mad with joy': EvA to LB, 14 Nov 1918. **p.164** 'You will think me a great shilly shallyer': EvA to Bertrand Russell, 10 March 1919. BRA. **p.165** 'I think I'm going to have to leave Dad': EvA to LB, 1 Feb 1919. **p.165** 'You know what he was like at San Ysidro': EvA to LB, 1 Feb 1919. **p.165** 'I now so thoroughly know': EvA to LB, 31 March 1919. **p.166** 'In a world where there are so many furies': *The Athenaeum*, 11 April 1919. **p.168** 'little savage from New Zealand': Margaret Scott (ed.), *The Katherine Mansfield Notebooks: Volume 2*, 31. **p.169** 'I keep thinking of Elizabeth's hands': KM to Ottoline Morrell, 27 June 1919, in *The Collected Letters of Katherine Mansfield: Volume 2: 1918–1919*, 335. **p.169** 'saying very much the same things': KM to Ottoline Morrell, circa 25 June 1919, ibid, 333.

Chapter 13 Mountain solace

p.171 'I have done my best with both of you': Bertrand Russell to Frank Russell, 19 May 1919. BRA. **p.172** 'It is quite hateful to think': Bertrand Russell to EvA, circa July 1919. CRP. **p.173** 'wretchedness could be packed so tight': *All the Dogs of My Life*, 152. **p.173** 'He at least is simple & kind': EvA journal, 6 March 1920. **p.174** 'I'm afraid of loneliness': *In the Mountains.* **p.175** 'It invariably conquers.': ibid. **p.175** 'Du forgive me, will yiu?': Beverley Nichols, *Being a Young Man's Candid Recollections of his Elders and Betters*, 80. **p.176** 'I didn't know men *had* so many places': ibid, 82. **p.177** 'oh the horror!': EvA journal, 23 May 1920. **p.177** 'intimate insults': EvA to Bertrand Russell, 9 July 1920. **p.177** 'I had a savage letter from Frank': Bertrand to EvA, 13 Jan 1921. CRP. **p.178** 'wicked lying abuse': EvA to Bertrand Russell, 15 Nov 1920. **p.178** 'How I wish we could at least be friends': EvA journal, 4 July 1920. **p.178** 'a thousand devils are sending Elizabeth': KM to Violet Schiff, circa 20 May 1920, in Vincent O'Sullivan & Margaret Scott (eds), *The Collected Letters of Katherine Mansfield: Volume 4: 1920–1921*, 13. **p.178** 'She has no use for a physical lover. I mean to go to bed with': KM to JMM, 7 Nov 1920, in Antony Alpers, *The Life of Katherine Mansfield*, 316–17. **p.179** Alexander Stuart Frere Reeves is sometimes spelled Alexander Stewart Frere Reeves. **p.180** cataloguing and arranging her books: Frere to EvA, 14 Feb 1920. Frere offered in his letter to come to London for an interview so she could meet him and see if she considered him suitable. Her diary records an appointment with a Mr Reeves on 19 March 1920, which is likely their first meeting. **p.181** 'I take no notice of my guests': EvA to LB, 20 July 1920. **p.182** 'I wanted to, yet I hated to': *Regurgitation*, (account of the pilgrimage to Nassenheide), unpublished manuscript, circa 1920. CRP. **p.183** 'Look at the lines on the faces': EvA to LB, 21 Dec 1920. **p.183** 'determined that my sunset shall be calm': EvA to LB, 16 Nov 1920. **p.183** 'of which there is much': EvA to LB, 8 Dec 1920.

Chapter 14 Do not marry a novelist

p.189 '[We have] occasional long talks': KM to Ottoline Morrell, 24 July 1921, O'Sullivan & Scott, op. cit., vol. 4, 252. **p.189** 'Breathes there the man, do you think': KM to EvA, 22 Aug 1921. CRP. **p.189** 'She appeared today behind a bouquet': KM to Dorothy Brett, 1 Oct 1921, O'Sullivan & Scott, op. cit., vol. 4, 287. **p.189** 'She is certainly the most fascinating small human being': KM to Dorothy Brett, 25 July 1921, ibid, 254. **p.190** 'She looks about 35': KM to Vera McIntosh Bell, early Nov 1921, ibid, 309. **p.190** 'They *exude* so': KM journal, Aug 1921, de Charms, op. cit., 222. **p.190** 'You are a loathsome reptile—I hope you will die': in Alpers, op. cit., 310. **p.191** 'I was horribly ungracious to you': KM to EvA, 30 Aug 1921, O'Sullivan & Scott, op. cit., vol. 4, 272. **p.191** 'I have drunk in new life': KM to EvA, circa July 1921. CRP. **p.191** 'there *is* something of the boss': Hugh Walpole, 29 Aug 1921, Hart-Davis, op. cit., 210. **p.192** 'slimy blandishments': *TLS*, 22 Sept 1921. **p.192** 'one of the most successful attempts': *The New Statesman*, 15 Oct 1921. **p.192** 'raised me to my feet': EvA to JMM, 17 Sept 1921. **p.192** 'Have you ever known a Wemyss?': KM to Dorothy Brett, 22 Dec

1921, O'Sullivan & Scott, op. cit., vol. 4, 346–7. **p.193** 'I expect he will admire': KM to EvA, 23 Oct 1921. CRP. **p.193** 'On the crest of *Vera*': EvA to KM & JMM, 16 Oct 1921. **p.193** 'It is as though she dwelt': Nichols, op. cit., 79. **p.194** 'It was extracted from me by torment': EvA to LB, 19 Dec 1921. **p.194** 'The description of his freaks of temper': Wells, op. cit., 91. **p.194** 'Do not marry a novelist': *Autobiography of Bertrand Russell*, op. cit., vol. 2, 224–5. **p.195** '*Poor* little thing': EvA to LB, 19 Dec 1921. **p.195** 'No doubt Elizabeth is': KM to Dorothy Brett, 1 Oct 1921, O'Sullivan & Scott, op. cit., vol. 4, 286. **p.195** 'A sort of awful innocence': EvA to KM & JMM, 5 Oct 1921. **p.195** 'I think of you often': KM to EvA, 16 Oct 1921. CRP. **p.196** 'Doesn't he belong to the intelligentsia': EvA to KM & JMM, 16 Oct 1921. **p.196** 'I seem always to be at my solicitor's': EvA to KM & JMM, 7 Nov 1921. **p.196** 'more discussed and less bought': EvA to KM & JMM, 7 Nov 1921. **p.196** 'Don't you get Wemyss-ing me': EvA to KM & JMM, 7 Nov 1921. **p.196** 'Only one thing, my hand on heart': KM to Dorothy Brett, 22 Dec 1921, O'Sullivan & Scott, vol. 4, 346–7. **p.198** 'He was composed': EvA to LB, 26 Nov 1921. **p.198** 'bless God for Sinner': EvA journal, 25 Nov 1921. **p.199** 'Cruel, terrible Death!': KM to EvA, 29 Nov 1921. **p.199** 'You should see me now': EvA to KM & JMM, 20 Dec 1921.

Chapter 15 Cousin Katherine

p.201 'She spoke of my "pretty little story"': 11 Jan 1922, in John Middleton Murry (ed.), *Journal of Katherine Mansfield*, 284–5. **p.201** 'Good God!': KM to EvA, undated circa 12 Jan 1922. CRP. **p.202** 'ashamed of what I said': 15 Jan 1922, Middleton Murry, op. cit., 286. **p.202** 'We are solitary creatures *au fonds*': KM to EvA, undated circa Jan 1922. CRP. **p.202** 'A strange fate overtakes me': 27 Jan 1922, Middleton Murry, op. cit., 291. **p.202** 'She suggested that if I did become cured': 14 Jan 1922, ibid, 286. **p.204** 'Aren't I fruitful since I left Frank': EvA to Bertrand Russell, 11 Feb 1922. **p.205** 'Oh, *that* book, my mother has it': Frere to EvA, 13 Jan 1922. CRP. **p.205** '[I] felt so proud of you': EvA to Mansfield, 1 March 1922. **p.205** 'kept taking peeps at it all day': KM to EvA, 6 March 1922. CRP. **p.205** 'I'm beautifully proud of her': EvA to Frere, 1 March 1922. **p.205** 'hotted up inside': KM to EvA, 6 March 1922, in Vincent O'Sullivan & Margaret Scott (eds), *The Collected Letters of Katherine Mansfield: Volume 5: 1922–1923*, 90. **p.206** 'Are you busy writing': EvA to KM, 24 April 1922. **p.206** 'it only wakens the Furies': KM to EvA, 23 April 1922, O'Sullivan & Scott, op. cit., vol. 5, 154. **p.206** 'walking up the path to the chalet': EvA to KM, 7 May 1922. **p.206** 'nothing will induce me to read a thing': EvA to JMM, 22 May 1922. **p.207** 'I suppose my enthusiasm': KM to EvA, undated circa early June 1922. CRP. **p.208** 'I am too much of a bother': ibid. **p.208** 'He ought to divorce me': ibid. **p.209** 'John, who is my one comfort': EvA journal, 5 July 1922. **p.209** 'What a pity I wasn't so lucky': EvA to LB, 6 July 1922. **p.211** 'Who wants to write, or think, of ancient griefs?': *All the Dogs of My Life*, 152.

p.212 'You've lent that £100': KM to EvA, circa 10 Aug 1922. CRP. **p.212** 'I hate to think you are nowhere': EvA to KM, circa 28 Aug 1922. CRP. **p.212** 'hissed out annoying political theories': EvA journal, 26 Aug 1922. **p.212** 'Bertie, that great brain': EvA to LB, 22 Aug 1922. **p.213** 'It's like a thin flute': EvA to Frere, 7 Sept 1922.

Chapter 16 Mortal longings

p.214 'dear little women': *New Statesman*, 2 Dec 1922. **p.214** 'fatuous beatitude': *The Spectator*, 11 Nov 1922. **p.214** 'a gentle assertion of the claims of life against duty': *The Nation*, Jan 1923, vol. 116, no. 3004. **p.215** 'letters are such laced-in things': EvA to KM, 12 Oct 1922. **p.215** 'Won't you send me one little line?': EvA to KM, 3 Jan 1923. **p.216** 'A black fit came on me': KM to EvA, 31 Dec 1922. CRP. **p.217** 'There *is* nothing to be said': Eva to JMM, undated Jan 1923. **p.217** 'All my friends are dying': EvA to LB, 15 Jan 1923. **p.218** 'cannibal yearning': EvA to LB, 2 July 1923. **p.218** 'she might just as easily not have had': EvA journal, 1 July 1923. **p.220** 'Tell Doris I love her very much': EvA to Frere, 12 June 1923. **p.220** 'what I want *really* want': EvA to Frere, 12 July 1923. **p.220** 'quite strangely bad': EvA to Frere, 7 Sept 1922. **p.221** 'submerged in that ugly treacle of bad things': ibid. **p.221** 'How *nearly* he was great': EvA to Frere, 12 Jun 1923. **p.221** 'I really don't know what I'll do': EvA to Frere, 3 Feb 1925. **p.221** 'outlived the alien authority of husbands': EvA to LB, 24 March 1924. **p.221** 'He is always tiresome here': EvA journal, 19 Aug 1923. **p.221** 'He is on the way to greatness': EvA journal, 5 Oct 1923. **p.222** 'Why did I ever come?': EvA journal, 22 Dec 1923. **p.222** 'It really is rather unfair': EvA to Frere, 9 Jan 1924. **p.223** 'Dried up English people with colonial accents': EvA to LB, 23 Jan 1924. **p.223** 'I'll never go away again': EvA to Frere, 15 Jan 1924. **p.224** 'Darling little house of happiness': EvA journal, 4 June 1924. **p.225** 'It was like a dream': EvA journal, 14 July 1924. **p.226** 'When one thinks of K.M.': EvA to Frere, 24 Sept 1924.

Chapter 17 A wormy business

p.228 'From her writing one would suppose': EvA journal, 20 Sept 1924. **p.229** 'Did you get my Love?': EvA to H.G. Wells, undated circa April 1925. **p.229** 'so painful one shudders to think': *TLS*, 26 March 1925. **p.229** 'a pessimist by conviction': *John O'London's*, 25 April 1925. **p.230** 'I am afraid I was pleased': EvA journal, 12 June 1925. **p.231** 'It is a wormy business digging up past': EvA to Margery Waterlow, 10 Sept 1925. **p.231** He hit back in the *Daily Express*, 16 Jan 1926. **p.232** 'How am I going to make a living': *NYT*, 12 Feb 1926. **p.232** 'I am a Quaker': *Daily Express*, 15 Feb 1926. **p.232** 'I was going, however, to suffer dumbly': *Daily Express*, 19 Jan 1926. An edited version ran in the *NYT* the same day. **p.233** 'But why should they know?': *The Delineator*, May 1926, 7–8. **p.233** 'It is too impertinent of them': EvA to LB, 15 Feb 1926. **p.234** 'You do burn my letters': EvA to LB, 11 March 1926. **p.234** 'These are bits out of some love letters': Fragments of love letters. CRP. **p.234** 'I have a most deeply rooted aversion': EvA to Mr Milne, 9 Sept 1924. Private collection. **p.235** 'Very few people have ever managed': Nichols, op. cit., 82–3. **p.235** The drawing was of British art historian: *TLS*, 2 Jan 1987. **p.235** 'the divine should be veiled in mystery': 'The Anonymous in Poetry', undated essay. CRP. **p.236** 'I shall be told I'm vulgar': EvA to Frere, 6 June 1926. **p.236** 'It seems to me it totally without any love making': EvA journal, 18 Oct 1925. **p.237** 'vulgar': *New Statesman*, 23 Oct 1926. **p.237** 'a little coarse': *The Spectator*, 16 Oct 1926. **p.237** 'airily malicious portraiture': *TLS*, 30 Sept 1926. **p.238** 'Made up my mind flight was essential': EvA journal, 27 Dec 1926. **p.239** 'Head of a genius': EvA to Frere, 14 Jan 1927. **p.240** 'If Tolstoy had written operas': EvA journal, 31 July 1927. **p.241** 'English by birth but nothing else': EvA journal, 1 Aug 1927. **p.241** 'She held a black fan': EvA journal, 7 Aug 1927.

Chapter 18 A vulgar little mind

p.242 'No one, I think, who wasn't acquainted with madness': EvA to Frere, 29 June 1927. **p.242** 'a vulgar little mind': KM journal, Aug 1921, Middleton Murry, op. cit., 259. **p.242** 'If it is true, was I not born with it?': EvA journal, 7 Sept 1927. **p.243** 'If only I hadn't been so much *afraid*': EvA to JMM, 8 Sept 1927. **p.243** 'I do know K.M. was fond of me': EvA to Frere, 15 Sept 1927. **p.243** 'It is somehow disgraceful that Middleton Murry': EvA to LB, 2 July 1929. **p.244** 'awful adventure': EvA to Frere, 10 Jan 1927. **p.244** 'black despair comes & perches like a crow': EvA to Frere, undated circa 12 June 1926. **p.244** 'My way of working is to spill freely': EvA to Frere, 4 June 1926. **p.244** 'Writing is the best fun in the world': EvA to Frere, 3 Sept 1927. **p.245** 'He told me things which were distressing': EvA journal, 29 Oct 1927. **p.246** 'A serpent masquerading as a dove': *Expiation*, Persephone Books, London, 2019, 150. **p.246** 'a one-sided quarrel': *Punch*, 6 Feb 1929. **p.246** 'graceful garden attitude': *The Yorkshire Post*, 20 Feb 1929. **p.246** 'as a squirrel stores nuts': EvA to LB, 3 April 1929. **p.249** 'How *happy* I've been!': EvA journal, 11 Oct 1929. **p.249** 'That has been a funny business!': EvA journal, 16 Oct 1929. **p.250** 'My father was terror itself': EvA to LB, 21 April 1929. **p.250** 'With no book learning to hamper me': EvA to LB, 21 May 1936. **p.250** 'Rooms don't make writers': *The Graphic*, 21 Dec 1929. **p.251** In it, Woolf described: Virginia Woolf to Ethel Smyth, 1 March 1930, Nicholson, op. cit., vol. 4, 147. **p.251** 'Amazed, horrified and shocked': EvA journal, 5 March 1930. **p.252** 'real fierce feminist': EvA journal, 5 March 1930. **p.252** Woolf considered some of Elizabeth's writing: Virginia Woolf to Ethel Smyth, 5 Sept 1930, Nicholson, op. cit., vol. 4, 209. **p.253** 'One marvels how ever one could': EvA journal, 9 Dec 1930. **p.253** 'I loved her so very much': EvA to Walpole, 9 Jan 1931. **p.254** 'one of the most charming men': *The Times*, 5 March 1931. **p.254** 'blessed release from a wicked cruel man': EvA journal,

9 March 1931. **p.254** 'I've always feared he might do you': Charlotte Waterlow to EvA, 5 March 1931. **p.254** 'Santayana later sent Elizabeth': See George Santayana to EvA, 10 Nov 1931. CRP. **p.255** 'How characteristic of Frank': EvA to Bertrand Russell, 14 March 1931.

Chapter 19 Dog days

p.256 'She is violently prejudiced': *The Illustrated London News*, 9 May 1931. **p.256** 'Read it, and dislike it—as I have always done': EvA journal, 25 March 1931. **p.257** 'half her mind': *The Daily Telegraph*, 10 April 1931. **p.257** 'the finest literary miniature artist': *The Sphere*, 4 April 1931. **p.257** 'Gracious heavens how angry K.M. would be!': EvA journal, 29 Oct 1933. **p.257** 'MM [Middleton Murry] is Lawrence's Judas': EvA journal, 17 April 1931. **p.259** 'all conquering oriental male': EvA journal, 2 Jan 1932. **p.259** 'Lord, what a fool I was!': EvA journal, 11 Feb 1932. **p.260** 'Moral is never be kind and generous to a young man': EvA journal, 12 Feb 1932. **p.260** 'We sat in the hall till after midnight smashing': EvA journal, 22 March 1932. **p.260** 'This is my final cutting off from him': EvA journal, 8 April 1932. **p.261** 'I might be back in Nassenheide': EvA to LB, 10 July 1932. **p.261** 'I believe Germany, as always, is the danger': EvA to LB, 22 May 1932. **p.262** 'H.B. & I are as happy': EvA to LB, 24 July 1932. **p.263** 'I feel that this house': EvA to LB, 9 Dec 1930. **p.263** 'cloistered slug, bursting out': EvA to Henry Norman, 11 Dec 1932. Henry Norman Papers, Huntington Library. **p.263** 'How happy I am now': EvA journal, 28 April 1933. **p.263** 'I'm so glad it is she and not I': EvA journal, 26 June 1933. **p.263** 'first whole year since I was sixteen': EvA journal, 31 Dec 1933. **p.264** 'Thank God for Pa's blood': EvA journal, 9 April 1933. **p.264** 'Alas, I cannot claim to be an Australian': EvA to E. Morris Miller, 30 Jan 1936. National Library of Australia, Canberra. **p.264** 'embedded in jasmine': EvA to Kathleen Arnold, 2 Aug 1931. **p.265** 'Trix writes that she can't understand': EvA to LB, 7 May 1933. **p.265** 'while people are being whipped to death': EvA to LB, 11 Feb 1934. **p.266** 'I ought to have snatched him': EvA journal, 11 Oct 1933. **p.266** 'alas, the unintelligent men are too many': EvA journal, 11 March 1934. **p.267** 'If I had known he would mind': EvA to Orlo Williams, 24 Nov 1934. **p.267** 'She sees the husbands of her friends suddenly disappearing': EvA to LB, 12 Oct 1934. **p.268** 'It's like a barrel of gunpowder': EvA to LB, 18 Nov 1934. **p.269** 'It is distressing to hurt him,': EvA journal, 3 Feb 1935. **p.269** 'I could spank you': H.G. Wells to EvA, 22 Jan 1935. (Wells has misdated this as 1934). CRP. **p.269** 'His gift is being funny': EvA journal, 7 Dec 1934. **p.270** 'How these men love to talk about themselves!': EvA journal, 31 Oct 1934. **p.270** 'uncrowned king of Greece': EvA to LB, 15 April 1935. **p.270** 'a most delightful mind. A most peculiar heart': EvA to Evi von Arnim, 1 Sept 1937. **p.271** 'He had eyes and heart only for me': EvA journal, 26 Aug 1935.

Chapter 20 Hell is loose

p.273 'little breathing space from torment': EvA journal, 27 Dec 1935. **p.274** 'I don't see how we are going to dodge': Eva to LB, 17 April 1936. **p.274** 'Have I finished forever?': EvA journal, 28 Feb 1936. **p.274** 'Why should I have to go': EvA journal, 15 April 1936. **p.275** 'Poor little Tit so shaken': EvA journal, 21 June 1936. **p.275** 'Am now definitely an old woman': EvA journal, 31 Aug 1936. **p.275** 'I count over my past and present happinesses': EvA to Maud Ritchie, 1 Sept 1936. **p.275** 'A pleasing contrast to the underdone old men': EvA journal, 31 Aug 1936. **p.276** 'But hardly anyone can do that': EvA to LB, 5 May 1936. **p.277** 'The style is that of a clear, small voice': *The Sunday Times*, 11 Oct 1936. **p.277** 'not all the days of her life': *NYT*, 27 Dec 1936. **p.277** 'Dearest but very inaccurate little e': H.G. Wells to EvA, 19 Sep 1936. CRP. **p.278** 'King chucked us for Mrs Simp.': EvA journal, 10 Dec 1936. **p.278** 'To those who know what Mrs Simp. is like': EvA journal, 11 Dec 1936. **p.278** 'I've grown so old—it's dreadful': EvA journal, 28 Nov 1935. **p.279** 'for then I wouldn't': EvA to Bertrand Russell, 6 April 1937. **p.279** 'Frank as a boy seems just like what he was later': Bertrand Russell to EvA, 9 April 1937. CRP. **p.279** 'Imagine having barbed wire in one's blood': EvA journal, 12 Nov 1937. **p.279** 'lovely, spacious past before 1914': EvA to Wells, 23 Jan 1937. H.G. Wells Papers. **p.279** 'for there is still a pleasant backwash': EvA to Wells, 26 Sept 1937. H.G. Wells Papers. **p.279** 'Most old men are bores': EvA journal, 15 May 1937. **p.280** 'Of course if she had two more legs': EvA to Beatrix von Arnim, 5 Aug 1937. **p.281** 'smoothed out': EvA journal, 6 April 1901. **p.281** 'All the old dodderers': EvA journal, 17 Nov 1937. **p.283** 'What I really am by nature is an Escapist': EvA to Liebet, 8 Jan 1938. **p.283** 'Of what is going on in the world I say nothing': EvA journal, 19 March 1938. **p.283** 'That small, sly Jane, scribbling away': EvA journal, 8 March 1938. **p.283** 'I expect you are horrified by the news': EvA to LB, 22 March 1938. **p.284** 'it would be absurd to take trouble': EvA to LB, 23 March 1938. **p.284** 'the incapacity of men': EvA to LB, 18 May 1938. **p.284** 'I can't help being distracted': EvA journal, 23 Sept 1938. **p.285** 'Profoundly distrusting Hitler and his crowd of gangsters': EvA journal, 30 Sept 1938. **p.286** 'no one wants a lipstick': EvA to LB, 26 Oct 1938. **p.286** 'She got a real scare & is going to be very careful': EvA to LB, 10 Nov 1938. **p.286** 'I, who was born in Australia': EvA to LB, 28 Nov 1938. **p.287** 'Hell is loose': EvA to LB, 22 Jan 1939. **p.287** 'The French would hurl themselves': EvA to LB, 25 Feb 1939.

Chapter 21 Life beneath the smiles

p.289 'Have you sent a copy to Hitler?': EvA to Wells, 30 March 1939. **p.289** 'I would prefer that Mr Wells': *The Age*, Melbourne, 7 Jan 1939. **p.290** 'Usual peaceful evening': EvA journal, 12 April 1939. **p.290** 'The plight of refugees is not for me': EvA to LB, 14 April 1939. **p.290** 'Hitler shan't come between me & it': EvA to LB, 14 April 1939. **p.290** 'usual imprisoned evening': EvA journal, 23 April 1939. **p.291** 'I can't go on living in Germany': Sybilla von Hirschberg to EvA, 19 April 1939, de Charms, op. cit., 388. **p.291** 'You should see my garden now': EvA to Teppi Backe, 1 May 1939. **p.292** 'Would that he could put me [down] too': EvA journal, 14 May 1939. **p.292** 'Which did you like best?': EvA journal, 17 May 1939. **p.293** 'These entries are very like Louis XVI's': EvA journal, 10 Aug 1939. **p.293** 'Your views on Jews shock me': EvA to LB, 3 Aug 1939. **p.294** 'I'm so happy for little Billy': EvA to LB, 3 Aug 1939. **p.294** 'England in the war': EvA journal, 3 Sept 1939. **p.294** 'It's so odd how what I write in my stories': EvA to LB, 21 Sept 1939. **p.296** 'In spite of the war horrors and the evil': EvA journal, 31 Dec 1939. **p.297** 'Elizabeth at her best': *TLS*, 27 Jan 1940. **p.297** 'I do not think it is good manners': *The Spectator*, 2 Feb 1940. **p.297** 'begins as a cream puff and ends as a bomb': *NYT*, 6 April 1940. **p.298** 'seven years—no eight—stuck on': EvA journal, 11 April 1940. **p.298** 'having some amusing experiences': EvA to Maud Ritchie, 6 April 1940. **p.301** 'Here, in the pinewoods of the deep south': EvA to H.G. Wells, 11 Nov 1940. H.G. Wells Papers. **p.301** 'Meditated on the growing silence and solitude': EvA journal, 1 Dec 1940. **p.301** 'Those who would beget anything must turn their attention': Foreword for Omnibus edition of three novels. CRP. **p.302** 'God's blessing on all I love': EvA journal, 31 Dec 1940. **p.302** 'Not very bad—really hardly at all': Eva journal, 17 Jan 1940. **p.302** 'No wonder he wouldn't marry her': EvA journal, 25 Jan 1941. **p.303** 'passion for secrecy and anonymity': *NYT*, 10 Feb 1941. **p.303** 'her early books were marked by charm': *New York Herald Tribune*, 10 Feb 1941. **p.304** 'Everything that "Elizabeth" wrote was interpenetrated': *The Times*, 11 Feb 1941. **p.304** 'amused, cynical, ironic, loving, gay, ferocious': Walpole, *Daily Sketch*, 24 Feb 1941. **p.304** 'judgments of men and women': Frank Swinnerton, *The Observer*, 16 Feb 1941. **p.304** 'What a devil she was, but *what* good company!': Stern to Hugh Walpole, 24 Feb 1941. CRP.

Appendix The Beauchamps and the Lassetters: their Australian beginnings

p.308 An anonymous correspondent: *The Cornwall Chronicle*, 15 April 1837. **p.308** 'slumbering on their pillows': *The Cornwall Chronicle*, 29 April 1837. **p.309** 'Reverend Mr Light-weight': *The Cornwall Chronicle*, 9 June 1838. **p.309** 'manifested sorrow for being married': Anne Valeria Bailey, 'Launceston Wesleyan Methodists 1832–1849: Contributions, Commerce, Conscience,' PhD thesis, University of Tasmania, Oct 2008, 245. **p.310** 'Go into that business': *The Sydney Mail*, 22 June 1910.

INDEX

The Academy 53–4
The Adventures of Elizabeth in Rügen 61–2, 66–7, 79, 88
Aga Khan 259
All the Dogs of My Life 49, 102, 270, 276–7
  reviews 277
Allen, Clifford 179
Allen, James Lane 154
Amberley, Viscount 108
animal welfare 265, 299
'The Anonymous in Poetry' 236
Anstruther, Roger 74
anti-German rhetoric
  British government 157–8
  Christine 153–5, 157
anti-Semitism 59, 241, 265, 268, 273–4, 282, 286, 287, 293
The April Baby's Book of Tunes 51, 57
Arlen, Michael 264
Arndt, Marie 265, 268
Arnim, Beatrix (Trix) von 34, 93, 94, 100, 116, 117, 129, 138, 301
  Chalet Soleil, at 173, 224–5, 249
  children 181, 218, 268, 280
  Elizabeth's visits to Germany 218, 231, 258, 261, 281–2
  First World War, during 124, 131–2, 140, 141–2, 143, 155, 163
  Forster as tutor 69, 72
  marriage 173
  Mas des Roses, at 276
  Nazi Germany, in 265, 267–8, 281–2, 285–7, 291–2, 297
Arnim, Count Harry von 26, 29, 32
Arnim, Elizabeth (Liebet) von 33, 34, 91, 93, 95–6, 100, 102, 114, 116, 132, 137–8, 183, 209, 234, 280, 305
  America, in 135–6, 141, 148–52, 156, 177, 247–8, 293, 295, 299–300, 302
  Chalet Soleil, at 224–5
  children 160–1, 174, 258, 276
  death of Elizabeth 303
  First World War, during 120, 124, 128, 130, 135–6, 143, 163
  Forster as tutor 69, 72
  Mas des Roses, at 258, 276
  Switzerland, fleeing from 118–19
Arnim, Elizabeth von (nee Beauchamp) 3, 7, 97, 183–4, 256 *see also* Beauchamp, Mary Annette (May)
  America, in 147–52, 291–4, 298–302
  ashes 305
  Australia, and 221, 264, 306
  Cape Town, visit to 222–3
  celebrity 298–9
  character 160, 176, 209–10, 234–5, 235–6, 242–3, 248, 275, 283, 303–4
  death 303
  dogs 32–3, 49, 87, 90, 103–4, 117, 118, 173, 200, 253, 259, 262, 265, 270–1, 275–6, 279–80, 283, 289, 291–3, 295, 299
  driving lessons 128
  England during First World War, in 119–21, 125–9, 289
  financial issues (post-war) 173–4
  French Riviera, on 238–40

INDEX

Greece, in 270
illness 222, 302–3
Italy, in 104, 113–14, 186–8, 203, 268, 283
Lausanne, in 210–11
letter-writing 220, 234
music 113, 127, 168, 197, 217–18, 240–1, 280
obituaries 303–4
parenthood, reflecting on 250
privacy 233–6, 298, 303, 306
psychic divisions 126–7
publishers, conflicting 155
religion 281
rose 306
second marriage 137–9, 140–1, 145–7, 159–60, 165–6, 234
serialisation of works 74, 224, 227, 233, 244, 246, 249
silence 116, 161, 211, 235–5
Switzerland, in 96–9, 102–4, 115–19
writing, on 244, 301

Arnim, Eva (Evi) von 33, 39, 77, 85, 86, 91, 93–5, 117, 138, 233
America, in 136, 140, 141, 148, 156, 173, 247, 293, 302
First World War, during 120, 124, 131, 135–6, 143
Forster as tutor 69, 72
marriage 181, 237
Switzerland, fleeing from 118–19

Arnim, Felicitas (Martin) von 49, 65–6, 85, 100, 113–14, 117, 125, 129, 210–11
character 114
death 142–5, 149, 168, 173, 199
First World War, during 124, 140, 141–2
grave 231
theft, accused of 115–16

Arnim, Henning Berndt (H.B.) 64–5, 66, 90–1, 99, 174, 176–7, 295
America, in 177, 207, 247, 284, 293–4
financial concerns 261, 284
First World War, during 132, 143, 147–8, 159
Mas de Roses, at 260–2, 284

Arnim-Schlagenthin, Count Henning August von 26–9, 30, 63, 73, 74, 83, 188, 207, 210, 250
character 71
death 94–5
domestic violence 40
financial troubles 85–7, 91, 261, 284
fraud charge 50–2, 213
illness 91, 92, 94–5
marriage 31, 33, 34, 38–43, 46, 49, 57–8, 66–7, 94
Nassenheide, at 36–40, 42, 70–1, 85–7, 90–1
son, birth of 64–5

Arundel Castle (RMS) 222

Ashton, Winifred (Clemence Dane) 197
A Bill of Divorcement 197

Astor, Nancy 164

Atherton, Gertrude 154

August of Prussia, Prince 224, 265

Austen, Jane 46, 48, 60, 82, 190, 192
Pride and Prejudice 283

Austin, Alfred 37, 44, 82
The Garden that I Love 37, 44, 82

Australasian Steam Navigation Company 5

Austria, annexation of 283, 284–5

Authors' Manifesto 157–8

Backe, Teppi 69, 70, 71, 79, 86, 90, 95–6, 100, 114
Chalet Soleil, at 105, 221, 249
Elizabeth's visits to Germany 218–19, 258, 261
First World War, during 117–18, 129, 132, 142, 144
Mas des Roses, at 287
Nazi Germany 283

Baker, Ida 189, 202, 209, 222, 224

Barrett Browning, Elizabeth 270

Barrie, J.M. 157

Bayreuth 27, 28

Beauchamp, Annie 45

Beauchamp, Arthur 20–1, 312

Beauchamp, Charlotte (Shad) *see* Waterlow, Charlotte

Beauchamp, Connie 21, 178, 288

Beauchamp, Craddock 20, 312

Beauchamp, Emma 6, 18

Beauchamp, Harold 20, 45, 193

Beauchamp, Harry 3, 22, 23, 24, 38, 167, 198, 312

Beauchamp, Henry Herron 1–2, 4–5, 29, 34, 42, 51, 55, 62, 83–4, 141
Australia, voyages to 15–18, 19–21, 306, 311
businessman, as 311–12
character 7, 12–13, 15, 17, 22, 84, 284
death 84–5
Elizabeth's writing, on 46, 48–9, 60, 75
England, move to 6–10, 11
Italy, in 14–15, 25–7
London, in 11–14, 18–19, 21–3
marriage 4, 312
Mary, relationship with 13, 15, 17, 18, 21–2, 45–6, 7–8, 65, 75, 84, 250
Switzerland, in 14–15

Beauchamp, Horatio 15, 19, 21, 312

Beauchamp, John 311–12
Beauchamp, Kathleen *see* Mansfield, Katherine
Beauchamp, Leslie (Chummie) 168
Beauchamp, Louey (nee Lassetter) 2–3, 4, 12, 21, 47, 95, 100, 309
  birth 308
  character 7, 8–9, 28
  Continental tour 27–9
  death 165
  London, in 11, 19–20
  marriage 4, 85, 312
  Mary's betrothal 27–9, 30
  Mary's second marriage 137, 139
  Switzerland, in 14–15, 17–18
Beauchamp, Mary Annette (May) 21 *see also* Arnim, Elizabeth von
  Berlin, life in 34–5, 37
  betrothal 27–9, 30–1
  birth 2–3
  Blue Hayes, at 87–8, 90
  caravan holiday 80–3
  character 18, 22, 76–7, 78, 134–5
  childhood 3–4, 5, 12–13
  children 32–4, 39, 49, 64–5
  Continental tour 25–9
  education 18–19, 20, 23
  England, visits to 6–10, 11, 33–4, 38–9, 49, 57–8, 64–5, 80–3, 91, 98–9
  fame 67, 68
  father, relationship with 13, 15, 17, 18, 21–2, 45–6, 48–9, 57–8, 60, 75, 84–5, 250
  identity, speculation about 47, 52–7, 60, 63–4, 68, 153–4
  marriage 31–3, 38–41, 42–3, 46, 57–8, 63
  music 22, 23–4, 26–8, 31, 39, 168
  Nassenheide, at 36–43, 45–6, 50, 57–8, 69–71, 78–9
  novelist, as 58–60
  presentation at court 30
  reading 37, 46
  Rügen, on 61
  silence 51, 62, 70, 77, 95
  Switzerland, in 14–15, 18
  Treibhaus 72–3, 98
  tutors, treatment of 68–9, 76–7, 78, 304
  undercover research 73–4
  wedding 31
  Who's Who 68
  writing, early 34–5, 40–1, 43, 45–6
Beauchamp, Ralph 3, 11, 14, 22, 39, 93, 198–9, 284, 312
Beauchamp, Sir Sydney (Sinner) 3, 14, 22, 23, 31, 33–4, 64, 162, 176, 178, 197, 203, 312
  death 198–9, 217, 305
Beauchamp, Walter 3, 22, 23, 24, 25, 83, 312
Beaumont, Harry 215
Beaverbrook, Lord 279
Bedford, Elizabeth 307, 309
Bedford, Georgina 307, 309
Beecham, Thomas 261
Beerbohm, Max 187, 268
Bell, Clive 100
Bell, Gertrude 99
Bell, Joseph 309
Bell, Vanessa 100
Belloc, Hilaire 176
Belloc Lowndes, Marie 176, 194
Belsize Park 11, 15
The Benefactress 58–60, 67
  play 151
Bennett, Arnold 157, 196
Bernhardt, Sarah 108
Beulah 3, 5, 6, 15, 19, 306, 313
Bigelow, Poultney 64, 135, 141, 231–2, 293
  Seventy Summers 231, 232
Billy 280, 292–3, 295, 298
Binyon, Laurence 158
Birrell, Augustine 99, 128–9, 179, 219
Birrell, Francis 179
The Birthday Party 274, 284
Bismarck, Otto von 29, 31–2
Black Prince, sinking of 142
Blood, Florence (Baby Blood) 114
Bloomsbury set 74, 100, 158, 162, 167–8, 192, 196
Blue Hayes 87–8, 90
Blythewood House 18
Bonny Hall 295
Book of the Month Club 296
Bott, Milly 245–6
Bowden, George 167
Brett, Dorothy 192, 195, 211
Brook, Peter 215
Brooke, Rupert 100
Burne-Jones, Philip 99
Butler, Samuel 179
Butterworth, Ann 276
Butterworth, Corwin 152, 174, 177, 247, 276, 293
Byrdcliffe 148

Callil, Carmen 305
Cammeraygal people 2
Cannes viii, 252–3, 262
The Caravaners 88–90, 99, 111, 123, 185, 214, 251, 301
Casaubon, K. *see* Arnim, Elizabeth von
Castle Hill plantation 300

INDEX

Cazalet, Thelma 218
Chagall, Marc 282
Chalet Soleil 102–4, 107, 132, 172–3, 185–92, 200–4, 207–9, 224, 248–9
  flight from 117–18
  guests 104, 111–12, 117, 179–82, 191–2, 211–13, 219–21, 225, 230, 248
  sale of 248–9, 258, 294
Chamberlain, Neville 285, 299
Chanel, Coco 239
Chanler, Beatrice 302
Chanterai Ma Chanson (I will Sing My Song) 181
Chaplin, Charlie 282
Charlottesville 299–300
Charms, Leslie de *see* Arnim, Elizabeth (Liebet) von
Château de Coppet 18, 223–4
Chesterton, G.K. 157
Cholmondeley, Alice 150
  nom de plume, as 153–4, 156–7
Cholmondeley, Christine 149–50
Cholmondeley, Mary 91, 156
  Sir Charles Danvers 156
Christine 149–50, 151, 158, 166
  identity of author 153–6, 234
  reviews 153–5, 157
Christmas in a Bavarian Village 282
Christopher and Columbus 149, 166, 214
  reviews 166–7
Chunkie 253–4, 259, 262, 292
Churchill, Lady Randolph 52, 176
Churchill, Sir Winston 52, 176, 299
Circular Quay 2, 6, 306, 311
Cobden-Sanderson, Anne 179, 230
Cobden-Sanderson, Thomas James (Cobbie) 99, 111, 112, 121, 134, 137, 177
  Chalet Soleil, at 179, 181
  death 213, 217
  diary 230
Coco 103–4, 117, 118, 173, 185, 189, 200, 276–7
coercive control 186
Conan Doyle, Arthur 157, 306
Connaught, Duke of 239
Constable, Captain Charles 12
Constable, John 12
Cornelia 32, 33
Cornwallis-West, George 52
Cornwallis-West, Mary Theresa Olivia (Daisy) 52
Cornwallis-West, Shelagh 52
Cosmic Anatomy and the Structure of the Ego (M.B. Oxon) 191, 215
Cowper Powys, John 270
Cunard, 'Emerald' Lady Maud 164, 176, 261
Czechoslovakia 285, 287

Dane, Clemence *see* Ashton, Winifred (Clemence Dane)
Darwin, Charles 61
Davis, Bette 299
de Staël, Germaine 223
Dean, Alexander 25
Dean, Isabel 25
The Delineator interview 233–4
Der Stürmer 282
Dexter, Lady Caroline 204
divorce 109, 156, 172, 197
Dix, Otto 282
domestic tyranny 40, 115, 145–7, 185–6
Doubleday, Florence 182
Doubleday, Frank N. 135, 155, 182, 230, 262
  The Memoirs of a Publisher 155
Doubleday, Nelson 262, 294–6
Doubleday (publishers) 155, 262
Dremmel, Ingeborg 122–3, 186
Dremmel, Robert 122–3
du Maurier, Daphne
  Rebecca 186
Dunbar 8
Duncan, Isadora 111

East Lodge 22, 206–7
Easton Glebe 99
Edward, Prince of Wales 273, 277
Edward VIII, King 277–8
Einstein, Albert 61, 265
Eliot, George 151
  Middlemarch 151
Elizabeth and Her German Garden 44–5, 46, 52–3, 69–70, 92, 205
  early MS 40, 43
  identity of author 47, 52–7, 60, 63–4
  reviews 44–5
Ellen and Arbuthnot 164
Ellen in Germany 151
Emily 276, 292
The Enchanted April viii, 164, 187–8, 204–5, 209, 213, 216, 301, 305
  movie versions 215, 305
  opera 305
  pictures 219
  play 305
  reviews 214–15
Entartete Kunst 282
Entwhistle, Lucy 185–6, 192
Estcourt, Anna 58–9

Etain 217
The Eternal Jew 282
Expiation 245–6, 247, 273
  reviews 246–7

Fabian Society 91, 97, 164, 278
Fairfax, James R. 23
Fanny 284, 290, 296
Father 249–50, 256–7, 269
  reviews 257
Fell, Rosemary 201
female independence 59, 227–8
feminism 250–2
  feminist publishers 305
Ferdinand, Archduke Franz 116
Festing Jones, Henry 179
Ffrangcon-Davies, Gwen 217, 225
Fidelio (Beethoven) 280–1
Filson Young, Alexander 129
First World War 118–19, 123–4, 128–9, 132–3
  Armistice 163–4
  outbreak 116–18
Fitzgerald, F. Scott 239
Fitzgerald, Zelda 239
Fleming, Peter 282
Forbes-Robertson, Norman 129
Forster, Edward Morgan (E.M.) 67–72, 77–8, 91
  caravan holiday 82
  Howards End 71
  The Longest Journey 77–8
  Nassenheide, at 67–72
  Where Angels Fear to Tread 71
Fräulein Schmidt and Mr Anstruther 74, 75
Frederick the Great 26
Frere, Elizabeth 279
Frere, Mary Stewart 180
Frere Reeves, Alexander Stuart (A.S.) 179–81, 218, 226, 236, 254, 262, 267, 275, 279
  'Doris' 220–1
  Elizabeth, relationship with 184, 187, 191–2, 198, 204–5, 206–7, 211, 214, 219–21, 230, 237, 243–5, 258, 260
  marriages 245, 264
Friedrich, Caspar David 61
Fullerton, Jinnie 288

Galli-Curci, Amelita 225
Garsington Manor 162, 163, 167
Gaskell, Elizabeth 37
  The Life of Charlotte Brontë 37
George V, King 159, 273
German militarism 89, 149–50, 283–7
Ghyka, Jeanne 114
Gibbes, William 3
Gibbs, Sir Philip 233
Gielgud, Sir John 93, 225
Goddard, Captain 7, 12
Goebbels, Joseph 274, 282, 302
Gold Eagle Tavern 295, 298, 299
goldfields (Australia) 310
Gordon Square 138, 140–1, 159, 162, 165, 170, 278–9
Grahame, Kenneth 80
  Wind in the Willows 80, 264
Graves, Eustace 181, 237
Graves, Robert 249
  Goodbye to All That 249
Greenaway, Kate 51
Grove, Sir George 24, 25
Guinness, Benjamin 253
Guinness, Bridget 239, 252–3
Gurdjieff, George Ivanovich 215

Haggard, H. Rider 158
Halcyon Inn 300
Hardy, Thomas 157
Hazel Cottage 30, 207
Heinemann (publishers) 267
Henry of Pless, Prince 52
Henry of Pless, Princess 52–7
Henry of Prussia, Princess 56
heroines 249–50
Hirschberg, Anton (Tony) von 173, 276
Hirschberg, Sybilla (Billy) von 280, 290–1, 294
Hitler, Adolf vii, viii, 264–5, 273–4, 283–5, 289, 299, 302
  Austria, annexation of 283, 284–5
  Czechoslovakia 285, 287
  Mein Kampf 241, 266
  Nuremberg Rallies 280, 284
Hogarth Press 163
Holmes, Sherlock 140
Holtermann, Bernhardt 16, 22
Holtermann Nugget 16
Hordern, Anthony 313
Hotel Château de Bellevue 96
Huxley, Aldous 239
The Immortal Hour (Rutland Boughton) 217–18, 225, 228

In the Mountains 174–5
Ingraban 49
Ingram, Edward 123S
Introduction to Sally 230, 233, 236–7, 242
  reviews 237
Iredale, Charlotte *see* Lassetter, Charlotte

INDEX

Iredale, Kezia 307–8, 310, 311, 312
Iredale, Lancelot 308, 310
Iredale & Co 310, 311
Isherwood, Christopher 61

James, Henry 99, 100, 221
The Jasmine Farm 263, 266–7, 269
Jellaby 88–9, 99
Johnstone, Harry 179
Joyce, James 206
  Ulysses 206
Junkers 26, 32, 87, 149, 166
Jutland, Battle of 142, 145, 275

Keun, Odette 239–40, 253, 259, 263, 269
Kipling, Rudyard 158, 306
Kirribilli Point 2–5, 15, 306, 312–13
Klee, Paul 282
Knobbie 253, 259, 262, 292
Koteliansky, Samuel 196
Kristallnacht 287

La Hogue 6–10, 12
Lamb, Charles 266
Lassetter, Annie Mary 308, 309, 312
Lassetter, Arthur 84, 263
Lassetter, Charlotte (nee Iredale) 11, 14, 20, 311
Lassetter, Elizabeth Waite *see* Beauchamp, Louey
Lassetter, Frederic 3, 4–5, 11, 12, 14, 23, 28, 84, 100, 132, 223, 313
  background 307, 309, 310–11, 313
Lassetter, Frederic M. 132
Lassetter, Reverend Matthew 4, 6, 7, 307–9
Lassetter's Pennies 310
Lassetters (store) 4, 263, 311
Lausanne 14–15, 210–11
Lawrence, D.H. 162, 168, 221, 239, 257–8, 306
  Kangaroo 221
  Lady Chatterley's Lover 258
  paintings 257–8
  Women in Love 162, 190
Lawrence, Frieda 168, 190, 239, 257
Lee, Vernon 114, 117, 248, 268
Leslie, Shane 219
Leviathan (SS) 247
Lindsay, Norman 260
Liszt, Franz 26, 27
Lloyd, George A. 310, 313
Lloyd George, David 164
Lloyd Wright, Frank 215
Lohm, Axel von 59

Lou Pidou 238, 258–9, 269
Love 227–9, 237
  reviews 229
Lusitania, sinking of 132
Lyons, Joe 289

MacDonald, Ramsay 254
Maclise, Daniel 110
Macmillan, Sir Frederick 237, 267
Macmillan (publishers) 154–5, 158, 194, 267
Magnolia of Mass 54, 55
Malleson, Lady Constance 163
Mallet, Marie 188, 208, 209, 219, 254
Man of Wrath 40–1, 47, 57, 71, 75
Mann, Thomas 61
Manoukhin, Dr Ivan 202–3, 211
Mansfield, Katherine viii, 20, 45, 65–6, 114, 163, 229
  'A Cup of Tea' 201
  'At the Bay' 200, 203
  'Bliss' 196
  'The Daughters of the Late Colonel' 205, 289
  death 217
  'Die Einsame' 66
  Elizabeth, relationship with 167–9, 178–9, 188–91, 195–7, 200–3, 205–6, 211–12, 215–16, 224, 242–3
  'The Garden Party' 203
  The Garden Party and Other Stories 205
  grave 225
  illness 168, 178, 188–91, 202, 205–6, 207–8, 211–12, 215–17
  In a German Pension 167
  journals 242, 257
  'The Life of Ma Parker' 205, 289
  memorial 288–9
  music 167, 168
  Prelude 163, 168
  review of *Christopher and Columbus* 166–7
  Something Childish and Other Stories 226
  Switzerland, in 188–91, 195, 200–3, 207–9, 211–12
  Vera, on 192–3
  'The Voyage' 203
Mas de Notre Dame de Vie 253
Mas des Roses vii–viii, 252–4, 258, 264–5
  Elizabeth's flight from 291–2
  French soldiers 290
  garden 262–3
  guests 258, 268, 272, 275–6, 280
Masterman, Charles 157–8
Maugham, Somerset 99, 239, 261, 264, 269
Melba, Dame Nellie 259–60
Melchior, Lauritz 240, 247

Meynell, Alice 298
Miklouho-Maclay, Nicholas 16–17, 306
Miles, Miss 6, 8, 14
Mondrian, Piet 282
Moore, George 122, 218
Morel, E.D. 130
Morrell, Lady Ottoline 133, 162–3, 169, 189
Morris, William 148
Mort, Thomas 19
Mougins viii, 252–4, 289
Mount Temple, Molly 264
Mr Skeffington 284, 294, 296–9
  movie 298–9
  reviews 297–8, 301
Munich Agreement 285, 287
Murry, John Middleton 167, 178, 202–3, 206, 212, 216–17, 219, 225
  Katherine's journals 242–3, 257
  Son of Woman 257
  Switzerland, in 188–90, 192–3, 195–6, 207–9
  The Voyage 226
Mussolini, Benito 240

Napoleon 223–4
Nassenheide 36–40, 42–3, 45–6, 50, 57, 90–1, 225, 253, 282
  destruction of 306
  Elizabeth's visits 182–3, 231
  fire 58
  Forster at 67–72
  life at 70–1, 79, 125
  sale of 85–8, 91
  Walpole at 76–7
Nazis 261, 265, 267–8, 273, 280–2, 289, 296
Neilson-Terry, Phyllis 93
New Zealand 20–1
Newell, Mike 305
Nichols, Beverley 175–6, 184, 193, 234–5
  Evensong 259–60
North, Marianne 61
  Recollections of a Happy Life 61

O'Brien, Kate 297
O'Niel, Colette *see* Malleson, Lady Constance
Otter, Amy Elizabeth 255
Ottringel, Baron and Baroness von 88–9

Paget, Violet *see* Lee, Vernon
Pankhurst, Emmeline 251
Parkes, Sir Henry 22
Parratt, Walter 24
The Pastor's Wife 33, 113, 117, 122–4, 129, 139, 185, 186, 244
  reviews 122, 123–4
Picasso, Pablo 239, 253, 282
Pincher 253, 259
Plowright, Joan 305
Poore, Charles 297
Portofino 187, 204, 219, 305
Priestley, J.B. 246, 264
Prillwitz, Elise von 26
Prince 87, 90
The Princess Priscilla's Fortnight 73, 79
  play 88, 92

Queen Mary (RMS) 292–3

Rains, Claude 299
Rayne, Jessica 245
Récamier, Juliette 223–4
Redleaf 84, 100
Reeves, Alexander Wilfred 180
Reeves, Amber 97
Richardson, Henry Handel 241
Richardson, Miranda 305
Ritchie, Anne Thackeray 60, 228
Ritchie, Maud 179, 191, 219, 294, 298
Ritchie, William 294
Rives, Amélie 299–300
  The Quick or the Dead? 300
Roberts, Cecil 257
Rockefeller, J.D. 268
Roddice, Hermione 162
Roosevelt, Ted 295
Roosevelt, Theodore 295
Ropes 90
Royal College of Music 23–4
Rügen 61
Russell, Bertrand (Bertie) 7, 108, 125, 170–1, 254–5, 278–9, 293, 305
  Amberley Papers 279
  Author's Manifesto 158
  character 159
  Elizabeth, relationship with 129–30, 133–4, 135, 137, 139, 161–3, 172, 177–8, 197, 204, 212, 259
  Ellen and Arbuthnot 164
  Introduction to Mathematical Philosophy 161
  Katherine Mansfield, and 168
  pacificism 108, 130, 160–3, 283
  Vera 194
Russell, Countess Mary (Elizabeth) *see* Arnim, Elizabeth von
Russell, Dora 197, 212, 278, 305
Russell, John Francis Stanley (Frank) 107–11, 279, 281
  affairs 164–5
  America, in 150–1

INDEX

bigamy trial 109–10, 213
character 108, 112–13, 130, 139, 145–7
death 254–5
Divorce 141
domestic tyranny 115, 145–7, 185
drug use 139–40
Elizabeth, relationship with 111–13, 115, 120–1, 125–7, 130–1, 133–6, 156, 170–1, 173
gambling 130, 140, 165
marriage to Elizabeth 137–9, 140–1, 145–7, 152, 159–60, 161, 165–6, 210, 213, 305
My Life and Adventures 213
separation from Elizabeth 170–2, 177–8, 196
South Africa, in 132, 133
Vera 194
Russell, Lord John 107
Russell, Mollie (nee Somerville) 109, 111, 138, 213
divorce 113, 132, 133
Five Women and a Caravan 111

Sandhurst, Lady Nellie 219
Santayana, George 111, 115, 146–7, 159–60, 177, 254, 268–9
Sargent, John Singer 235
Schlagenthin 26, 85, 86, 94–6, 100, 144
Schmidt, Rose-Marie 74, 75
Schwitters, Kurt 282
Scott, Mabel 109
Sgambati, Giovanni 25, 26
Shakespeare, William 37
Shaw, George Bernard 91, 158
Shepard, E.H. 264
Winnie the Pooh 264
Sherman, Vincent 299
Simpson, Wallis 277–8
Skeffington, Job 296, 297
Skeffington, Lady Fanny 296–7
Smythe, Ethel 248, 251–2
The March of Women 252
The Wreckers 248
Snow White and the Seven Dwarfs 287
The Solitary Summer 46–9, 53
identity of author 63–4
Somerville, Mollie *see* Russell, Mollie
Spade House 82, 89
Spence, Patricia 279
Spenser, Edmund 37, 52
Stanley, Kate 108
Steinweg, Herr 69
Stern, Gladys B. 277, 304
Strong, Charles 268–9
Strutt, Emily 187
Stuart, Charles Erskine 78, 79, 99, 104, 117, 141
death 151, 173
Sudetenland 285
suffrage 251–2
Swinford Manor 82
Swinnerton, Frank 41, 47, 160, 179, 304
Sydney 1
nineteenth-century, in 1–2, 19–20, 308

The Tea Rose 43
Telegraph House 125, 130, 133, 135, 138, 141, 143, 146, 147–8, 159, 163, 170, 177, 278
Terry, Ellen 93
Thackeray, William Makepeace 60
Threlkeld, Lancelot 23
Törring-Jettenbach, Countess Anna von 26
Toscanini, Arturo 280
Travers, P.L. 215
Trevelyan, Robert 179
Trotsky, Leon 282
Tuppence vii, 289, 292

Usborne, Karen 235

Van Diemen's Land 308
Vaughan Williams, Ralph 99
Vera 164, 185–6, 187, 188, 192–5, 196, 204, 205, 246, 257, 301, 305
reviews 192–4, 214
Vesuvius (eruption) 14–15
Vickie 275, 292
Victoria, Queen 30, 139, 187, 208, 239
Villa Gamberaia 114
Villa Isola Bella 288–9
Villa Le Fontanelle 113
Virago (publishers) 305

Wagner, Cosima 27–8, 241
Wagner, Richard 27, 197, 218, 240, 261, 300
Das Rheingold 197
Die Meistersinger von Nürnberg 176, 280
Götterdämmerung 245, 302
Liebestod 184
Nazism, and 280
Parsifal 240, 260
Siegfried 240
Tristan und Isolde 247
Wagner, Siegfried 240–1
Wagner, Winifred 241
Wallace, Edgar 263
Wallace, Patricia 263, 275, 279
Walpole, Hugh 75–7, 91, 99, 111, 120, 125, 198, 219, 240, 253

Chalet Soleil 191
Elizabeth's obituary 304
The Golden Scarecrow 77
Nassenheide, at 76–7
Waterlow, Cecil (Puddle) 128, 238, 267, 272–5, 284
death 275
Waterlow, Charlotte (nee Beauchamp) 3, 15, 18, 68, 95, 98, 109, 137, 148, 177, 183–4, 198–9, 230, 254, 281, 312
Chalet Soleil 191
First World War, during 125, 127–8, 130, 132–3, 135, 142–5
French Riviera, on 238, 239
marriage 19, 21, 62, 90
Puddle, concerns about 267, 272–5
teenage pregnancy 17–18, 33, 250
Waterlow, Commander John Beauchamp 128, 142–5, 173, 275
Waterlow, George 19, 21, 62, 90
death 230–1, 275
Waterlow, Guy 230, 275
Waterlow, Margery 80, 98, 132, 142, 179, 181, 198, 260
Waterlow, Nick 19
Waterlow, Sir Ernest 19
Waterlow, Sir Sydney 18–19
Waterlow, Sir Sydney (Monarch) 68, 100, 111, 120, 142, 178, 193, 246, 270, 275, 278, 284
Waterlow, Zoe 21
Way, Oliver 250–1
Webb, Sidney 91
Welles, Orson 300
Wellington House meeting 157–8
Wells, Herbert George (H.G.) 80–1, 89, 123, 131, 137, 145, 184, 192, 269–70, 279
America, in 300
Bigelow, conflict with 231–2
British war propaganda 157
Elizabeth, relationship with 99–106, 109, 173, 176, 229, 269, 277
Experiment in Autobiography 269
The Food of the Gods and How it Came to Earth 66–7
France, in 238–9, 253, 258–9, 263
H.G. Wells in Love 101–2
The Holy Terror 289
The Island of Dr Moreau 81
Marriage 104
The New Machiavelli 97, 99
The Time Machine 81
Vera, on 194
The War of the Worlds 81, 300
The Wonderful Visit 82
The World of William Clissold 239
The World Set Free 105
Wells, Isabel Mary 81
Wells, Jane 81, 97, 99, 105, 131, 145, 176, 191, 239–40
Wemyss, Ellen 164
Wemyss, Everard 185–6, 192–3, 301
West, Anthony 131, 259
West, Rebecca 104–6, 131, 192, 214, 256, 259
The Judge 220
Wharton, Edith 253
White Gates 230, 244–5, 250, 251, 253, 258, 260
White, Patrick 90
Whitehead, Jane 148
Whitehead, Ralph 148
Whyte, Lady Maude 85
Wilde, Oscar 92
Wilhelm Heinrich August, Prince 26
Wilhelm II, Kaiser 32, 64
William, Orlo 266
Winkie 262, 270–1
Wister, Owen 154
Woolf, Leonard 100, 163, 266
The Intelligent Man's Way to Prevent War 266
Woolf, Virginia 74, 78, 100, 163, 168, 248, 251–2
Flush 270
Room of One's Own 250–1
To the Lighthouse 242
Woozie 262, 266, 270, 271, 276–7
Wordsworth, Dorothy 37, 266
Wordsworth, William 37, 266
World War I *see* First World War
World War II 294, 299
Wortley, Clare Stuart 235
Wotonga 3, 5, 313

x-ray treatment 205–6, 216, 229